FRAMED

*The New Right Attack
on Chief Justice Rose Bird and the Courts*

by
BETTY MEDSGER

Foreword by Richard Reeves

THE PILGRIM PRESS

NEW YORK

Library of Congress Cataloging in Publication Data

Medsger, Betty.
Framed: the new right attack on chief justice
Rose Bird and the courts.

Includes index.
1. Bird, Rose Elizabeth.   2. California. Supreme Court.
3. Judicial power—California.   4. Political questions and
judicial power—California.   I. Title.
KFC960.M43   1983   347.794'03534   83-2216
ISBN 0-8298-0655-5   347.94073534

The Pilgrim Press, 132 W. 31 Street, New York, New York 10001

To the loving memory of
Sue, Karen and Michael

Contents

Acknowledgments

In *Absence of Malice* Paul Newman tells the reporter played by Sally Field that ". . . things aren't always what they seem."

Many journalists, still basking in the glow of *All the President's Men,* were shocked that Hollywood just a few years later would make a film that portrayed reporters as being less than saviours of the Republic. The professional ox gorers did not like being gored.

This book is, in large part, an examination of a series of events that were not what they seemed to be, were not what the journalists and politicians said they were. My investigation of that illusion of truth would not have been possible without the information and insights provided by the hundreds of persons I interviewed. They helped me get beyond the illusion of truth. I am grateful to all those sources, even the very few who tried to mislead me. To those who took great personal risk by providing me with confidential documents, no words are adequate and no public praise is possible. I hope they find reward in knowing they helped contribute to the revelation of the truth and to the vindication of persons falsely accused.

I also want to thank Jon Swan, senior editor at *Columbia Journalism Review,* who encouraged me, the Ottinger Foundation for supporting initial research, and Peggy Harrison, who transcribed my tapes. Thanks to Esther Cohen, my fine editor, and thanks to my colleagues at the Department of Communication at Stanford University and at the Department of Journalism at San Francisco State University.

Loving thanks to those persons closest to me who supported me in this long project, even when they didn't want to hear another word about courts—Ben Bagdikian, Lynn Kidder, and Valerie Miner. And thanks to M².

Betty Medsger
San Francisco, 1983

Foreword

One July day in 1978, I set out in search of a political conglomerate which operated under a long and impressive list of divisional titles. The Law and Order Campaign Committee, the Free Market Political Action Committee, the Gun Owners of America—those organizations and more operated out of a small town in California, Arcadia.

And I found what I was looking for—sort of. Like Dorothy when, at the end of her travels, she discovered the Wizard of Oz—an "ordinary man" pulling levers behind a curtain. In my quest—I was writing a column then for *Esquire* magazine—the organizations were the curtain and the man was a California state senator, a Republican, H. L. Richardson.

Richardson, though, was not ordinary enough for my tastes. He was a smart, tough and cynical political operator with an idea whose time he thought was coming. The idea, as he defined it, was to get political control over state and federal judges. That definition was bad enough, but, in my mind, Richardson was trying to do more—and worse. He was clumsily attempting to undo what Americans like James Madison had done just about 200 years before. In a little office building on the outskirts of Los Angeles, I was talking with a guy who was trying to change the United States of America from a government of laws to a government of men.

He assumed, foolishly, that the new governors, in capitols, assembly chambers and courtrooms, would be his kind of men. More impressive Americans had tried the same thing before, making the same assumptions. In 1937, a President, Franklin D. Roosevelt, concocted a plan to expand the membership of the United States Supreme Court to suit his own political priorities of that moment. Their politics were different—Richardson, an aggressive conservative, would have loved the Supreme Court justices FDR wanted to neutralize—but their ambitions were the same. Each of them wanted to bring courts and judges under greater political control, assuming that they, Roosevelt or Richardson, would exercise that control. "The goal," as Betty Medsger writes in this important case-study, ". . . is to intimidate judges into making judicial decisions according to political pressures."

I had sought out Senator Richardson because he was then, through his paper organizations, computerized mailing lists and a sure instinct for the frailties of the body politic, raising money to finance a campaign to defeat the Chief Justice of California in the referendum state law requires for the approval of judges appointed by the governor and confirmed by the Commission on Judicial Appointments.

Richardson failed in that effort. But it came close enough to success to frighten anyone who understands that democratic voters, bless them, tend to vote *against* somebody or something rather than *for* dedicated and lovable public servants and altruistic, civic–minded proposals and propositions. There were two cunning edges to Richardson's campaigning. First, it would be easy to get large numbers of voters annoyed at a judge, but relatively difficult to excite equally large numbers to develop such devotion to jurists that they would take the trouble to come out and vote and then search out obscure ballot lines. Second, the prospect of such campaigning would almost certainly persuade some other judges that the road to professional survival might be paved not with good intentions but, rather, a protective regard for the interests and opinions of the Law and Order Campaign Committee and anything else connected with the computer fund-raising lists in Arcadia.

"We're not playing patty-cake," Richardson told me that day in his office. "We're talking about the ideological direction of the court, and we've got to grab peoples' attention with tough talk."

Tough talk is cheap. And courts will always be a target for it. Judges are always "soft" on something—Roosevelt thought they were soft on what he called "economic royalists," Richardson thought they were soft on criminals—because courts must operate within a different time-frame than the other two branches of U.S. government. In the jargon of electronics, American courts are always "out-of-sync" with the political process. Within a few months of my meeting with Richardson, I happened to be in the office of a justice of the United States Supreme Court, Potter Stewart. He pointed to the rows of bound volumes on shelves behind him, copies of every Supreme Court decision back to 1790. "They reflect," he said, "nothing more than what was on the mind of contemporary America. Those decisions are a reflection of American morality with a time lag."

The "time lag" sometimes means that court decisions will not be particularly popular at a given moment. But that lag, the inevitable delay between the time of complaint or conflict and the time of ad-judication and resolution, is at the very center of the workings of the American democratic system.

Democracy has to be slowed down. Men whose ideas were a little more profound than Richardson's, the men whose ideas got us this far, spent a lot of their time trying to figure out how to slow down the processes of democratic government. In the Federalist Papers, James Madison worried about protecting people against themselves, of safe-guarding the citizens of a democracy "against the tyranny of their own passions." The United States of America, as a government, was deliberately designed to be cumbersome. Checks and balances and laws piled upon and modified each other so that governing would not be done until the mob dispersed, until people went home.

Slowing down. Separation of powers. Time—time to consider and reconsider. All that has become more important as technologies, from television in Manhattan to computers in Arcadia, has tended to speed up the passions and actions of democratic government. So, the movements and the ideas Betty Medsger writes of here are critical to the continuing American experiments in self-government and self-discipline. It is ironic that the people and movements and ideas that Medsger examines in "Framed" are described as "conservative." In their passion, they are anything but conservative. The Americans who would make judges as "accountable" as politicians do not understand the American experience well enough to know what is truly worth conserving—it is not the whims of men but a working system of en-forced justice.

Richard Reeves
New York City, 1983

Introduction

California has been the scene of an ominous dress rehearsal. Since 1978 the New Right has been refining its plan to revolutionize the nation's courts by attacking the California courts. The national proponents of the plan include powerful figures in the Reagan administration who helped design and execute the California dress rehearsal.

A California state senator, financed in his election by State Senator H. L. Richardson, the leader of the movement against the California judiciary, was candid in 1981 about the attack on the California courts:

"This is an attack on the state courts, and tomorrow we will attack the federal courts."

This book is the story of the dress rehearsal. It is a story of treachery and tragedy. It is a warning of the techniques planned for the destruction of independent courts in the United States. Thanks to the movement's substantial financial backing, its ingenuity and radical revisionism, it has been able to undermine public belief in the honesty and legality of the courts. It has had a profound impact on the traditional independence and unparalleled past good reputation of the courts in California. It has plunged the court system into high-finance politics and, in some instances, coerced decision-making. Wittingly and unwittingly, most of the state's news media have been manipulated so as to create a picture of dishonesty and chaos in the largest court system in the world, a court system that for many years has been very highly regarded among respected legal scholars.

The goal of the enemies of the courts is to intimidate judges into making judicial decisions according to political pressure, to fear partisan money being used against them in elections. More important, they are trying to coerce courts into abandoning the traditional dictates of the Constitution, the law, and the evidence in individual cases. "Giving the courts back to the people," is the enticing slogan used by the executive director of the Law and Order Campaign Committee, the central organization in the California anti-court coalition. "Democratization of the courts" is the cynical slogan of Randall Rader, counsel for the Constitutional Subcommittee of the United States Senate Judiciary Committee. Along with Patrick McGuigan of the Judicial Reform Project of the Free Congress Foundation, a New Right–funded organization that is working to change federal courts, Rader has edited *Blueprint for Judicial Reform.*

If successful, this movement would bring about two basic changes. First, it would remove the judiciary from its historical and constitutionally required position as an equal third branch of government and make it subservient to the legislative and executive branches. This diminishing of status would be initiated by legislation removing certain issues from the jurisdiction of federal courts. The issues the reformers now want to remove are busing, school prayer, and abortion. Any ideologically motivated group could remove issues of its choice later. There were about three dozen bills in Congress in 1981 and 1982 advocating the removal of particular issues from the jurisdiction of federal courts.

The second basic change would be the destruction of a fundamental principle of American justice, namely, that the accused is innocent until proven guilty. The rhetoric of the new reformers publicly classifies judges according to their percentage of convictions, their obvious ideal being 100 percent. It is a clever political device, labeling judges "pro-defendant" or "pro-victim," but it attacks the responsibility of the court to treat each defendant as an individual whose case is to be tried on the merits of the evidence rather than on the basis of the public sympathy or public anger of the moment. It was precisely fear of such political pressure and emotion of the moment that led the founders of this country to create an independent judiciary. The present movement has not limited itself to public rhetoric and highly financed campaigns against individual judges. For five years anti-fair-trial observers have been sitting in California courtrooms with the admitted goal of intimidating judges, and through judges juries, into convicting and giving maximum sentences to defendants in criminal cases.

Another part of the plan to diminish the power of the judiciary is the phasing out of life appointments of federal judges and the requirement that all federal judges face voter approval periodically. The election of judges is not new in state courts. In many states, including California, trial judges are elected by the voters, usually after being appointed by governors. In some states even appellate judges may have opponents on the ballot. But the difference promoted now by the New Right is that the election of judges at all levels would become just another political race. In most states that have judicial elections, it is assumed that judges should be inspected by the voters for their fairness and integrity on the bench. The New Right would have judges become politicians who, like legislators and elected executives, must raise large amounts of money and run on platforms. They would be asked to promise what kind of rulings they would make in specific kinds of cases, especially criminal cases. In most states, that kind of electioneering by judicial candidates would require judges to disqualify themselves when such cases came before them. But, as envisioned by the New Right reformers, it would qualify rather than disqualify judges.

This movement would do nothing short of having the majority—or a vocal minority that claims to represent the majority or is capable of mobilizing the majority—rob the individual or a minority group of their rights. But the judiciary is supposed to be different from the other two branches of government. It is not supposed to be controlled by the opinion of the majority. Our country's founders wisely understood the necessity of having one branch of government that stood between the government and the governed, between the individual and the mob, between the minority and the majority. The judiciary is supposed to remove some issues from the reach of the majority. As Laurence Tribe, Professor of Constitutional Law at Harvard Law School, has said, "When people complain about this, they're really saying they don't agree with the decisions the [United States] Supreme Court has made. In fact, they're calling for a radical change in the kind of country we've had, with its independent judiciary protecting the rights of the minorities against the majority."

From the beginning, Americans have been somewhat ambivalent about an independent judiciary. The concept has been both enshrined and spat upon. This is not to suggest that judges are truly independent and isolated from the reach of the citizenry. They are not and should not be. But the reach of the citizenry should be limited, as it has been. Judges make rulings that are required of them by the law as it is written by the legislators, who are elected by the people. They interpret the law as set forth in the Constitution, which was adopted originally and amended later by the people. It is here, in this interpretation, that the independence of judges has been crucial. It is here that judges have sometimes made the difference between justice and mob rule, between justice and suppression of minority groups.

There is no doubt that without a strong and independent judiciary black people and other minority group Americans would not today be recognized as having equal rights under the law. It took a war to free the slaves. It took an independent judiciary to eliminate the legally required segregation that kept black Americans in an economic and educational caste not far removed from slavery nearly a century after the war that freed them. What the Bill of Rights guaranteed, elected governors and presidents ignored and delayed because of personal opinion or political expediency. Only the branch of government furthest removed from political expediency, the judiciary, had the courage to protect the minority from the majority.

Many Americans bristled in the 1950's after the U.S. Supreme Court outlawed forced segregation and required law-enforcement officers not to break the law in the course of their work. "Impeach Earl Warren" signs blossomed in many parts of the country throughout the 1950's and early 1960's. Chief Justice Warren became the symbol of the courts of his day. Rose Elizabeth Bird, the Chief Justice of the California Supreme Court, has become to the New Right what Warren was to the old right. The California dress rehearsal has focused on her.

Now the movement against the courts flourishes again, as it did in the 1950's, but more intensely and with more sweeping goals. In 1982 it figured prominently in political campaigns in both California and New York. Armed with New Right money and considerable public fear about a rising crime rate, the leaders of this movement use false information to manipulate a public that is largely uninformed— thanks to the news media—into thinking that making the judiciary "responsive" to public opinion is correct in a democracy. They have successfully hidden the fact that they are talking about a radical idea: the alteration of American society by making the judiciary subject to political expediency rather than to the Constitution.

FRAMED

CHAPTER 1

Chief Symbol Rose Bird

In 1982 Rose Elizabeth Bird, Chief Justice of the California Supreme Court, was a major issue in the California governor's race, the U.S. Senate race for Sam Hayakawa's seat, and the race for the office of State Attorney General. Since Bird was appointed in 1977, becoming the first woman ever to serve on the state's highest court, there have been repeated attempts to remove her, including five unsuccessful recall campaigns that never made it to the ballot stage. But, in late 1982, Howard Jarvis, one of the men who brought Californians the tax-slashing Proposition 13 that was much imitated in other states, threw his influence and money behind a campaign to have a special election in 1983 to recall Bird from the bench. Not enough signatures were gathered. If one of these recall campaigns ever gets to the ballot stage, it will be the first time in history Californians have been asked to vote on whether to recall a member of the Supreme Court, long considered one of the most respected appellate courts in the nation.

Who is this judge, this woman? How did she manage to become a more sensational election issue in 1982 than the highest unemployment rate in either the state or the country since World War II? How did she become more sensational in election rhetoric than a controversial statewide gun-control initiative?

Since 1977 Rose Bird has come to symbolize the liberal judge, living proof of the New Right's contention that judges are primarily the defenders of criminals, not of all citizens. In California, at least, Rose Bird has been made as strong a symbol of what's wrong with the courts as motherhood and apple pie are symbols of Americanism.

She is such a strong symbol that the Republican candidate for gov-

3

ernor in 1982, State Attorney General George Deukmejian, repeatedly told voters that one of the major faults of his opponent, Los
Angeles' Mayor Tom Bradley, was that Bradley was a "strong supporter" of Rose Bird. The Republican candidate for the U.S. Senate, San
Diego's Mayor Pete Wilson, not only repeatedly drew attention to the
fact that his opponent, Governor Edmund G. (Jerry) Brown Jr., had
appointed Bird Chief Justice, but also took the unprecedented elec-
tion-year step of announcing as part of his senate campaign that he
favored her recall from the court unless she voted to uphold a controversial anticrime measure then pending before the state's Supreme
Court. A prestigious statewide publication, *California Magazine,*
claimed that Brown's appointment of Bird to the court was such a
strong liability that it could cause his defeat. The article was accompanied by a sketch that showed Bird pushing Brown under water.

Recall is supposed to be an extreme act. It asks the voters to perform major political surgery on their own earlier decisions. Usually it
is used only when an official has engaged in serious wrongdoing. But,
in Bird's case, politicians seem to speak of this drastic political action
as easily as they might vote to thank the Senate chaplain for his pray-
ers. They say Bird should be recalled because they disagree with her
judicial opinions. Without blushing, they say they want to use recall in
order to replace her with a judge of their ideological persuasion.
They do not blush because they apparently feel assured that they
have succeeded in recent years in inducing public amnesia about the
fact that the United States and California constitutions both provide
for an independent judiciary. Those who are now attacking the courts
would eliminate this concept and practice and have their judges beholden to them. As this book will show, they learned this attitude at
Ronald Reagan's knee in 1973.

George Nicholson, the candidate whom high officials in the White
House supported for State Attorney General in the 1982 election,
distributed a letter during his campaign calling for Bird's recall. The
letter was remarkable in two ways. First, candidate Nicholson sent the
mass mailing in his capacity as a spokesperson for the Recall Rose
Bird Alliance, but he put it on a letterhead that reproduced the state
seal and listed his title in the Department of Justice, Senior Assistant
Attorney General. Obviously, Nicholson meant to make it appear that
Bird's recall was urged by him in his official capacity. That, of course,
would be highly improper, if not illegal.

In case his letterhead was not sufficiently misleading, this candidate
for top law enforcement official in the largest state in the nation went
further. He lied. He wrote in the letter that "the Bird Court has
decided that rape and forced sodomy constitute 'trivial and
insignificant' injury." The court never issued such a decision, and no

justice on the court has expressed such a view. But the Republican candidate for Attorney General was quite likely to be able to persuade the unsuspecting thousands who would receive his letter of the opposite. He went on to repeat a claim that others in the New Right have made repeatedly: "In case after case, Rose Bird's court has ruled in favor of the rights of criminals and against the rights of the victims of crime." This claim has been made so often by California politicians and so often reported without being checked by journalists, that by late 1982 it was generally assumed to be true. The truth is that more than 90 percent of all criminal convictions appealed to the State Supreme Court are upheld by that court.

Truth has been treated very casually by those who attack the courts. The philosophy that has permeated the campaign started against the California courts when Ronald Reagan was Governor is perhaps best exemplified by a comment made by gubernatorial candidate Deukmejian's 1982 campaign manager, Bill Roberts. In *Book of America* by Neal Pierce and Jerry Hagstrom, Roberts is quoted as saying, "I'm opposed to putting a lot of rules and restrictions on campaigning. I think I ought to have the right to lie to you if I think it will help me win. I think you have the right to detect my lie and vote 'no' when you go in the polling booth."

It was precisely that philosophy of lies and dirty tricks which permeated the campaign that started against Rose Bird in 1978. But the public has never learned that. It has been kept a secret, mainly because those whose job it is to uncover secrets, the journalists, were part of the deception.

Bird had been appointed and confirmed as Chief Justice in the spring of 1977. As is the practice in California, at the next statewide general election after a judge is appointed, the judge must face the voters for approval. Appellate judges are unopposed on the ballot and always win easily. Not one has ever lost. But in November 1978 Rose Bird won by only 1.7 percent, the lowest margin of victory of any appellate judge in the history of the state.

That election was very important. What began at the time of the 1978 campaign, when Bird was narrowly approved by the California voters, and continued through the 1982 election, when she was used as a weapon by every major Republican candidate in the state, was the significant evolution of Bird as symbol of "what's wrong with the courts." And the courts were portrayed during that time as what was wrong with society. They were perceived as the last bastion of liberals, particularly on the federal level. The attack against California courts at all levels, went the New Right reasoning, would provide a model that could be exported to other states and then used to combat the federal judiciary. If California could export Proposition 13, hot tubs, and Ronald Reagan to the rest of the country, then perhaps it could also nurture in the hothouse of its politics a plan to convince the country that an independent judiciary was a blight on the land.

There seemed to be support for such a plan, not only at the White House but also in Congress. In 1982 there were more than thirty bills pending in Congress that would remove certain controversial issues— abortion, school prayer, and busing among them—from the purview of the federal courts. These proposed laws were an astonishing intrusion by the legislature, one of the three co-equal branches of government, into another, the judiciary. The executive branch watched with approval from 1600 Pennsylvania Avenue as this mangling of the Constitution was proposed. Of this Congressional attempt to usurp judicial power, American Bar Association President David Brink said, "If we shut off our access to the courts, we shut off our constitutional rights. . . . If Congress can shut off these particular rights, a future Congress can shut off other constitutional rights." Such legislation, he said, is a "weapon by which our free government can be destroyed."

As a state senator who supported the attack on the California courts and saw its larger implications said in 1981: "This is an attack on the state courts, and tomorrow we will attack the federal courts."

As the head of the Law and Order Campaign Committee, the most powerful of the organizations that have been campaigning against the California courts, told me about the New Right emphasis on Bird: "We use her because it's easier to grasp a symbol. . . . She is no different than the men on the court. She is simply a convenient focus. She's a perfect symbol."

Though many people will be indirectly affected by the outcome of the New Right's attack on the courts, the future careers of two people in particular are intimately tied to this outcome. They are Chief Justice Bird and William P. Clark, the former California Supreme Court justice who is now National Security Adviser to the President.

Some of the architects of the plan to unseat Bird are now in the White House. If they and the President have their way, Bird will continue to be used as a symbol of what is wrong with the courts and, if they succeed in removing her, as a symbol of what a powerful threat this anti-court movement can be to judges who do not knuckle under to the demands of the New Right.

If the movement succeeds, Clark's destiny would, of course, be quite different from Bird's. Clark was appointed in 1973 by then Governor Reagan to the California Supreme Court. How he has functioned since then is important to this story because of his present power, his past power, and his expected future power. As a justice on the State Supreme Court in 1978 and 1979, Clark played a central role on behalf of the New Right political forces. His role then and earlier on the court has never been carefully examined.

William Clark is now one of the most powerful people in America, perhaps in the world, for he may be the only person besides Nancy Reagan who has the ear of the President. He is the closest aide of a president who Clark himself has said values loyalty more than competence. Clark's loyalty to the President has been richly rewarded. He arrived in Reagan's Sacramento administration with little political experience and perhaps even less knowledge of the law. But he has gone far. Astute observers of the Reagan administration in Washington speculate that the President wants to reward Clark with the highest position the President could give him: an appointment to the United States Supreme Court. In fact, there is speculation that the President will appoint Clark Chief Justice of the United States when Warren Burger retires. Given Clark's background and his activities on the California Supreme Court, it is an astonishing possibility.

Most of Clark's career has been spent in service to Ronald Reagan, first in Sacramento, then on the state courts, and now in Washington. In all these jobs, he was intellectually unprepared and unknowledgeable. But he is charming, shrewd, shy, and perhaps sly. He has combined these qualities to serve the Governor and now the President in essentially two capacities: as super–office manager, reducing the information and insights of others so Reagan can understand them, and as spy.

To put it mildly, William Clark has been very useful to Ronald Reagan. How well he served the Governor while he was on the court has not been known until now. How well he and others now in high positions in the White House have served the New Right in its attempts to subvert the judiciary also has not been known before. Clark is a combination of contrasting images. Were his opinions concise because he easily and brilliantly got to the point? Or were they concise because he was incompetent and didn't know what to write? Or, were they concise because he only cared about expressing his own angry views and those of Reagan?

There are also conflicting descriptions of the other judge whose destiny is tied to the attack on the courts. Rose Bird is viewed by admirers as courageous, pleasant, brilliant, thorough, and kind. Detractors label her vindictive, stubborn, aggressive, abrasive. For those New Righters who were looking for a symbol for their attack on the courts, the appointment of Rose Bird as Chief Justice of the California Supreme Court must have seemed like a dream come true. She already had an impressive list of enemies among the state's agricultural interests, which are of considerable importance to the state's law-and-order movement. In Brown's first cabinet, she had been

Secretary of Agriculture and Services, then the largest agency in the state government. Soon after taking office she was responsible for prohibiting the use of the short hoe, a humane reform that agricultural interests and the Reagan administration had successfully blocked for the previous eight years despite considerable medical evidence that using this tool, because it requires a perpetually bent back, is lethal to farm workers. Bird was also a key architect of the Agriculture Labor Relations Act, legislation that probably will be called Brown's most significant accomplishment in his eight years as Governor. This guaranteed farm workers the right to organize and negotiate labor contracts. It also guaranteed Bird the permanent enmity of agribusiness, probably the most powerful lobby in California.

Her nomination to the Supreme Court by Brown won her immediate opposition from agribusiness interests. Many others too were amazed that someone without any judicial experience could be appointed to the state's highest court, let alone the highest position on that court.

At age 40 she was young, as judges and popes go. She was an aggressive administrator, the cabinet member in the Brown administration responsible for the largest portion of the state budget, twelve departments. Nearly her entire career before working in the Brown administration had been spent working as a public defender. She was a liberal. She had never been a judge. All these things increased her value as a symbol and, eventually, as a scapegoat. So did the fact that she was a woman, the first woman ever on the high court. She was no more, no less liberal than some of the other liberals on the court. The Law and Order Campaign Committee admitted that she was simply a much more effective symbol than any of the men. Bird was the object of selective harassment. Male judges are often best described as gray. They resemble each other in appearance. They do not stand out in this world of powerful video images. They are not the stuff of which feature magazine articles are written. A far cry indeed from this tall, reddish-brown-haired woman who likes to wear bright blouses with her suits and robes. A woman, moreover, who speaks her mind quite clearly, even when she knows it might be used against her. From the standpoint of an advertising campaign—which is what the attack against the courts was, albeit without the truth-in-advertising requirement—here was a perfect target, particularly since she was required, as a judge, not to explain her judicial opinions other than in their written form.

In fairness, it was not only the New Right that saw Bird as a symbol. In her first three years as Chief Justice, she was also a strong symbol to many of the judges in the system she now administers. When Jerry Brown became Governor in 1975, he gave judges the distinct impression he did not like them. During his first years in office he gave speeches throughout the state saying judges were lazy and didn't deserve a raise. Worst of all, after he became Governor, when the first 70 vacancies occurred on the bench because of death and retirement, Brown refused to fill them. Many months passed. He said he wouldn't fill the vacancies until the judiciary reformed itself. Brown never said what he meant by "reform," nor did anyone on his staff. It was an unreasonable and contemptuous attitude. Neither he nor anyone else offered evidence to justify his criticism and much harm would come from it. His failure to fill vacancies helped paralyze the movement of cases through the state's most crowded courts in Los Angeles. In 1981, he would wait many months to fill two vacancies on the seven-member Supreme Court, also causing the flow of cases there to slow down.

Because Bird had been in Brown's cabinet, perhaps its most visible member, she was seen as his close ally, as someone who probably shared his taunting approach to the judiciary. Consequently, some of the judges who had been the butt of Brown's thoughtlessness saw her, as she later put it, as the "worst joke yet" that Jerry Brown had pulled on the judiciary. What they didn't know was that she shared none of Brown's flippant attitudes toward the judges who were on the bench before Brown became Governor.

"I didn't agree with his attack on the judiciary," she told me. "I had come out of Santa Clara County, where judges worked very hard, long and hard. . . . I didn't agree with that [his attack] and I basically always believed that an attack on the judiciary ends up as an attack on the Constitution and the Bill of Rights. . . . But I was not consulted by the Governor, and it was not my field in Sacramento." But when he appointed her to the court, she said, "I became a symbol of a governor whom the judiciary felt was an enemy. . . . I became a symbol of being thrust down their throats [by him]. I was the ultimate insult to the entire judiciary." The judges, said Bird, felt that by "putting someone like me into a position like that you demean them because 'If she's the head, what am I?' "

But the strongest animus expressed toward Bird from inside the judiciary came from those judges who wanted to be Chief Justice. Their feelings were not known to her until after the fight over her confirmation. The strength of the animus of one of them became startlingly obvious after the 1978 election. Bird won't say what it was that Supreme Court Justice Stanley Mosk said to her on her first day at the court, but the story is widespread, largely because Mosk himself has said essentially the same thing many times in private. The most charitable version I have heard of what he said to her that first day is that it was a harsh variant of what each of the three bears said: "Somebody's sitting in *my* chair." But this Goldilocks at the court, unlike the one in the children's story, did not run away. She did, however, discover that there were several bears in the woods, mostly Brown bears, judges who had been appointed to the Superior Courts or the Courts of Appeal years earlier by Governor Edmund G. (Pat) Brown Sr., Jerry's father, and who were confident now that Brown the son would give friends of Brown the father nice promotions when he became Governor. More than one had expected not only to be elevated but to become Chief Justice. One of these judges pounded Jerry Brown's desk furiously, cursing the Governor for not appointing him Chief Justice.

Some people were disturbed by Brown's commitment to appoint women and minorities to the bench. Though white men make up the majority of Brown's appointments, he did appoint more women and minorities than any previous governor, perhaps in any state. They made up a minuscule portion of the judiciary when he came to office in 1975. By the time Brown left office, 17 percent of his appointments to the California judiciary were women and 27 percent of his appointments were minority group members.

At the same time Brown appointed Bird to the court, he appointed Wiley Manuel, a black man whose entire career had been spent in the Attorney General's office until Brown appointed him to the Alameda County Superior Court a year earlier. Until Manuel and Bird were appointed, neither a woman nor a minority group member from any race had ever sat on the Supreme Court. After Manuel died in 1981, Brown appointed another black to the court and later appointed the first Hispanic. There were a lot of comments at judges' and lawyers' meetings about the fact that this governor couldn't be expected to appoint anyone if they weren't from "the three B's"—blacks, browns, and broads. Which led one person to suggest that he should have a fourth "B"—bigots. The fact is that Brown's appointments have started to integrate the judicial system. By and large he has found qualified people, no matter what their sex or race.

The loss of the Chief Justice's chair to Bird probably angered the old boys' network more than any appointment, judicial or otherwise, that Brown made as Governor. It is unclear why he chose Rose Bird as Chief Justice, the most coveted place on the bench. There were a number of women in California whom Brown could have chosen for the high court. Several had been on law school faculties for years. One, Shirley Hufstedler, had been appointed to the federal court by Lyndon Johnson and was appointed the first Secretary of Education by Jimmy Carter. It was widely assumed that she would become the first woman on the U.S. Supreme Court, and she probably would have, had Carter had an opportunity to make an appointment to the high court.

There were several women trial court judges in California. Instead of choosing any of these, Brown chose Rose Bird, a woman who had never sat on the bench. Even some admirers of Bird say the Governor did her no favor, that he should have made her an associate justice with an eye toward elevating her to Chief Justice a few years later, upon the death or retirement of one of the other justices. An argument against that alternative is that when Brown appointed her in 1977 it was not clear that he would win re-election in 1978 and, assuming he thought it was important that she become Chief Justice, he needed to seize the opportunity when it existed in 1977.

There was an indignant outcry when her appointment was announced. Most of it came from conservatives who had not liked her agricultural policies. Some people didn't like her sex. And some people didn't like her age, because they thought the appointment belonged, if not to them, then at least to their generation.

Wrote one Superior Court judge to the three members of the Commission on Judicial Appointments that would vote whether to confirm the Governor's appointment of Bird: "I have been on the bench in California for over 15 years, having been initially appointed by former Governor Pat Brown. I've always been proud of the California judicial system. I hope we will have a new Chief Justice that I can be proud of. I hope you will vote against the confirmation of Ms. Bird."

Another judge wrote a public letter to the commissioners that claimed the Santa Clara public defender's office once considered firing Bird for improper activity on the job. No such thing had ever happened or even been considered. A phone call from the judge to her former employer, the public defender, would have clarified the matter. But that careless accusation was a forerunner of what was to come—the handing of false charges to the press with the hope that they would generate the kind of negative publicity that would destroy Bird's credibility. A prime ingredient in much of the attack against Bird and the courts in general has been the use of discredited information to discredit. The irony was often missed.

The letter to the Commission that got the most attention was one from Roger Mahoney, a Catholic bishop from Fresno and a former member of the state Agriculture Labor Relations Board (ALRB). His letter to the Commission questioned Bird's "emotional stability" and called her "vindictive." His letter became the centerpiece of the early attack on her. If Bird had exhibited those qualities, the Bishop, some thought, was courageous to write the letter. He had asked that it remain private, but letters to the Commission may not remain private, a fact he must have known. His perception of Bird was not shared by his colleagues at the board. All past and present members of the ALRB, plus past and present general counsels of the board, all of whom had worked with both Bird and the Bishop, jointly announced immediately after his letter that they strongly disagreed with Mahoney.

Mahoney and Bird had often disagreed over her view that he was careless with the board's budget, which was always in danger of being reduced by the legislature. Some members of the legislature had an intense desire to abort this labor board they had reluctantly helped conceive. But even the Republican Attorney General, Evelle Younger, a member of the Commission on Judicial Appointments who was looking for a solid reason to vote against Bird, would tell me four years later, "I couldn't take the letter [from Mahoney] that seriously. I learned that the problems between them were more his fault than hers." Though the Bishop's letter did not prevent Bird's appointment to the court, his claims that she was emotionally unstable and vindictive would be resurrected by others little more than a year later when she had to face the voters in 1978.

Some felt that Rose Bird's appointment was to Jerry Brown what William Clark's appointment had been to Reagan: an affront to both the judiciary and the public. One law school professor compared them and noted that both had become successful as a result of education rather than old family connections. It was true that neither of them came from elite backgrounds—Clark's family was in farming and law enforcement, and Bird's mother was a factory worker. But it was not true that both judges made their way to the bench on the basis of educational achievement. Whereas Clark flunked out of both college and law school, Bird graduated from both with distinction: *magna cum laude* and "most outstanding senior" at Long Island University in 1958, and honors prizes for best oral advocacy and brief writing at Boalt Hall School of Law at the University of California at Berkeley in 1965. Neither had graduated from the twin schools of elitism often cited as "good background" in California, Stanford (the best of the West) and Harvard (the best of the East). But their educational experiences were vastly different. About the only similarity was that both had worked their way through school.

When they arrived in Sacramento to work for their respective governors, both Bird and Clark had been in law practice for eight years. But their experience had been quite different. Clark had a small practice that required routine work and few appearances in court. During her first five and one-half years as a public defender, Bird handled an average of five hundred cases a year. They included felonies, misdemeanors, juvenile, mental illness, and appellate cases.

During those years she made 8,207 separate court appearances. Later she created the Public Defender's Appellate and Motions Division and handled over 600 motions and appeals.

The dean of the law school that Clark attended asked him to leave, to try another line of work. W. James Hill, the associate dean at Bird's law school, recommended her for her first job by saying, "I cannot speak too highly of her. . . . She was the best who had been through Boalt Hall in a long time."

When some critics complained in 1977 that Bird should not be appointed to the high court because she had no previous judicial experience, her supporters were quick to point out that some eminent jurists on both the California Supreme Court and the U.S. Supreme Court were not judges before being appointed to those illustrious benches. For instance, six of the fifteen chief justices of the U.S. Supreme Court never had judicial experience before their appointments. One justice who achieved considerable respect for his work was Potter Stewart. President Eisenhower lifted him from the Cincinnati City Council rather than from a judicial bench when he appointed him to the U.S. Court of Appeal in 1953 and, two years later, to the U.S. Supreme Court. One letter to the Commission spoke strongly on the subject: "California Republicans did not squawk about the appointment of a fellow California Republican with no prior judicial experience as chief justice of the United States Supreme Court— Earl Warren. I say that genitalia structure as well as taint by Democratic affiliation are the true covert reasons for Republican rejection. In order that the humane philosophy of Earl Warren be perpetuated, I recommend Rose Bird be confirmed by you."

Some of the women who were considered likely choices instead of Bird wrote to the Commission in her defense. Their letters were a sharp contrast to the letters and private comments of some of the men who had hoped to get the job. Dorothy Nelson, then dean of the law school at the University of Southern California and later appointed a federal judge by President Carter, wrote Bird at the time of her appointment: "I can't tell you how delighted I am that you have been selected by Governor Brown to serve as our next Chief Justice. This is truly an historic event made even more important by your obvious qualification for the position."

When she graduated from law school in 1965, Bird applied at the public defender's office in Sacramento. The man who interviewed her said he would not hire a woman. He said he had never seen a good trial attorney who was a woman, ". . . except one . . . and she ended up a terrible alcoholic." Bird smiles her ironic smile as she tells the story. She applied next to the Santa Clara County public defender's office and found a non-sexist public defender, Donald Chapman. She became that office's first woman attorney. When Chapman asked the staff of ten attorneys how they felt about having a woman on the staff only two voted in favor. Bird now laughs about the men's attitudes, but her laughter has a tinge of sadness. "They thought a woman would be a killjoy. They were afraid they wouldn't be able to continue their Friday afternoon get-togethers. Whoever won a case during the week would buy a bottle and they'd sit around and tell their war stories. They thought if a woman was present they couldn't swear." She won cases and she bought bottles for the Friday afternoon gatherings.

Bird's lifelong tenacity was shaped in part by a mother who saw education as a means of guaranteeing never having to do menial work and never having to be dependent on anyone. The three Bird children—Bird has two brothers—were taught to train their minds. Special advice was given to the daughter, who Mrs. Bird knew would be treated differently than her two sons. The Chief Justice recalls that her mother told her as an adolescent "to get a good background in everything and to not listen to the advisors in high school who would say, 'Don't take advanced math because you're not going to be an engineer. . . .'

"I knew that because I had no money that if I were going to go to school I had to make my own way and I had to rely on scholarships. I'd lost my father when I was young, and I saw my mother, a very intelligent woman, have to work in a factory and slowly destroy her health. It was brought home to me very early that you are dependent on yourself, not on anyone else. She would say, 'You're not going to have somebody who's going to take care of you. The most important thing for you to do is to find work that you enjoy and not be stuck having to do manual labor.'"

It's unlikely that Ann Bird, who lives with her daughter in a small home in Palo Alto, ever thought that an alternative to being a factory worker would be being Chief Justice of the California Supreme Court. But her early lessons and example undoubtedly helped shape the mind and talent that eventually led Jerry Brown to tap her daughter for this prestigious job.

When Rose Bird went to law school, professors tried to discourage her from becoming a trial attorney. It was difficult, if not impossible, for women to get those jobs, they said. She was not deterred. By then Bird knew what she wanted to do. After graduating from college she had worked briefly as a secretary and then come to California to study political science in the graduate school at Berkeley. A year later she was one of ten students who won Ford Foundation scholarships to be interns for a year in the California legislature. Until then she had wanted to be a journalist. Her work in Sacramento focused her interest on law. While working on the staff of Assemblyman Gordon H. Winton, she wrote a report that led to Winton's bill establishing statewide testing of elementary and secondary students.

In part, Bird entered public defender work because the door was open there when it was closed elsewhere to women lawyers. "It was almost impossible for a woman, even in 1965, to find a law firm that would allow you to be a litigator in the civil field," said Bird. "If you wanted to be a litigator, the only opportunity was in the criminal field." Fortunately, she also had a natural interest in the work. "I felt comfortable defending indigent people accused of criminal offenses. I felt it was important that they got good representation."

She anticipated that they might try to create a "woman's" niche for her at the public defender's office, so she immediately told them she didn't want to be put in juvenile work. "I knew that in some places where there were women public defenders they put them in juvenile court. Why? Because they were considered good social workers or good with children, and that's where they belonged. I didn't want that." She eventually did juvenile work, but she did every kind of work that was available in the office. By successfully asserting herself at the beginning, she avoided the stereotype of the woman lawyer.

This quality—it is called stubbornness, commitment, inflexibility, depending on how the speaker feels about Bird—has been a pattern throughout her career. She brought it to her work as a lawyer, as a state administrator, as a judge. She is not one to settle in and passively accept existing standards and habits. She evaluated each new situation she entered, took the long view of where the course was leading, and, if she didn't think the course served the public well, she cut a new path. She did not change for change's sake, but usually because she thought it would increase the effectiveness of whatever institution she was in.

As the day for the vote on Bird by the Commission on Judicial Appointments approached in 1977, it became clear that her appointment as Chief Justice had generated more public response than any in the history of the court. Some of the letter writers agreed with the late Oliver Wendell Holmes, who claimed that women shouldn't even be jurors, let alone judges. Women's service on juries, the eminent jurist had said, would lead to two things: first, they would take up the smoking of cigars; secondly, because women were so weak, they would acquit criminal defendants. The modern-day version of Holmes's opinion came in a letter from Daniel M. Arteaza of Richmond, California: "As a woman she has the natural sensitiveness, tipical [sic] of her sex. She lacks the maturity needed to sit in judgement in a court where critical cases at every level of criminal and civil jurisdiction are to be decided. There is no reason for senamentalism [sic] in the courts."

Some letters had a desperate quality. "Don't do it, Mr. Younger. Please don't do it! If you do, the average guy like myself is going to lose again and the crooks are going to win again. . . . You should at least be listening to the voices of those to whom you claim a strong bond, the men and women of law enforcement."

In February, as the hearing date grew closer, the sharp comments of Bishop Mahoney—that Bird was vindictive and emotionally un-stable—hung over the upcoming hearings like a winter cloud. They were accusations that had to be taken seriously. An impressive num-ber of letters claimed the opposite of what the Bishop claimed. One was particularly interesting because it came from a Catholic priest who claimed Bishop Mahoney had expressed quite different views to him. This unsolicited letter was sent before Mahoney's. "I have fond memories of a rather lengthy meeting we had a year ago in Governor Brown's office with reference to the farm labor problems," wrote Monsignor George Higgins, a Washington, D. C., official of the United States Catholic Conference, in a letter congratulating Bird on her appointment. Higgins had worked for decades on labor issues. He concluded his letter of congratulations on the appointment by saying, "I have also heard our mutual friend Bishop Mahoney speak of you in the highest terms on more than one occasion."

Because it was her administrative skills that Mahoney had attacked, saying she was emotionally incapable of being a good administrator, the letters sent to the Commission by long-time Sacramento adminis-trators who had worked under Bird and several earlier bosses were important.

"During the past two years I have enjoyed a close working relation-ship with Ms. Bird in my capacity as Director of the Department of Industrial Relations," wrote Donald Vial. "These have been two of the most productive and satisfying years in my working life primarily because of the leadership qualities and administrative skills of Ms. Bird . . . a brilliant individual whose sense of purpose and per-sonal integrity extract the highest level of performance from those who are associated with her. . . . These qualities are buttressed by her sheer competence—her ability to cut through complex issues, then make tough decisions—and balanced by her compassion for human beings. . . . [She has a] commitment to make government truly acccess-ible to all people. . . . In these and other respects, Ms. Bird is the antithesis of the arrogant administrator 'who knows it all,' and it is beyond my comprehension how anyone who knows her can even repeat such an outlandish charge."

Here's a letter that must have made Younger think his hopes of finding clear evidence that the nominee was an incompetent administrator were dashed: "I am a Reagan appointee, I am from industry, and I am conservative in my political views," wrote A. W. Turner, Chairman of the Occupational Safety and Health Standards Board. "I have had the opportunity to observe Rose Bird as an administrator, as a problem solver, and as a person. In my mind, she is superb in all these categories. Although we supposedly occupied opposite ends of the political spectrum, I have never observed Ms. Bird demonstrate the slightest anti-industry or any other bias. It is for this reason, and because of the high esteem in which I hold her as a person, that I unhesitantly support Ms. Bird for Chief Justice of the California Supreme Court."

Until the last moment, it was unclear what the vote of the Commission on Judicial Appointments would be on Bird's nomination. The three-member panel that would vote included Younger, the Attorney General; Justice Mathew O. Tobriner, the senior justice on the court, Acting Chief Justice and, as such, the Chairman of the Commission; and Parker Wood, the senior justice on the Court of Appeal. It was assumed that Tobriner would vote for Bird's appointment, though early in the selection process he had urged the Governor, as outgoing Chief Justice Donald Wright had, to appoint Stanley Mosk to be the next Chief Justice. But in the end, Tobriner voted for Bird.

Justice Wood was expected to vote against Bird. But a couple days before the voting, he sent an emissary, another Court of Appeal justice, to tell Bird that if she would have a Protestant minister testify before the Commission that she was a "fine Christian" and attended church every Sunday, he might vote for her. She thought this highly improper and refused to do it. Justice Wood voted against her.

That meant her confirmation rested with the third member of the panel, Evelle Younger. At the time of the confirmation hearings in the spring of 1977, Younger already was hoping to become the Republican opponent of Brown the next year in the gubernatorial race. All attention at the confirmation hearings was on Younger, the conflicted commissioner, and on Bird, the first woman nominated to the court. Previous judicial confirmation hearings had been perfunctory events held in small rooms with perfunctory statements made about the sterling character of the person whose confirmation was a foregone conclusion. The appointees usually were not even present. Bird's confirmation had generated so much attention that it was held in the court's large hearing room in San Francisco and was televised live. Fervent speeches were made for and against her, just as hundreds of fervent letters had poured into the Commission before the hearing.

Midway through the second day of testimony, Younger announced that he had heard enough and was ready to vote. He voted yes, he would confirm her. But Younger immediately lamented publicly that the Commission, as he interpreted its mandate, must approve a nominee even if she were "merely qualified" rather than the "best qualified" person for the job. Perhaps that lamentation accompanying his yes vote was the first sign of what would happen the next year: after voting for Bird's confirmation as Chief Justice in 1977, Younger would make her one of his campaign issues in 1978 when he ran for governor against Brown.

A letter to the Commission from an official of the Educational Employment Relations Board made this observation about Bird: "I have been impressed and even startled by her acumen both in administrative efficiency and legal versatility. She possesses a unique combination of compassion and, for lack of a better word, toughness."

She needed that toughness soon after she moved into her chambers at the Supreme Court's headquarters in San Francisco. In just one year, some members of the Supreme Court staff would claim that Bird was destroying morale at the court, even destroying the court itself. By 7 November 1978, the date Bird's name appeared on the ballot, some members of the court staff were hoping that she would lose the election. Some felt so strongly about it that they walked their precincts and asked people to vote against her. Some of them, it would become clear later, took even more drastic steps in their efforts to defeat her.

On election day morning, not only Bird, but also the much-respected senior justice of the court, Justice Tobriner, came under fire. Tobriner was accused in the press that day of unethical behavior on behalf of Bird's election. Defenders of Bird and Tobriner would claim that the accusations were a political dirty trick. But the voters of California were forced to ask themselves: Had one or more California Supreme Court justices become a judicial crook?

Given the nature of the accusations, the question needed to be asked. It also should have been asked several years earlier, for the seeds of the movement that had its most dramatic success on the morning of election day 1978 were sown during Ronald Reagan's years as Governor of California. They were sown after Reagan discovered that Donald Wright, his appointee as Chief Justice of the State Supreme Court, had written a majority opinion saying the state's death penalty was unconstitutional. Reagan mistook Wright's integrity for disloyalty.

CHAPTER 2

After Governor Reagan Gave Up Merit Selection of Judges, He Appointed William Clark

When Ronald Reagan became Governor, he appointed judges on the basis of merit. His first legal affairs secretary, Paul Haerle, was committed to the idea that brilliance and fairness, rather than mere ideology or personal loyalty, were the prerequisites for judges. Such a policy led to the elevation of Donald Wright in 1970 from Superior Court to Court of Appeal to Chief Justice of the California Supreme Court. Wright was Reagan's first appointment to the high court. He was a widely respected chief justice.

But Reagan became mighty disappointed with Wright, just as President Eisenhower had been profoundly disappointed with his choice of Earl Warren as Chief Justice of the United States Supreme Court. Reagan had assumed Wright would be "his man" at the court. Wright reveals now for the first time that Reagan met with him once, in the presence of Edwin Meese and Herbert Ellingwood—then aides to Governor Reagan and now high officials at the Reagan White House—to try to influence the Chief Justice on a case then before the Supreme Court. On numerous other occasions, Wright told me, officials from the Governor's office spoke with Wright about cases before the court, passing along the Governor's advice. Wright said he was always deeply irritated at such improper attempts to influence him. In 1972 Wright wrote the majority opinion when the Supreme Court ruled that the state's death penalty law was unconstitutional.

Reagan was so angry he attacked the Chief Justice's opinion publicly. He said he was "deeply shocked" at Wright's court opinion and told reporters the opinion was "one more step toward totally disarming society in its fight against violence . . ." Shortly before leaving office, Reagan begged Wright to retire so he could replace him before Brown was inaugurated. Wright refused.

But in 1973, Reagan found just the man he needed for the Supreme Court: William P. Clark, the strongest influence on Reagan from the first year of his governorship. As a member of the Commission on Judicial Appointments at the time Reagan nominated Clark to the California Supreme Court, Wright voted against Clark.

On 2 January 1973, California Supreme Court Justice Raymond Peters died. A member of the Supreme Court since 1959, he was deeply respected and admired by his fellow justices. They went to his funeral on a Saturday. The next day they flew to Los Angeles for the court's monthly public hearings. They were surprised to discover in the Monday morning newspaper that Governor Reagan had already nominated Peters' replacement, William P. Clark.

Wright remembers that his immediate response when he read of the appointment was to welcome the new nominee. Wright told me he thought that day of what had happened to him on the day he was nominated Chief Justice by Reagan. The Supreme Court had been on circuit in Los Angeles then in the same courthouse where he sat as a Court of Appeal justice. "Only one [Supreme Court] justice, Justice Louis H. Burke, came in to see me. The other six justices just walked right past my door. I thought that was strange. So when we were in Los Angeles and Clark's appointment was announced, I laughed and told the other justices, 'You wait right here. We're not going to do to him what you guys did to me.'

"I went to Clark's office and brought him up to meet the court. He shook hands all around. It was very friendly. Justice Tobriner was the first person to speak up. He said to Clark, 'It's so good to have another Stanford man on the court,' and then Justice Burke smiled and said, 'Well, I'm glad to have another Loyola Law School graduate on the court.'" Within a few days they would look back on their innocent schoolboy remarks with a wince. They had read of his school background in that morning's paper. "Everyone was cordial," recalls Wright. "I invited him back into my chambers. When we were alone, I told him I would do what I could to get an early confirmation hearing, that we needed a full court to work well.

"While the court was still south, the Santa Monica newspaper ran a story . . . that indicated Justice Clark was not a graduate of Stanford, had only gone two years. It said his departure was brought about by scholastic deficiencies and he flunked out of Loyola Law School. I began to wonder. I could not blame him for not speaking up in front of all the justices, but I felt that when he and I had our private talk, he should've said something. When the announcement came from the Governor's office, it had indicated he was a graduate of both schools."

Wright was concerned. As chairman of the three-member Commission on Judicial Appointments, he would be voting on this nominee. In an unprecedented action, he asked the State Bar's Board of Governors to prepare a detailed report on Clark's background. Reagan was furious and denounced Wright publicly. (Such reports by the bar on nominees are now required.)

Four years earlier, when Clark was appointed by the Governor to be a Superior Court judge in San Luis Obispo, he had become the most visible exemplification of the Governor's changed policy on judicial appointments. Early in his first administration, Reagan had asked the legislature to approve a merit system for choosing judges. When the legislature refused to approve it, saying it would simply substitute bar politics for the politics of the Governor, Reagan said that he would maintain a merit system of selecting judges on his own. Wright says that this attitude originated primarily from Paul Haerle, the Governor's first legal affairs secretary (a post designed to help the California governor select judicial appointees). "Paul told me he hated his job selecting judges," Wright told me, "because he would rather be in 'good fighting politics.'" But Haerle felt there was no place for that in selecting judges. He looked for people who were highly qualified as lawyers and judges, not people who were qualified only by ideology. But that all changed, said Wright, when Herbert Ellingwood and Edwin Meese took over. Ellingwood was the Governor's legal affairs secretary during his last six years in office and Meese was his chief of staff, having succeeded Clark when Clark became a judge. "Herb saw that Reagan put no one in but hard-nosed, dyed-in-the-wool Republicans, law-and-order Republicans," Wright told me.

Reagan was at least as partisan as all governors in appointing judges. In his first 25 months in office, 85 percent of the judges he appointed were Republicans. But most of them were Republicans who were respected for their competence and evenhandedness. Only later, said Wright and other close observers, did the litmus test become whether a prospective judge was a strict law-and-order believer. Indicative of this change was the plucking of Clark, a man with very limited legal experience, from a position as Reagan's chief of staff, and his appointment in 1969 as a Superior Court judge. Reagan moved him through the chairs quickly, to the Court of Appeal in 1971 and thence to the Supreme Court in 1973.

When the State Bar report on Clark was completed for Wright, it confirmed Clark's embarrassing academic record. But it also confirmed that Clark had perhaps never lied on any records about his background. In some instances, at the Governor's office for example, he had apparently permitted mistakes to be made but did not make them himself. On his State Bar application card, which he filled out after passing the State Bar examination on the second try, instead of writing "none" he crossed out "graduate of" and listed the two schools where he had flunked. He never graduated from any law school.

As it turned out, the "education" that mattered most in Clark's life was described best in a satirical column written by Herb Michelson in the *Sacramento Bee* during the 1979 investigation of the California Supreme Court. Describing each of the major figures in the investigation, Michelson wrote: "William Clark also is an associate justice who thought that maybe if Brown had gone ahead with naming Tobriner as Chief Justice and Rose as only associate justice then when Evelle Younger became governor and Tobriner retired, the chief justiceship would go to William Clark, who attended the Ronald Reagan School of Law." This bit of satire would seem even more interesting a year later when presidential candidate Reagan announced that he was considering appointing some non-lawyers to the Supreme Court. So far as we knew, Reagan, unlike Michelson, was not speaking satirically.

Many letters were written to the Commission when Clark was nominated. Some were from Clark supporters. They said they had appeared before his bench and found him a fair and honest judge and thought the fuss about his academic background was unfair. One writer reminded the Commission of the words of former U.S. Senator Roman Hruska who, arguing a short time earlier in defense of the Nixon nomination of G. Harrold Carswell to the U.S. Supreme Court, had said that the Carswell appointment should be approved because he was mediocre and mediocre people had not yet been represented on the high court. The writer asked that mediocrity not now be an accepted criterion for the California Supreme Court. Another letter urged the Commission to note Clark's former association with people in the John Birch Society. This writer was referring to the last paragraph of an Associated Press story printed shortly after Reagan announced his appointment. Clark was quoted as saying he had never been a member of the John Birch Society but had clients who were. Clark told the reporter he "agreed with some of the group's concepts" in the early 1960's. Urging the Commission to vote against Clark, the letter writer went on, "I would feel the same way about a person sympathetic to the KKK, the American Nazi Party, the Communist Party or any other fringe organization." This was written by a refugee from a Nazi concentration camp.

A letter writer from Morro Bay, a small coastal town just north of

San Luis Obispo, said he thought a speech by Clark before the village's Rotary Club in 1969 demonstrated that he was capable of "unjudicial and unethical" behavior. The judge had been asked to talk about campus unrest. His speech, said the writer, was "almost inflammatory. . . . He charged that students were being funded by foreign countries to carry on . . . treasonous activities." The writer said Clark was publicly asked what countries were supplying funds to fuel American protest. "He replied that because an investigation of the matter was still in progress, he couldn't reveal anything. To this day I haven't heard a sliver of verification of that charge," the Rotarian wrote in 1973. "I was appalled that a person who had conducted himself in such an unrestrained, unjudicial fashion was sitting on the bench of the 'Hall of Justice.'" Such extreme remarks were not unusual during that period. But most of the people who made them were not judges. And surely none of them might have been expected someday to become Deputy Secretary of State, let alone National Security Adviser.

While some people thought it was outrageous to appoint a person to the Supreme Court who had not graduated from either college or law school, others objected only to the possibility that Clark had lied or purposely misled the public about his educational background. These people made the laudable argument that it is possible, for a variety of reasons, for a bright person to do poorly in school and later, on his own, become an educated and competent lawyer.

Donald Wright prefers that justices of the Supreme Court have fine academic records, but he says he would have been quite willing to accept a self-made excellent nominee without the usual degrees. But Wright did not believe Clark was such a nominee. If Clark had been misleading about his background, as the Chief Justice feared, he thought that this raised serious questions about Clark's integrity. While he thought one could serve on the Supreme Court without formal educational credentials, he did not think a person should serve on the Supreme Court if his integrity was in question. Later, Wright would have questions about the appointee's competence as well as his integrity.

In 1970, Clark distributed an apparently misleading campaign brochure when he ran for the Superior Court judgeship Reagan had appointed him to the previous year. In it Clark put facts about his past in the form of questions: "Has family background in law enforcement and agriculture?" "Earned his way through college and law school?" "Has presided at more than 60 trials?" The question mark after the one about school seemed significant and perhaps provided the rationale for the entire question-mark format. Under the circumstances, it seemed likely the question mark was purposeful, clever, and misleading. The information seemed designed to create a specific impression: that Clark had graduated from college and law school. And the question mark seemed to be part of a design to leave Clark technically not a liar.

When Wright received the report from the State Bar's Board of Governors, it said Clark was not considered a "leading lawyer," perhaps not even a good one, in the small community of Oxnard, north of Los Angeles. His only years of law practice had been eight years in Oxnard before he went to Sacramento to work for Reagan after running the Governor's Ventura County campaign. He had specialized in real estate and other business law. He seldom went into court. He wrote contracts, leases and wills. Some lawyers who examined his work told the State Bar Board of Governors that the documents prepared by Clark were "short and concise, but often too short and too superficial to handle the problems that the transactions contemplated." He did not have an adequate degree of intellectual depth, these colleagues said.

There was a similar analysis of Clark's work on the state Court of Appeal. While some praised his capacity for brevity, others said his brevity actually pointed to his incapacity as a judge. They said the few opinions he published were superficial, failed to treat the important issues in the cases, were not supported by adequate or competent legal authority, or overlooked applicable authority. Significantly, some people said his opinions showed a "lack of understanding of fundamental judicial process."

The Bar Board concluded that it found nothing that would "disqualify" Clark from being appointed to the Supreme Court. The lack of education was not an automatic disqualifier. There was no clear evidence that he had lied. He had passed the bar examination on the second try and had been a lawyer the requisite number of years. But the report from the Board also said a summary of the views of Clark by colleagues was that he "has not demonstrated that he has . . . present experience and capacity to handle complicated or difficult matters with that degree of skill which should be expected of Supreme Court justices." After Clark had been on the Supreme Court a while, some of his colleagues thought the earlier assessment had been an elaborate understatement.

During the weeks before Clark's confirmation hearing, Wright also did his own investigation of Clark. "I thoroughly investigated him . . . I phoned lawyers and judges in Ventura County [where Oxnard is located] myself and I found out he had a very limited practice. . . . He had not done much when he was on the Court of Appeal.

"Ev Younger [the Attorney General then, as at the time of Bird's confirmation four years later] is a very cagey politician, so I thought I knew how he would vote—for Clark. And I thought the other member of the commission would do the same thing."

There was testimony at the hearing from both opponents and proponents of Clark. One who spoke particularly forcefully against Clark, James L. Blawie, a professor at the University of Santa Clara Law School, began by saying, "I teach such old-fashioned subjects as real property and equity, so you can see I am by no means one of the fellows who teaches these poverty laws and that sort of thing. . . . Large numbers of my law students have reported to me in the last couple of weeks that they are in a state of demoralization as a result of this nomination. . . . It is one thing to say that this knowledge can be acquired by practical apprenticeship and private study. . . . But it is quite another thing to say that, where a person has demonstrated as a result of study in a practitioner's metropolitan law school that he is unable or unwilling to acquire such theory and knowledge and fails to demonstrate even minimum competence in the course of study, that he is nevertheless competent to serve as attorney, let alone as appellate judge. . . . It is a standing insult to a generation of superb California attorneys of Republican political persuasion that this was the best nominee that the governor could find for appointment to one of the outstanding appellate tribunals of the English-speaking world."

"I could not bring myself to believe he was qualified to become a member of the Supreme Court," Wright told me in 1981. "I knew I would be defeated, but I felt I had to oppose him. This was probably the first time a Chief Justice had voted against a nominee for the Supreme Court."

At the conclusion of the confirmation hearing on Clark, Wright read a prepared statement: "My decision to vote against the confirmation of Justice William P. Clark, Jr. is one of the most difficult decisions I have been called upon to make since my appointment to the Supreme Court. . . . Having carefully considered . . . all . . . matters presented to us, I am of the opinion that as of now he is not qualified by education, training, and experience to be confirmed as an associate justice of the Supreme Court."

San Luis Obispo was proud of its adopted son William Clark. An overflow crowd was present on 23 March 1973, for his swearing-in as the newest State Supreme Court Justice. When Clark stepped to the microphone, he got a standing ovation. Supreme Court Justice Marshall McComb was there to welcome Clark to the high court. "I have heard over and over again that this was one of Governor Reagan's finest appointments," said McComb. (It was unknown to the public and probably to Clark at the time, but Justice McComb already constituted a secret crisis at the court because of his debilitating senility dating from a few years earlier.)

Reagan flew to the ceremony from Sacramento to tell Clark and his admirers that his appointment of Clark to the State Supreme Court "is one of my most satisfying acts since becoming governor."

He probably felt confident that appointing Clark to the Supreme Court was going to be a lot more satisfying than his appointment of Wright had turned out to be. By this time, Reagan strongly regretted his appointment of Wright. California court aficionados are fond of saying that Chief Justice Wright was to Reagan what Chief Justice Earl Warren was to President Eisenhower. Each embittered the chief executive who appointed him to a high bench. An additional ironic connection between the two men is that Wright would probably never have become Chief Justice in California except for a last-minute act by then Governor Warren before he went to the United States Supreme Court.

Donald Wright was a lawyer in Pasadena in 1953 when Earl Warren told him he wanted to appoint him to the Municipal Court. Wright asked for a week to think about it, he told me, because he had no desire to be a judge. But Warren said he couldn't have that long. What Wright didn't know was that U.S. Attorney General Herbert Brownell was then in Sacramento waiting for Governor Warren to say whether he would accept the nomination as Chief Justice of the U.S. Supreme Court.

Like Reagan with Wright, Eisenhower often profoundly disagreed with the opinions of the man he had appointed Chief Justice. In his memoirs, Warren describes finally having personal confirmation of what Eisenhower had reportedly said privately—"that his appointment of me as Chief Justice 'was the biggest damn fool thing I ever did.'"

Seated next to Warren aboard *Air Force One* on the way to Winston Churchill's funeral in 1965, Eisenhower said he had been disappointed in both Warren and William Brennan as U.S. Supreme Court justices. He said he had mistakenly thought they were moderates. Warren told him he still considered himself a moderate, and asked the former President what court decisions he had in mind. "Oh, those Communist cases," said Eisenhower. "What Communist cases?" asked the Chief Justice. "All of them," responded Eisenhower. Prodded by Warren, Eisenhower mentioned a specific case that involved Communists in California. "I tried to explain," wrote Warren after he left the court, "that in the judging process we were obliged to judge Communists by the same rules that we applied to all others. He refused to accept this statement, and I asked him:

" 'What would you do with Communists in America?'

" 'I would kill the S.O.B.s,' he said."

"Perhaps that could be done in the Army," Warren recalled telling the former President, "but it could not be done through civilian courts."

Eisenhower waited until he had been out of office five years before he told Warren of his disappointment with him. Reagan didn't wait, nor was his criticism always private. He publicly rebuked Wright for his judicial opinions. More importantly, he took the extraordinarily unethical step of seeking to intervene in the judicial process. As Governor, he tried to tell the Chief Justice how to vote on particular cases while those cases were pending before the court.

Both Wright and the bailiff who drove him to Sacramento remember one of these instances well. "He called me and invited me to lunch in Sacramento," said Wright. "He said he believed it would be good if we got a little acquainted with each other. The two of us, the Governor and I, went to lunch with Herb Ellingwood and Ed Meese." The former Chief Justice laughs at this point in his account. "I remember really enjoying the lunch. We had small loin lamb, which I like very much, but because it was so expensive I never ordered it. I enjoyed the food very much."

But, says the former Chief Justice, he did not enjoy the conversation. It still evokes consternation in him. Not much was discussed. One topic was the apparent sole reason for needing to get "acquainted." "The governor told me his stand on reapportionment. He went on and on, told me why he had felt compelled to veto the bill. I made no comment. Then I said, 'You understand the matter is before us, and it would be inappropriate for me to comment about it.' I said, 'I'm working on that opinion right now.' " There was an awkward silence, as Wright remembers the occasion. Then the Governor turned to Meese and said, "Ed, would you get the gift?" Meese produced a nicely wrapped box. The Chief Justice opened it and found cuff links, each engraved, "To Don from Ron." Years later Wright laughs gently and shakes his head as he completes the story.

The bailiff who drove Wright that day recalls that when the Chief Justice got in the car after the lunch with Reagan he was livid. He told him what Reagan had done and then angrily declared, "How can they be so crazy to bring me up here to discuss a case?!"

And on more than one occasion, Wright told me, Reagan's appointment secretary in Sacramento, Ned Hutchinson, "would say to me, 'The governor didn't like that opinion you signed (or authored).' I told Ned in certain terms that I was sorry but I could not be convinced by it and that it was not the prerogative of the executive branch to have anything to do with our opinions."

It was the 1972 death penalty case, *People* v. *Anderson,* that most provoked Reagan's public anger at Wright. By a 6–1 vote, with only McComb dissenting, the California Supreme Court declared the death penalty unconstitutional under the California Constitution. And the judge Reagan had earlier thought would be "his man" on the court had written the majority opinion. "This is when the Governor first got mad at me," Wright said. "I think I was much more liberal than he was inclined to be. He was surrounded by people like Ed Meese and Ellingwood who are law-and-order–minded." It is true that they would not make the kind of humane comments Wright makes about that death penalty case: "It was a labor of love and that's all. It was something that had to be done. We could not allow the number of inmates on death row to grow and grow with no conclusion [about what would happen to them]." At the time there were 105 prisoners on death row in California.

During Chief Justice Wright's hard times with Reagan, Wright came back from lunch one day and his secretary told him that the Chief Justice was waiting in Wright's chambers. Being the Chief Justice, Wright was a bit confused by her statement. He decided that Roger Traynor, his predecessor, must have stopped by. When Wright entered his chambers, he was surprised when this "big bear of a man," Earl Warren, jumped up and "put his arms around me." The two men had a pleasant chat. "When I appointed you," boomed Warren with great pride, "I certainly bought myself a pig in a poke." Reagan might have said the same thing about his appointment of Wright, but in a considerably different spirit. On another day the two Chiefs went to lunch, and the bailiff who drove them remembers Wright movingly recounting to him, after they dropped Warren at his hotel, that Warren had told him that day that the thing he regretted most in his life was his decision, as Attorney General of California in the 1940's, to intern Japanese Americans in concentration camps during World War II.

Reagan wanted to get rid of Wright. On one occasion he said that if he had appointed him he could un-appoint him. In fact, he could not do so without Wright's cooperation. He tried to get Wright to say he would step down in late 1974. At Reagan's request, the Chief Justice met again with Reagan in the lame-duck Governor's office. A couple of years earlier, Wright had had a heart attack and said that if his health didn't improve, he might want to retire early. His health improved substantially. Once again he became the lively, smiling man who whistled themes from *Don Giovanni* as he came to work each morning. Reagan still wanted him to retire early so he could replace him before Jerry Brown became Governor. "He said he wanted a younger man with longer life expectancy, longer judicial life expectancy. I could understand his point," said Wright. "I told him I'd think it over, but I said, 'I might as well tell you that I'm not interested in retiring. I like the job.' I could tell he didn't like what I said. I don't remember whether he started eating any jelly beans, but it was clear he didn't like it." Wright would not be moved. He didn't retire until early 1977, long after Reagan had left Sacramento.

Reagan and his closest aides remain furious about the opinions Wright wrote or joined at the court and about his not leaving when Reagan asked him to go. Meese said during the 1980 presidential campaign that, before appointing Wright, "We scrutinized every one of his opinions and thought he had a favorable judicial philosophy." What they didn't take into account, apparently, was that an independent legal mind, even a Republican one not deeply steeped in liberal philosophy, may decide from time to time that the Constitution does not endorse Ronald Reagan's interpretation of the law, based as it is— like the philosophy of today's New Right advocates of radical change in the courts—on the supposed need for harsher penalties and the removal of defendants' rights.

Such fine points being lost on Meese, he preferred to attribute Wright's lack of malleability to psychological and intellectual shortcomings: "Wright was given every possible review and every possible test except a psychological test—he didn't have the psychological stamina to stand up to people like [Justice Raymond E.] Peters and other very liberal justices up there, and the liberal intellectual community. He just didn't have the intellectual stamina."

William Clark did not do well in tests in college and law school. In contrast to Wright, however, he passed the Reagan administration's tests with flying colors. The value of Clark to Reagan was established very early on in Sacramento, where he organized the Governor's office. Early in the first Reagan administration, Clark established a procedure that proved to be invaluable to the Governor. He issued a rule that no one in state government should send the Governor a memo or report more than one page long. Clark specified that a memo should contain only four paragraphs and he described the function each paragraph should serve. If the Governor wanted or needed more, Clark directed, he would ask for it.

Reagan and Clark genuinely admired each other. They had common interests. Each loved to ride the range. They valued precious weekends at their ranches, Reagan's in the hills above Santa Barbara and Clark's, a 900-acre grain-and-cattle spread where his wife and children lived, in San Luis Obispo County. But the affinity of the two men went beyond Clark's ability to bring coherence to Reagan's work life and beyond their common interest in the land and horses. They were soul brothers, they agreed on issues. Clark found it natural, for instance, to echo Reagan when, in the first Sacramento administration, the Governor opposed the continued federal funding of California Rural Legal Assistance (CRLA), which provided legal assistance for the rural poor, including many Mexican-American farm workers. As was true later, when he was a judge, Clark often did not consider the human effect of his positions. He supported Reagan's determination to get rid of CRLA and wrote a memo saying that "the encouragement of litigation has perhaps opened the door too wide to the indigent client. They have imposed burdens in the rural courts by their incursions into social legislation." At that time there still were a few Republicans who stood up to Reagan and told him they thought he was wrong, that he was going too far. Houston Flournoy was one, during the threat to kill CRLA. State Controller at the time, and in 1974 the unsuccessful Republican candidate for governor, Flournoy wrote to Clark: "It has appeared to me that one of his [Reagan's] gravest concerns has always been the potential oppression of big government against individual citizens. It has never been, to my knowledge, qualified by the requirement that those individual citizens must have sufficient resources of their own to independently pursue redress."

At the time Reagan was trying to kill CRLA, lawyers from the organization were suing to reverse his administration's decision to reduce the state's medical insurance program for the poor. CRLA was also fighting the Governor's approval of the use of Mexican braceros as harvest laborers in California. Reagan backed off and permitted the federal funding of CRLA. His opposition to the organization continued into his presidency. Shortly after he was inaugurated, Reagan renewed his efforts to kill CRLA. Several months after he became President, according to White House aides, he decided to appoint one of the longtime archenemies of CRLA, Ron Zumbrun, a former official in Reagan's Sacramento administration, to be president of the federal Legal Services Corporation (LSC) in order to destroy that agency from within. Zumbrun did not accept the appointment. (LSC grew out of the 1960's war on poverty; it is the funding agency for CRLA and other local agencies throughout the country that serve the poor. The President has continued his efforts to destroy LSC by appointing to its board people who are opposed to government funded legal aid for the poor.)

Clark obviously had great skill at echoing Reagan's opinions, perhaps even at shaping them. And he was an excellent office organizer. Still, his rewards seem extreme—a seat on the Supreme Court of California, Deputy Secretary of State, National Security Adviser, and a widely held assumption that he eventually will be appointed to the U.S. Supreme Court. (Clark reportedly turned down an offer to go to the Court at the time the President appointed Sandra Day O'Connor.) It is difficult to find any justification for these plum appointments in the record of Clark's public service. Some people believe he won Reagan's strongest loyalty and gratitude as the result of his role in ridding the Governor's office of homosexuals in 1967, Reagan's first year in Sacramento.

Someone on the Governor's staff was told that a member of Reagan's inner circle and three others on his staff and numerous other men outside his staff, including a man who is now a congressman from another state, were conducting homosexual orgies. After a series of keystone-cops–like attempts by staff members to record or photograph these "orgies" so the men would be arrested, eleven members of the Governor's staff told him about the matter and he promptly asked for and received the men's resignations.

When the dust had settled and the men were gone, there was a shake-up of Reagan's staff. William Clark, the man whose only previous political experience had been that he had delivered a hefty majority of Ventura County votes to Reagan in the 1966 election, was elevated from Cabinet Secretary to Executive Secretary, the title of the Governor's chief of staff. Clark and others in the Governor's office had gone to great lengths, including lying to the press and public, to save Reagan from what they and he considered an enormously embarrassing, if not politically fatal, episode. He was deeply grateful.

Shortly after the 1980 election, Chief Justice Bird introduced each of the Supreme Court justices at a luncheon meeting of the Sacramento Bar Association. The audience laughed a lot, but each justice must have been laughing on the outside and cringing a bit on the inside. When she introduced Frank Newman, for instance, the Chief Justice wondered aloud if anybody had noticed that Justice Newman wasn't smoking Tareytons anymore. "That's because he'd rather switch than fight," she said. Everyone understood. Just a few weeks earlier, Newman, who was usually part of a liberal majority on court decisions, had helped form a majority that voted to uphold the death penalty.

But her introduction of William Clark got the strongest laughter. "Bill, you know, is a good friend of Ronnie Reagan, so he was very pleased at his electoral victory," Bird told the audience. "He called his friend and lawyer, Ed Meese, and told him he would like to work for them full-time." Most of the audience understood the joke. It was widely known that while on the court Clark had not only continued his social contacts with Reagan and Meese, something to be expected, but from his judicial chambers had also been a source of political advice, both before and during the just-completed campaign. Clark's advice was pivotal in Reagan's decision to fire Washington lawyer John Sears as Campaign Chairman in the spring of 1980. And now, of course, it was assumed Clark would go to Washington. Bird's introduction of Clark continued: "Ed Meese asked him what kind of job he would like, and Bill replied that he would like to write the one-page memos for the President-elect. Only now, since he has been on the court, I think he has them down to one-half a page, including footnotes."

Clark demurred throughout November and December of 1980 when reporters asked him if he was going to be in the new Reagan administration. He said he liked being on the court, even said once it was a "good" court, and that he had no intention of leaving it. His comment that it was a "good" court was a surprise to those who knew he had been criticizing the court most of the time he was on it. Later, after he accepted a job in Washington, he said the President's transition team had asked him to be Attorney General, Director of the Central Intelligence Agency, or Secretary of Agriculture. Clark said he turned down all three. Then, in the first week of 1981, Meese dropped by Clark's chambers in San Francisco and asked if he would be Deputy Secretary of State, the second highest position in the State Department. Clark said he answered yes because Meese had told him that this request came directly from the President.

The appointment required Clark to appear before the Senate Foreign Relations Committee for a confirmation hearing. Clark was now 49. It was the first time in his public career he would have to be examined in a setting that would provide an opportunity for public assessment.

It did not go well. The part that caught the attention of the press was a quiz administered by Senator Joseph Biden (D–Delaware).

BIDEN: Can you tell me who is the Prime Minister of South Africa?
CLARK: No, sir, I cannot.
BIDEN: Can you tell me who the Prime Minister of Zimbabwe is?
CLARK: It would be a guess.
BIDEN: Can you tell me what the major bilateral issues are between the United States and Brazil at this point?
CLARK: I am unaware of the priorities.
BIDEN: What are the countries in Europe, in NATO, that are the most reluctant to go along with theater nuclear forces modernization? From what countries do we have the greatest difficulty getting

cooperation in the placement of long-range nuclear weapons on European soil?

CLARK: I am not in a position . . . to categorize them from the standpoint of acceptance on the one hand and resistance on the other.

BIDEN: . . . let's talk about England. . . . England is going through some difficult times. Can you tell us, just from accounts in the newspaper, what is happening in the British Labor Party these days?

CLARK: I don't think I can tell you with specificity what is happening in the British Labor Party these days.

Even when the senators' questions called for Clark's opinions and reflections, rather than specific information, Clark was an astonishingly incapable witness. Senator Randolph E. Boschwitz, a Republican, asked him for his viewpoints on détente and Russian-American relations. "I have not heard the term 'détente' for some time. . . . Like many other terms, 'Third World' being one," said Clark, "I am still trying to learn what are the definitions of those words at the moment. I have some idea of what they were from my reading of *Time* and *Newsweek*."

A few minutes earlier, Clark had expressed confusion about the "Third World." Democratic Senator John Glenn had asked him his views on the Carter administration's "global reconstruction" policy, a policy which according to Glenn was emphasized in relations with the Third World. Clark responded by saying that under one of the windows in the office of the Deputy Secretary of State "is the largest globe of the world I ever have seen. I have had occasion to look at it frequently during the past week as I have sat there, on the one hand, finishing my opinions as a California judge and also preparing for this position, if confirmed. I have great difficulty in finding the Third World any more as an entity. I have some idea of the genesis of it. Thus far in my study, I look at the globe as a one-world situation from the standpoint that I am just unable to cut it up in what started as academic terms."

Glenn asked him for his view of nuclear nonproliferation. "In honesty, I do not have a personal view," said Clark. Both Glenn and Republican Senator Charles Percy were incredulous.

"Nonproliferation is the law of the land and we are honor-bound to execute its provisions unless it is amended. Why, everyone has to have an opinion on that subject," said Percy.

Glenn said he didn't approve of the detail "quiz" Clark had been given by Biden. But the Senator said he felt it was necessary for the Committee to learn Clark's general opinions and knowledge on crucial foreign policy issues. Glenn told the witness he was going to ask him as general a question as he could think of: "What do you think should be the objectives of the U.S. foreign policy?"

CLARK: The prime objective announced by President Reagan is peace through strength.
GLENN: Can you give me a little more detail on that? . . . Strength can be defined in many ways—economic, military and in other ways. Can you define how you think "strength" should be defined?
CLARK: . . . I feel it would be presumptuous of me to give those priorities. . . . I am ill-prepared at the moment to answer that.

" 'Peace through strength' is a great line for a speech," said Senator Christopher Dodd, "but I would hope you would have a more in-depth sense of what our foreign policy ought to be under this administration."

"I certainly understand what appears to be the dilemma you find yourself in, Senator," replied Clark. "It is a value judgment that you must make (about me), as I must, as a California judge, and I have for the past twelve years each day."

Early in the hearing Clark made prepared remarks. In them he made a declaration that soon everyone would realize was not false modesty: "I bring to this committee and to the administration, if confirmed, no formal training in foreign policy."

But when Senator Dodd, within two hours of that comment by Clark, reminded him of what he had said, Clark protested, "I would respectfully disagree, Senator, that I have said that at any time. . . . I must respectfully for the record, disagree with your statement that I have at any time, today or whenever, [said I] had no foreign service background, if I am quoting you correctly, that I have no formal training in that subject." The future Deputy Secretary of State then cited trips he had taken abroad and the fact that he had once represented a Salzburg ski-binding company as evidence that he was qualified for the high level foreign policy job. "I realize this is hardly foreign affairs, but I am trying to give you a flavor of my background to show you my interest in people, in negotiation, and in diplomacy."

When his nomination to the State Department job was announced, Clark told reporters, with humor and considerable truth, that his foreign policy experience had been limited to "seventy-two hours in Santiago." Given the fact that he refused to answer most questions on foreign policy, most of the time saying he couldn't and sometimes saying he shouldn't, one of the few insights into his approach to foreign policy issues came indirectly from his explanation of his weekend in Chile in 1966. Before Reagan's first inauguration, the

Governor was asked to approve continuing "Chile-California." This was a program started during John Kennedy's presidency. The State Department provided funds and the State of California provided technical personnel for 22 development projects in Chile. At the Governor's request, Clark flew to Santiago to investigate the program. He said he tried to reorganize the program, but could not get the State Department to cooperate. On his recommendation, he said, California cancelled the program after shifting the "good" parts of it "into the private sector, with Sunkist, Bank of America, Del Monte Foods . . . , and they carried on the technical assistance to the host country without either governmental support or governmental interference."

The Foreign Relations Committee approved the nomination of William Clark by 10 votes to 4. The nine Republicans on the Committee plus Democratic Senator Alan Cranston of California voted for him. Four Democrats voted against him and three Democrats abstained. Glenn said the testimony showed Clark was completely unsuited for the job and that this would be the highest level of on-the-job training he had ever seen. Cranston said he was voting for him because he understood he "is a fast learner when he wants to be." Senator Jesse Helms of North Carolina chastised his colleagues: "There is nothing embarrassing about this man. He is a good American and he is dedicated to this country. . . . We have had too much pretentiousness in Washington, D.C., from people who pretend to know everything."

The most stinging criticism came from a senator who voted for the nomination, Senator Percy. He said he was voting for Clark only because Reagan, on his second day as President, asked Percy to meet with him and during that half-hour meeting told the Senator "in no uncertain terms how much he wanted Justice Clark in this job, and also how strongly he felt about his qualifications for it. . . . But never again can we accept a candidate who professes ignorance in an area where he is to be given responsibility." Percy had met with Clark several days before the hearing and advised him to prepare for it by reading the President's foreign policy statements, the agreements the Carter administration had recently made with Iran when the American hostages were released, and the text of Secretary of State Alexander Haig's confirmation hearings before the same committee. Amazingly, at the beginning of the hearing, Clark admitted he had read none of those documents and he even refused to answer questions about Haig's testimony, saying that it had not been indexed for him yet. Clark said he had not even seen the Haig confirmation hearing because "I was on the coast." (It was broadcast coast-to-coast, of course.) He tried unsuccessfully to add a touch of lightness to a pathetic moment: "In explaining that to him [Haig], I assured him that I had never seen a Ronald Reagan movie, either."

The next day the foreign press reacted to the Clark performance. One Amsterdam paper called him a "nitwit." Another Amsterdam paper headlined its story, "American Minister Knows Nothing." The *Citizen* in Johannesburg reported, "Don't Know Man Gets Nod for Reagan Top Policy Slot." The London *Daily Mirror* editorialized, "America's allies in Europe—Europe, Mr. Clark, you must have heard of it—will hope he is never in charge at a time of crisis." *Time* magazine quipped "A clean slate for State." But the *Telegram-Tribune* in San Luis Obispo, where Clark was once a trial judge, had this headline: "It was a bad day for our Bill Clark."

A couple of weeks later the president of Cafe de California, Inc., a Hispanic public employees' organization, said he identified with Clark's poor performance when he was tested by the Senate Committee. "I am convinced that he has the ability to do the job; he just needs the chance to show it. I am also convinced minorities have the ability to succeed as attorneys. We just don't test well. . . . We also don't have the confidence of the President. . . . But we do have the confidence of the California Supreme Court, as the court's decision in the *DeRonde* case reveals. In that case, decided . . . February 11, 1981, the court upheld the race-conscious affirmative-action admissions program at the University of California's Davis School of Law. Except, of course, for Justice Clark, who dissented."

A month after his confirmation hearing, Clark told *San Francisco Examiner* reporter K. Connie Kang that he had not been disturbed by the unfavorable publicity about his performance before the Foreign Affairs Committee. "It bothered my parents and children, but I was not concerned, feeling that it is part of the ritual one goes through back here. In fact, I rather enjoyed the process."

It is difficult to believe he "enjoyed" a process of public humiliation. It was certainly a painful process to watch, a person appointed to a job for which he was demonstrating he was unqualified and unprepared. In all his years of public service, he never faced public scrutiny until this Foreign Relations Committee hearing. The only prior public evidence of his work, his judicial opinions, is believed to have been largely the work of his law clerks. Former colleagues say he only provided general direction on what the outcome should be. He didn't appear at his confirmation hearing when he was appointed to the California Supreme Court. Consequently, his lack of skill for that job was never visible to the public, only to those justices and staff who would later work with him behind the closed doors of the court. Some of them would soon wonder why Reagan had done this to a friend, even if the friend had saved Reagan from scandal. If he was looking for a conservative ideologue, why didn't the Governor appoint an ideologue who was thoroughly knowledgeable about the law and intellectually brilliant? Surely California has many such people among its conservative lawyers and judges. A person who worked for Reagan and then for Meese in Sacramento, and later for Clark on the Court of Appeal and at the Supreme Court, has a theory: "The governor changed his mind after Wright. Intellectually bright people tend to be their own man. He feared they would be too independent. He appointed Wright and Wright did his own thing. After that Ronald Reagan decided to rely primarily on loyalty. . . . He knows Clark will be true to him."

Clark himself probably provided the most incisive explanation of his own ascent. In 1969, shortly after the Governor had made him a judge, Clark described as follows Reagan's attitude toward the people he appoints: "He values loyalty above competence."

By the end of 1981, after Clark had been in place at the State Department for eight months, John M. Goshko, a *Washington Post* State Department reporter, wrote that Clark "is widely regarded as the most influential and powerful man to occupy the State Department's second-ranking job since George Ball in the 1960's."

Within a month of that article's appearance, Clark moved to the White House to an even higher appointment in the Reagan administration. When Richard Allen was forced out of the White House, William Clark was moved in as National Security Adviser. The administration announced that now, with Clark in place, the power of the position would be increased. Unlike Allen, Clark would not report to the President through presidential counselor Edwin Meese, whom Clark had hired in 1967 to work for Governor Reagan in Sacramento. Instead, Clark would report directly to the President. He would be the President's eyes and ears on all foreign policy and would give him daily reports. His testimony a year earlier before the Senate Foreign Affairs Committee made it difficult to imagine what insight he would be able to give the President.

Some California judges guffawed on the morning of 12 January 1982, when they read in the morning newspaper that Clark, then newly in place at the White House as National Security Adviser, had written the order, just signed by the President, that required government workers' "contacts with news media in which classified National Security Council matters or classified intelligence information are discussed" to have the advance approval of a senior official. The Clark memorandum said all persons who grant interviews with reporters must submit a memorandum about what was discussed. He warned that "all legal methods" would be used to investigate government employees who talk with reporters without authorization. If only Chief Justice Bird had had such a policy in 1978 at the California Supreme Court. As a retired California judge put it the morning he read Clark's stringent anti-leaking policy, "Did you notice who is in charge of plugging leaks at the White House? Nothing like giving the job to a real expert!"

Given Clark's background, much of it either undiscovered or well concealed for years by journalists either friendly to him or uninterested in him despite his high positions, his appointment to the State Department and then to the pinnacle of American foreign policy as head of the National Security Council was astounding. But it was typical of William Clark's history. He had flunked out of college and law school, yet Governor Reagan appointed him to the respected California Supreme Court. He admitted he knew nothing about foreign policy, yet President Reagan made him his chief foreign policy adviser.

"I am here because the President asked me to take this position," Clark told the Senate Foreign Affairs Committee during his 1981 confirmation hearings in the Senate. "I prize our relationship and believe it will assist me in carrying out my responsibilities." At the time, some critics speculated that Clark was being sent to the State Department to be Reagan's friend at State. Others put it more harshly and said Clark was sent to the State Department to be Reagan's spy on Haig.

One thing about both Clark appointments in the Reagan administration seemed clear. They brought Clark closer to the image of national respectability that he needed if the President was going to appoint him later to the position that many close to the President believe is the most coveted goal he has for his friend Clark: not just a seat on the United States Supreme Court, but Warren Burger's seat as Chief Justice.

The possibility of Clark being on the nation's highest court is truly shocking. First there is the question of his ability. Then there is the question of his ethics. Those familiar with his work on the California Supreme Court believe he is as profoundly ignorant of the law as he was in 1981 about nuclear nonproliferation, the Third World, and other elementary aspects of foreign policy. Many of these same people believe he also was guilty of gross improprieties while on the Supreme Court in California, improprieties that have remained a secret until now. Among those improprieties are ones related to the suspicion that he originally was sent to the State Department to be Reagan's spy on Alexander Haig. If it is true that Clark's assignment at State was that of spy, it is a job that some past and present members and staff of the California Supreme Court told me they believe he was eminently qualified for. They think he was a spy for Reagan while he served on the California Supreme Court.

CHAPTER 3

Disorder in the Court Preceded Rose Bird

The California public has been led to believe that the State Supreme Court was a pure and uncorrupted institution until Rose Bird came along. Then, suddenly, with the hanging of plants in her chambers, the changing of locks, and new personnel policies, the high court became a place of intrigue and corruption. Such is the common wisdom.

What the public has never been told is that the recent troubles are rather minor compared with earlier ones. One justice was senile on the court for nearly a decade. He did not do his own work, instructed his staff to plagiarize opinions, fell asleep during public hearings, and during this entire time was unable to discuss any case before the court.

Even more serious than this senile justice's role on the court was the role of the man appointed to the court in 1973 by Governor Reagan, William P. Clark. Clark was apparently so incapable of understanding the law that he could not discuss cases even in the justices' private conferences. At public hearings, he sat mute, hardly ever asking a question. Clark delayed the completion and filing of numerous opinions, once taking more than two years to complete an opinion after it reached him.

At other times he was far from mute. Former Chief Justice Wright told me he believes Justice Clark was a spy for Reagan on the court, and that he called the Governor's office regularly with confidential court information. Furthermore, Wright believes that Clark went to people outside the court, former Reagan administration officials, for assistance in writing at least one opinion. Clark's secretary at the time also told me she thinks he took this extraordinarily unethical step.

As Chief Justice of the California Supreme Court from 1970 to 1977, Wright had, as he put it, "two major problems: Marshall McComb and William Clark."

The problem with Marshall McComb began for Wright as soon as he arrived at the court. By this time McComb, at 76, had been a judge since 1927 and on the Supreme Court since 1956. Wright noticed in his first weeks at the court in 1970 that at the weekly private conferences the justices held in the chief justice's chambers, McComb never said a word voluntarily about court matters. When asked to vote, McComb would ask, "How did Justice Burke vote? I'll vote the same." After Justice Clark joined the court, McComb would ask, "How did Justice Clark vote? I'll vote with him." Though he always seemed to have no knowledge of the cases under discussion, and moments later could not even remember his own votes, he did seem to know who was a liberal and who was a conservative and, therefore, whose vote he should imitate. "He was an ultra, ultra conservative," Wright told me.

McComb was usually in a hurry to complete the justices' long weekly conferences. They are a fundamental process of the court. More than 6,000 cases are appealed to the California Supreme Court each year. It accepts for consideration only about three percent of those it is asked to hear. The crucial decisions about which cases to accept have a profound effect on litigants and on the development of California law. These decisions on which cases will be heard by the court are made at the weekly Wednesday morning conferences. For some justices, preparation of written recommendations on whether to take particular cases, recommendations that are discussed at these conferences, takes up 60 to 75 percent of their weekly work time.

As the conversations on the crucial decision to grant or deny a hearing in individual cases went on each Wednesday morning, McComb, according to Wright, would sit in silence. When asked to report on the cases that had been assigned to him, he would usually refuse to talk and when pressed would impatiently say, "It's all in the memo." He was referring to memos that had been prepared by his staff—prepared, increasingly over the years, without any assistance from him. Occasionally he would impatiently urge his colleagues to hurry and would chastise them for engaging in "talk, talk, talk, squawk, squawk, squawk, yak, yak, yak." He angered them by getting up from the conference table and doing exercises in the middle of the room, or, even more annoying, going to the telephone on the Chief Justice's desk, just a few feet away from the conference table, and making long-distance calls to friends in Los Angeles. In a loud voice he would discuss the weather, usually inaccurately, Wright remembers.

Sometimes McComb's staff, with McComb's permission or at his direction, would write opinions that were verbatim copies of briefs filed by litigants. Other judges were so aghast at this plagiarism that they themselves would rewrite McComb's work or require one of his clerks to do so. His problems increased the other justices' workload and were also a deep embarrassment in private and in public. During monthly public hearings held with all judges sitting on the bench, Justice McComb invariably fell asleep. "I would nudge him," Wright told me, "but he would come to with such a start that I decided it was better to let him sleep." Occasionally McComb would leave the room while a hearing was in progress, return to the bench with a magazine and read it while an attorney was arguing a case. He performed eye and other physical exercises during proceedings. Other unusual behavior was documented by a 1976 investigation that recommended that he be retired or removed from the Supreme Court. It included his wearing pig earrings in the State Building and to a meeting at a San Francisco hotel. Once he brandished a police riot stick in a public building at San Francisco International Airport. He urinated in court bailiffs' cars without requesting a stop to relieve himself. He occasionally left the State Building and walked the streets of San Francisco in his judicial robes. "He loved to be driven every noon," said Wright, "to the Bohemian Club, where he would sit at the head table."

Wright said McComb's behavior was, to put it mildly, a complete surprise and shock to him when he arrived at the Supreme Court. Wright had not heard about it when he was on the Court of Appeal in Los Angeles. "It was obvious to me very quickly that he was senile. . . . Then I learned it had been true for many years. I went to see Chief Justice [Roger] Traynor [Wright's predecessor as Chief Justice from 1964 to 1970] and he said McComb had been that way for years—that for years McComb had not expressed an opinion.

"I was in a bind about how to get rid of him. I knew we could not let him stay on the court. His condition was not a secret. Most of the counsel who appeared before the court knew the situation, they had seen him. . . . I tried many times to get him to leave. He always said he was going to 'stay till I die.' I went to his family and asked for help. I talked with his son-in-law. He said he'd help, but later he said he couldn't, that he didn't have any power over him. . . . I thought I'd file a complaint myself," said Wright, "but my colleagues on the court discouraged me."

Finally, in early 1977, just as Wright was leaving the court and before Bird came on, McComb, then 82, was forced to retire because of senility. He died in 1981. His forced resignation came after an investigation by the State's Commission on Judicial Performance, the agency with which Wright had wanted to file a complaint. In the end, a local lawyer filed the complaint. A 1976 law specified that when the Commission finds that a member of the Supreme Court should be disciplined, instead of making the recommendation to the Supreme Court, which the Commission does in cases involving judges of all other courts in the state, it would make the recommendation to a special panel composed of Court of Appeal judges.

The man who was chairman of the Commission when it recommended that McComb be forced to retire, Court of Appeal Justice Bertram Janes, told a reporter in 1979: "Everybody was covering for McComb. Even you and I could tell by looking at him that he was senile. But we [the Commission] never got a complaint. . . . We were cowardly, you see. We didn't do it until we had to."

The protection of McComb was carried out by many people, and it was not entirely a humane act on his behalf. And it certainly did not serve the public well. It would, of course, have been sad to see his name tarnished by the inevitable headlines and news stories that would—and did—accompany a forced resignation. But surely it was worse to have one member of the court completely unable to function. In reality, a person whom the public thought was a justice was not a justice, and the seven-member court had only six justices. A man who could not function as a justice often was casting the decisive vote in close cases. Through the years innumerable reporters observed McComb's senile behavior at public hearings and heard about how he behaved in his chambers and on the streets of San Francisco. They knew about it and decided not to report that a member of the state's highest court was incompetent. Probably hundreds of lawyers argued before the court during the time he was senile and observed his behavior. They probably shared lots of chuckles about it. They, too, protected him.

The court protected McComb. But eventually it wasn't clear whether the court was primarily protecting McComb or itself. "The court was afraid of being lambasted in the press," said a former member of the court staff. "They were afraid that if the truth came out against McComb, the court as a whole would give up some prestige."

Beginning in 1968 an underlying fear at the court was Ronald Reagan. McComb did not do any of the work required of a justice, and he engaged in bizarre public behavior. But he looked fine. He walked straight and briskly. His eyes were lively. To see him walk the corridors, you wouldn't know there was anything wrong with him—unless you happened to notice his pig earrings. But another justice, Raymond Peters, a liberal, was becoming increasingly physically incapacitated. Peters suffered from a degenerative muscle condition.

He had to be helped during public hearings. With Wright on one side and Mosk on his other side, Peters would be lifted onto his chair in the hearing room. His spine was shrinking, so his worsening condition was evident to anyone who saw him. But Peters' mind remained sharp, and he continued to do his job with efficiency and brilliance. It was this peculiar situation of the two men—one whose body was fine but whose mind was disabled and the other whose body was disabled but whose mind was fine—that made the court fear Reagan. They feared that if anyone on the court, or anyone else for that matter, moved to force McComb to leave the court, then Reagan would move to force Peters out too. Several factors, including the court's fear of Reagan and its excessive fear that public shame to one justice would bring shame to the entire court, conspired to protect McComb for years.

A few years later this elaborate and long protection of a person who could not perform as a justice would seem quite strange. For years the press, the court justices, and the court staff had considered it proper to hide the fact that one justice was simply not functioning as such. The justices, the staff of the court, the press, and the part of social San Francisco that observed Justice McComb at the prestigious Bohemian Club all conspired to keep the situation, the truth of which was verifiable, from the public that paid McComb to be a justice. In contrast, by 1978, many of the same people who protected McComb—the press and some justices and some members of the court staff—would regularly engage in publicly spreading damaging, unverified information about other members of the court. They would eventually try to destroy the reputation of the entire court. By 1978 it seemed the court's era of self-protection was over and the era of false, malicious gossip had been ushered in.

What has not been revealed until now is that William Clark, Wright's second major problem while he was at the court, enjoyed protection for behavior some people on the court considered strange, unethical, and judicially shocking. Yet Clark was never charged or investigated. He came on the court in 1973 as the replacement for Justice Peters, the physically disabled justice. "The important thing to me when he [Clark] arrived," said Wright, "was that I now had two justices instead of one not participating. Both McComb and Clark would just sit there." McComb never asked questions of lawyers who argued before the court, nor did Clark. This was considered highly unusual. The justices spent considerable time preparing what they called calendar memorandums that outlined each case that would be presented at the public hearings. At the hearings the justices asked questions of counsel to probe weak legal briefs, or to challenge the lawyers to convince them on a given point. Supreme Court justices, as well as lawyers who have argued before the court, say Clark usually said nothing from the bench. In fact, there was a slight stir in the courtroom in June of 1980. People were surprised. Clark asked a question. Some present thought it might have been his first and only question in eight years on the Supreme Court. But another justice remembers that through the years there were a couple of other questions from Clark and that "they were so unclear that counsel was in some doubt as to what Clark was talking about."

One person said that when Clark would occasionally speak at the court's weekly private conferences, he would "argue for an ideological point, not a legal point. He could not substantiate his opinions with legal information." The justices were embarrassed. On one occasion one justice said to him, "We deal in legalities here. You have to have a basis for what you say." But Clark seemed lost. He often expressed admiration for McComb and for a while seemed not to realize there was anything wrong with the man. When Clark first came on the court, the most charitable explanation that some could find for his perpetual silence was that he was simply imitating the man on the court whose conservative opinions he most admired, Justice McComb.

The fact that Clark usually sat mute at the justices' weekly private conferences seemed even more unusual than his not asking questions at public hearings. These private conferences were often lively. Most members of the court were "brilliant and loved to talk across the conference table," said Wright. "He was no match for them, he was generally silent. When it came to solicitation of votes, frequently he'd say, 'I have to look into it further, put me in question mark,'" an indication that he hadn't made up his mind and was going to think more about the case, was going to ask his staff for advice, or, as some justices came to fear and believe later, was going to ask people outside the court for advice.

Before the end of Clark's first year on the Supreme Court, there was a persistent rumor that he either sought advice from one or more lawyers outside the court for one of his dissenting opinions or that he had asked someone outside the court, someone formerly in the Governor's administration, to write one of his dissents. The rumored unethical activity involved his dissent in a welfare case the Reagan administration cared about deeply, *Cooper* v. *Swoap*, one of a series of welfare cases that attacked the Reagan administration's attempts to reduce welfare payments substantially. (David B. Swoap was director of the State Department of Social Welfare under Governor Reagan, and served as under secretary of Health and Human Services under President Reagan in Washington until early 1983, when he returned to California to become Governor Deukmejian's Secretary of Health and Welfare.) The court's decision, written by Justice Tobriner, invalidated Reagan welfare reductions. In a little-noticed moment in Clark's Senate confirmation hearing in 1981, Clark was asked if he ever had outside help in writing a court opinion. He said he had not. Chief Justice Wright believes that that statement, made under oath, was not true.

I interviewed former Chief Justice Wright after those hearings and asked him if he believed Clark had ever had someone outside the court write an opinion for him. "Yes," he responded, "I believe he did on one that had to do with welfare. . . . It was my strong feeling that someone outside the court wrote that opinion. . . . I didn't like it. I was very upset . . . I never knew it for certain, but I believed it to be the case."

Speaking of the same case, Connie Cantrell, Clark's secretary at the time, told me she also felt certain that he had someone outside the court write his dissent in *Cooper* v. *Swoap*. Cantrell, who has a master's degree in English, was hired by Clark to write letters for Reagan early in his first administration as Governor. She also worked in Sacramento for Meese. When Reagan appointed Clark to the Court of Appeal in 1971, Clark hired Cantrell to work for him. She says he told her he needed help with his writing. "He wasn't illiterate," she said, "but he wasn't competent." The standard procedure in his office, she said, was that a law clerk would turn out a draft. Then it would go to Clark and he'd say whether it was on track. Then she would rework it, edit it, and type it. During the three years she worked with him at the two courts, the Court of Appeal and the Supreme Court, Cantrell believes he never wrote an opinion or did legal research. She told me he fired her in late December 1973, after she asked him if someone outside the court wrote his dissent in the *Cooper* welfare case.

"There was one instance where I was personally convinced he had an opinion written outside the court," Cantrell told me. She described the same opinion Wright had described to me. "He gave me one opinion that I'm sure did not come out of our staff. He said he had written it, but I had worked for these guys [Clark and his clerks] for three years by then. I knew their writing, and I was sure it had not been written by anyone in our office. When he gave it to me, it was clear it had been typed on a typewriter that did not exist at the Supreme Court. Besides that, the language was not a piece of legal work; it was a soapbox appeal. . . . My impression at the time was that it had come out of the Governor's office." Others believed the source was more likely to have been an attorney who recently had left the State Department of Welfare, a party to the suit being decided by the court.

"He gave it to me on a Monday morning," said Cantrell, "and asked me to retype it. I read it and went to him and said, 'What is this?' I told him that I thought it was not an opinion. He told me he had typed it over the weekend at his ranch." That was something Cantrell said he had not done before in the three years she had worked for him, though he spent most weekends at the ranch.

Wright was very troubled by the possibility of a justice going to someone outside the court for assistance with a court opinion. Especially troubling was the suggestion that the person he had gone to was Ron Zumbrun. Until the day Clark was confirmed as a Supreme Court justice, Zumbrun had been counsel to the State Department of Welfare, a party to the suit in question. Instead of confronting Clark directly, Wright told me, he asked a respected conservative on the court, Justice Burke, to go to Clark about the matter. Clark reportedly denied the accusation. In the end, Clark rewrote the dissent and said in it that he was relying on information written in a law journal—information written by Zumbrun and another colleague who had recently left the State Department of Welfare. On the same day Clark was confirmed as a justice of the Supreme Court, Zumbrun left his position in the Reagan administration and filed incorporation papers establishing the Pacific Legal Foundation, the first of a series of conservative public interest law firms that would spring up around the country.

Wright told me he received confirmation from a court employee that Clark engaged in yet another highly improper practice—regularly discussing pending cases with people outside the court. Clark was believed to be talking with people who had a particularly strong interest in the outcome of pending cases—people in the Governor's office. Cantrell said she was aware he called the Governor's office often but she never knew whether he talked to Reagan or others about pending cases. A judge who served with Clark on the Court of Appeal said Clark also spent much time while on that court calling the Governor's office, but added that he did not know if pending cases were discussed. Wright, however, said he received confirmation that such conversations had taken place. One morning a member of the court staff told the Chief Justice that Justice Clark usually came to work early and called the Governor's office nearly every morning before other court staff, including Clark's own staff, arrived. In these calls, Wright said he was told, Clark reported confidential activities of the court, including information about pending cases, to the Governor's office. The staff member told Wright he had actually heard the conversations.

Wright said he was angry at both the staff member and at Clark. He said he told the staff member to stop eavesdropping on Clark's conversations. But at the same time the Chief Justice was profoundly disturbed by the possibility that Clark was discussing confidential matters with the administration. "We had a very strict rule of confidentiality," said Wright. "It was almost as sacred as conversation between priest and confessor, between doctor and patient." Strict adherence to confidentiality is, of course, common practice on appellate courts. It has always been believed that the integrity and independence of a court would be severely damaged if the decision-making process was discussed outside the court. For one thing, such a practice could expose judges to pressure from parties with vested interests.

Robert Bolster, a former bailiff at the court who was Wright's driver (but who was not the staff member who overheard Clark's conversations with the Governor's office), remembers that one day Wright told him, "We have to be very careful about Mr. Clark." Bolster said he asked, "How do you mean?" And the Chief Justice replied, "I think we've got a spy in our midst."

The accusations against Clark were believed by the Chief Justice and by some other justices on the court. But the Commission on Judicial Performance, the proper agency to investigate such charges, was never asked to do so. Had the charges been investigated and determined to be true, Clark might have been removed from the court. Such violations of confidentiality are considered gross violations of judicial conduct standards. It is not clear whether the decision not to ask for an investigation of Clark, like the earlier decision not to file a complaint about McComb's incompetence, was more the result of a desire to protect the court itself from negative publicity or of a desire simply to protect Clark.

I sent Justice Clark a series of questions about the accusations others made against him. He did not respond to my questions. But my letter to Clark did prompt a response from Richard C. Morris, a law clerk to Clark at the Supreme Court since 1977 who went to Washington with Clark and now serves as his special assistant at the White House. Interestingly, Morris does not say he is writing on Clark's behalf or expressing Clark's views. In essence, Morris denies the accusations, but his answers to specific questions are oblique, if not evasive. The only instance in which he implies Justice Clark participated in formulating Morris's answer to me is one about the circumstances of Cantrell's dismissal. Morris wrote that she herself terminated her employment, that the reasons were "personal," and that "Judge Clark deems it improper to further comment on them."

In 1979, when all the justices on the court were being investigated as to whether one or more of them delayed a decision until after the 1978 election, no justice brought up the far more serious allegations they had long believed to be true about Clark, including the delaying of opinions. They remained silent. On the other hand, Clark, the only accuser then among all the justices, testified about old and new petty complaints—for instance, he said that his present secretary was unhappy that she had not received a carpet remnant from Bird's office when the Chief replaced her carpet. Before and during the hearings long newspaper profiles of Clark were written and apparently no reporter learned about Clark's alleged improprieties which, if true, made the alleged wrongdoing under investigation in 1979 look innocuous. By 1979 it could not be said that the justices were protecting the court from negative publicity. By the time they testified the court had become a public spectacle, a joke to some. It could be assumed that the justices, given the nature of the accusations they were then being investigated for, were being exceedingly humane in then not mentioning the far more serious allegations they could have brought up about the accuser in their midst. As he publicly catalogued petty accusations against fellow justices, Clark must have done so with confidence that his fellow justices' sense of dignity would not permit them to retaliate by pointing to his own more serious alleged indiscretions.

Justice Tobriner, who in 1978 was accused of delaying a decision for political purposes, was on the court when Clark arrived. The closest he came during the public hearings to mentioning any of Clark's alleged past wrongdoing was a brief reference to the fact that Clark had once shelved an opinion for many months. Though he had the most to lose if the 1979 investigation found the accusations to be true, Tobriner did not reveal in his testimony that Clark habitually delayed public release of court decisions. In the first half of his eight years on the court, three justices said, Clark kept some opinions in his office for more than a year, a few for more than two years, without taking any action and without sending them on to the next justice. Rather than assume that Clark was withholding the opinions for political purposes—the accusation against Tobriner in 1978—the justices assumed that Clark was delaying opinions because he was unable to write his dissents and carelessly let them accumulate. But they never were certain of the reason for the long delays. The problem did not ameliorate, justices say, until the last two years he was on the court. Then he increased the size of his staff, adding a former member of Wright's staff, Richard Morris, to his, and moved opinions at a more normal pace. Morris, now on Clark's staff in Washington, was a fast writer.

"We were held up on innumerable cases because of Clark's slowness," another justice told me long after the 1979 investigation of the court was completed. He said that when the problem became severe—15 or 20 cases piled up in Clark's office—the other justices discussed the problem with Clark at weekly conferences: "We tried, but quite unsuccessfully." Ironically, in the months just before the 1978 election, Clark gave public speeches condemning the backlog of cases at the court and complained about the slowness of his colleagues. Some of them were amazed that he would make such speeches. He must have been confident they would never reveal his history. "He himself was the culprit through the years," a justice told me soon after Clark left the court. "He was holding up our cases interminably."

Wright agreed. Sardonically, he told me he was amused to learn that Clark sat in judgment on his fellow justices during the 1979 investigation and claimed that Tobriner and Bird each had kept opinions inordinate lengths of time. Ironically, the opinions for which they were being investigated took less time from start to finish—from public hearing to filing of completed decision signed by all justices— than the time Clark kept opinions waiting in his office for him to complete a dissent or simply okay someone else's opinion.

"He was the slowest one on the court the whole time I was there," said Wright. "They [the boxes, each containing the complete record and opinions of a different case] would sit in his office. We often would tell him, 'Please pass it and the rest of us will work on it and send it back to you last.'" But although this method might speed up the work of the other six justices, it only changed the timing of the bottleneck in Clark's office. In 1979 Clark would publicly claim that for a case to take 10½ months from hearing to release of decision was highly unusual. It was curious that he would say that, considering that all the justices knew he often had delayed cases much more than 10½ months.

Wright evaluated the four years he was on the court with Clark and drew this important conclusion:

"I never heard him express himself enough to know what kind of legal mind he had. I cannot say that to you for anybody else I've ever worked with. There's nothing but a vagueness there on how he thinks. He leaves you not knowing what knowledge he has. He authored a very small number of majority opinions, many dissents, but they were very short. He offered no detailed breakdown on why he thought the majority was wrong. . . . I really don't know what kind of mind he has," said Wright. "It's astounding that you could work with someone for four years and not know whether they can think."

For these reasons, the former Chief Justice thinks that Clark should not become a member of the U.S. Supreme Court. "I don't think it would be a good spot for him," said Wright, shaking his head at the thought. It is assumed by Wright and others that Reagan intends to appoint Clark to the U.S. Supreme Court, and that his present position in the inner circle of the White House is merely an essential intermediate step on his path to the high court. While being Reagan's effective eyes beside Secretary of State Alexander Haig, Clark developed crucial positive relations with many members of the Washington press corps, relations that could be helpful if he is nominated to the high court and others try to draw attention to his lack of qualification, to the possibility that he might be unfit for the job. There was a hint of the subtle deception that may be employed then in a story by *The Washington Post*'s Lou Cannon, who has known Clark as a source since Reagan's first administration in Sacramento. The day after Clark was nominated to the State Department post, Cannon wrote, in stark contrast to what Chief Justice Wright told me, that Clark's judicial opinions, "though quite conservative, have rarely been faulted on intellectual grounds. And those opinions may one day be of great interest to legal scholars, since there are those in the Reagan entourage who expect to see Clark on the U.S. Supreme Court some day."

For those familiar with Clark's lack of judicial skill and his apparently near-total dependence on his law clerks—not to mention his alleged highly improper violations of the separation between the executive and judicial branches and his strange, if not unscrupulous, role in the 1979 investigation of the Supreme Court—the suggestion that he might become a justice on the highest court in the land seems outrageous.

CHAPTER 4

An Intruder in the Village of the Court

It would be a mistake to say that Rose Bird shares none of the blame for the troubles that have developed at the Supreme Court since her arrival in the spring of 1977. It would also be a mistake to ignore the fact that people, both in and out of the court, have gone to shocking lengths, including the use of lies and half-truths, to try to ruin her.

"If she had only crawled before she walked," said a former member of the court staff. His remark seemed particularly interesting in view of what Bird told me a few weeks later, that she had a transition team of four lawyers come to the court before her arrival "so I could come on board running."

Her swearing-in ceremony in Sacramento started the symbolism of radical change at the court that already had some members of the staff nervous. Traditionally, the Acting Chief Justice—it would have been Justice Tobriner in this case—swears in the new Chief. Jerry Brown had asked Bird if he could have the honor of swearing her in. "He wanted to do it, I think in retrospect, because it was historic. [She was the first woman justice.] Well, that was a breaking of tradition. And that was used as an example of how I didn't understand how the process worked. . . . But I felt I couldn't hurt his feelings, after he had made me Chief Justice, by saying, 'You can't swear me in.'" But for those who saw Brown as having disrespect for the judiciary, his swearing her in reinforced that attitude. As Bird put it more than four years later, it looked as though "an outsider was being brought in by an outsider."

The swearing-in was a festive occasion at the historic B. F. Hasting Building in Sacramento, the original headquarters of the Supreme Court. Many women couldn't help feeling good that another male bastion had fallen at last. This was a time to celebrate. Bird's mother and close friends were there. Many retired justices of the court came. And all the sitting justices were there except for Stanley Mosk and William Clark. Later, their absence then would seem significant. At the time, Bird didn't think much about it.

"Initially, everybody supported her," said a former staff member who was not aware of the fact that some people on the staff had worked against her confirmation from the beginning. "We were all proud of the court. It had a reputation. We felt we were going to do everything we could to keep it the way it was. . . . She had a golden egg. That staff was wonderful. Why, if I had been her, I would have just sat there and let the staff make me look good. It would have been smooth sailing."

The assumption seems to be that she was not capable on her own of "looking good," that she should have been dependent on others. But Rose Bird sails her own boat. She knew that there were administrative procedures, big and small, that she needed to know about before she got to the court, but she had only two weeks from the time she was confirmed until the time when she was supposed to arrive at the court and take over the reins of leadership. In those two weeks she had to wrap up her responsibilities as head of the Brown administration's largest agency, Agriculture and Services. She also had to consult with the Governor on his plans to break that agency into smaller units. All of which allowed her no time to learn the ropes at the court before she had to conduct her first weekly court conference. This meant the preparation of memorandums on numerous cases that she would have to be able to discuss. Throughout the second week on the job, moreover, she would have to preside over public hearings—the court's monthly calendar, as the hearings are called. Twenty-five cases would be argued before the court then, and she would be expected to be well acquainted with all of them.

So she hired what she called a "transition team," four lawyers whom she knew well, whom she considered bright and capable. As soon as she was confirmed, the transition team went to work at the court. They went to each office of the court—the court secretary's office, the clerk's office, the bailiffs' office, the Administrative Office of Courts—and learned the function of each, who was responsible for it, and what the Chief Justice's responsibility was toward it. She found their groundwork invaluable. "You need to know who are the people that are under you, the people you are responsible for. And what your duties are. You need to have that all laid out very carefully and efficiently for you so that when you go on board, you can come on board running instead of having to sit back and wait until you find out, 'Oh, my goodness, I should have done that,' or, 'Oh, my goodness, I'm responsible for that and it isn't done.' Also, I was coming into an extremely hostile environment."

She had learned during preparation for her confirmation hearing that some members of the court staff had worked against her confirmation. Also during the two weeks before she came to the court, Wiley Manuel, who was confirmed as an associate justice at the same time she was confirmed, called her one day and wanted to make arrangements for her to go with him to a lunch the Supreme Court justices had invited him to. Both she and he were surprised to learn that she had not been invited: this was a men's-only lunch. Manuel would later express slight irritation at the fact that he and Bird were considered "novelties" of the court, she because she was a woman, he because he was black—two biological specimens that had never sat on the California Supreme Court before.

With the help of Justice Tobriner and his staff, the transition team learned what Bird needed to know. "Even though I'd done extensive appellate practice, I didn't know that there was a conference memo or a calendar memo that was written on yellow paper," she says, giving a sample of the details she needed to learn. The weekend before her first day on the job, she sat down with her transition team and they gave her a massive briefing on administrative details she needed to know immediately and on the 25 cases the court would be hearing.

The very existence of a transition team shocked the court staff. Why did the new Chief Justice send in these young lawyers to ask them what they did? No one says they were rude. Rather, it was the principle of the thing. To those people on the court staff who had felt for a long time that they were running the court, merely being asked questions by the new Chief Justice's transition team seemed to imply criticism.

To understand this reaction, it is helpful to understand the special atmosphere of appellate courts. The reams of paper that come into such courts daily deal with the most turbulent issues, the most violent acts of society. But the atmosphere of an appellate court is one of calmness and virtual silence compared to the issues it must resolve and compared to the other two branches of government, the legislature and the executive. Legislators and chief executives hammer out compromises at noisy meetings where opposing parties forcefully challenge each other. They give up some of their goals, if not some of their principles, in exchange for an opponent giving up some of theirs. In the appellate court, judges and their clerks and other support personnel work alone in small, quiet offices. The parties to the disputes that are settled in the appellate court are admitted to the court only for a formal and highly controlled hearing. There is no horse-trading between the judges and the parties to the disputes. The judges may compromise with each other but not with the litigants.

Many people who work in an appellate court feel they work in a special place. They serve and they protect the judges who quietly resolve major disputes. They protect secrets every day, secrets they hear and secrets they see on paper. Workers at all levels of a court staff are entrusted with secrets that would be very valuable to litigants, politicians and others outside the court. Workers at the court are very close to power. Some of them hold that power in awe. And some of them feel deeply honored to be there.

The appellate court is a small bureaucracy. It is not the impersonal large office of the average corporate or government organization. Because an appellate court is small, the workers tend to know each other well. At the California Supreme Court, that closeness meant that mutual respect, even loving friendships, flourished for many years among some of the workers. This was especially important because the Supreme Court staff, like court employees throughout the state, are exempt from civil service protection. Many felt the atmosphere was so good that they didn't mind the lack of protection. They felt secure.

This court, like many appellate courts, was like a village. And as in a village, just as respect and admiration could grow there, gossip and meanness could also flourish in the midst of such relative isolation and secretiveness. Awe could be replaced by bitterness. Both old-timers and newcomers can too easily develop a siege mentality in an isolated village. That is what happened when Rose Bird went to the California Supreme Court. She was treated like an intruder in the village. Unlike her predecessors Bird had not been part of the upper echelons of the judicial fraternity of the state. She was not an insider. And she did not have the good grace, as an outsider, to settle in slowly. Instead of waiting for cues, she sent in a transition team. In a corporation or at any other government agency, it might have been considered a wise way to assume leadership. At the Supreme Court, it was considered insulting.

Perhaps no one was more insulted than Ralph Kleps. It was hardly any secret that many people in and out of the court considered Kleps to be the real power behind the California court system. Chief justices came and went, but Kleps remained. He had been hired in 1961 by former Chief Justice Phil S. Gibson to be the director of the Administrative Office of Courts (AOC). The court staff, as well as the 30-

member AOC staff, looked to Kleps as their leader. Gibson had enjoyed both the scholarly opinion-writing role of being a justice on the court and that of administrator of the state's entire court system, the largest court system in the world. He hired Kleps to be his right arm in the latter role and together they brought efficient organization to what had been an inefficient, disorganized state court. The AOC, as shaped by Gibson and Kleps, is responsible for the administration of all personnel and budget matters throughout the system, including the assignment of substitute judges when judges are sick, on vacation, or disqualified from hearing a case. The AOC staff of lawyers and statisticians also conduct studies of problems in the system and are the official record keepers for the thousands of cases that go through the California courts annually. Officially, the AOC is the administrative arm of the Judicial Council, a 21-member body that consists of judges, representatives of the bar and the legislature. But much of the policy and activity of the AOC approved by the Council during Kleps's years at the helm were initiated by him.

Gibson's first two successors, Roger Traynor and Donald Wright, were less interested in administration than Gibson had been. They were glad to have Kleps in place as an administrator. Traynor relied on him more than Gibson had, and Wright more than Traynor. Kleps probably assumed in 1977 that Wright's successor, Rose Bird, given her inexperience on the bench, would rely on him more than anyone had. He was wrong. More than any chief justice since Gibson, Bird would want to be deeply involved in the administrative responsibilities of her job, including her responsibilities as Kleps's boss.

Kleps told me he almost quit the day Bird asked him to authorize the hiring of the four-member transition team. Previous chief justices had relied on him, not on a transition team, to introduce them to the administrative nuts and bolts of the court.

At about the time Bird was asking Kleps to sign the requisitions that would put the team on the payroll, Kleps wanted the new Chief Justice's signature on some documents. She refused to give it. The court staff as well as the AOC were amazed that the new Chief did not automatically grant Kleps's request. The documents, if signed by Bird, would have delegated specific administrative authority to him, authority that automatically became hers upon becoming Chief Justice but which Kleps was used to having delegated to him.

To Kleps, the request was a simple one. It would keep him and his staff performing functions that he had performed for Wright without consulting with the Chief Justice. As he put it in a memo to Bird, her delegation of authority to him would "keep the machinery running."

To Bird, the request was premature and unacceptable. She also thought her agreement would be a negligent turning-over of her administrative responsibilities before she even knew what these were. "If I had signed those documents," she told me, "I would have turned over to him every power I had as chairperson of the Judicial Council."

Instead of signing the delegations of authority, Bird later wrote Kleps a memo informing him that "all delegations of authority, either verbal or written, granted to you by all former Chief Justices of the Supreme Court and chairpersons of the Judicial Council are hereby cancelled." The State Constitution and various statutes gave the administrative responsibilities to the Chief Justice. She told Kleps she'd be willing to delegate them after she fully understood them. In the meantime, she said, she would sign all documents herself. She started signing over some delegation of authority to him by two months after his original request. "Unless you understand what you're delegating, you're not fulfilling your proper responsibility," said Bird. "Now, perhaps you ought to delegate a lot of duties which you simply can't do. And I have done that since. But at that point when I was coming in, I didn't know what delegations I was giving because I didn't know what the responsibilities were of the Chief in these areas, and I wasn't about to turn them over to someone that I didn't know very well. . . . I don't do things blindly."

This naturally hurt Kleps. His history with the courts went back a long time. In 1941, the new Chief Justice, Phil Gibson, asked him to write his first speech to the Conference of California Judges. Kleps wrote it on "how to create an excellent staff structure in order for the Judicial Council to become a fine manager of the state courts." Kleps later felt he himself had built this management structure. Before Bird came to the court, he sent her "notes" that he had prepared in 1970 before it was known who would be the next Chief Justice. Kleps said that because Wright knew the system so well he never gave them to Wright, but now he was making them available to Bird. In those notes, he spoke of the need for "confidence. That means that the chief justice would have no hesitation in making a maximum delegation of responsibility to the Administrative Director of the Court and would not feel that he must undertake some particularly complicated issue personally because he could rely upon the Director and the staff to execute it discreetly, energetically and effectively." That this new boss should come in and demand that trust be built from the ground up instead of assuming his trust because of his long tenure in the job, was unsettling and, ultimately, unacceptable to Kleps. As Bird did it her way, gradually taking on each part of the administrative responsibility in order to comprehend it before turning it over to others, Kleps was afraid she would make serious mistakes. At a meeting with two members of her staff in early May, a month before he would resign, Kleps said, "Unless we work together jointly in this effort to protect her, we will wind up with all of our throats being cut."

It was as though Kleps had been run over with a bulldozer. He never expected to have his role questioned. He was a friendly person, a wise person. But he was also capable of being somewhat patronizing. In his first letter to Bird after she was nominated by Governor Brown, Kleps told her he was enclosing a "simplified description of the California judicial system that we use for public distribution. I know that this information is familiar ground for you, but you may find it a handy reference." Perhaps he meant well. But it was condescending to send such a brochure to the person who had just been nominated Chief Justice. Bird had a great deal of appellate experience and had been active in local and State Bar issues, sometimes in opposition to Kleps, for several years. She had never been a judge but, unlike many recipients of the brochure, she was not a high school civics student either.

While there is evidence that Bird and Kleps exchanged memos, sometimes sharply worded ones, there is little evidence that they tried to talk out their problems. Each of them made almost identical statements to me: each wondered why the other had not tried to talk to them. Both Kleps and Bird must bear some responsibility for this lack of communication.

"I knew he was unhappy," Bird told me. "He basically had the powers of the Chief Justice for a long time. . . . He didn't agree with a lot of things I had in mind."

By the time Bird became Chief Justice, Kleps was 62. He had served three chief justices and expected to serve a fourth until his retirement in a few years. But Kleps was soon certain that he did not have the confidence of the new Chief. There were the delegation-of-authority documents she refused to sign. She had also refused his request that she provide him with a rubber stamp of her signature for use on AOC documents. If Kleps felt his new boss had little confidence in him, he also had little confidence in her.

Kleps remembers that when he left his job in Sacramento as counsel to the legislature in 1961 to come to work for Gibson, some of his Sacramento colleagues thought his new job was "a job with no content. . . . One of my good friends . . . said, 'Why do you want to go down and just become Phil Gibson's errand boy?' And I said, 'I don't think that's what either the Chief Justice or I have in mind.' And of course that isn't the way it worked out," Kleps says. He speaks with pride of his accomplishments. California was the first state to have a statewide court administration. And because Kleps had been with it from the beginning and was identified so strongly with every facet of its operation, his advice was sought often by court systems in other states and by the federal judiciary. He was also widely respected in the California judiciary, so much so that many judges were shocked that Bird had done anything to offend or alienate him. But some judges also felt that Kleps, in the last half of his leadership of the AOC, had become too powerful, particularly under Wright. When he started the job in 1961, some thought he was going to become the Chief Justice's errand boy. But when he left it in 1977 some people thought he had come to see himself as the shadow Chief Justice.

Soon after Kleps left the court, he began writing a regular column, "Focus on Court Reform," in the *Los Angeles Daily Journal,* a large statewide legal affairs newspaper. Until his death in the summer of 1982, hardly a column by Kleps didn't take a swipe at Bird. Given the wide circulation of the paper among lawyers and judges, it was a particularly potent forum for him.

For her part, Bird had some strong ideas on changes that she thought would improve both the Supreme Court and the judiciary as a whole. She might have been more acceptable if she had come to the office with no ideas and only a question, "What do I do now?" She might have saved herself some agony by being less abrupt and more diplomatic before she instituted her changes. Be that as it may, she started right away. She had been noticing more than the rulings on her cases during those eight years she appeared in court as a public defender. She had been evaluating the system as a whole. She felt that trial judges should have the opportunity to sit temporarily on the Appeals Courts, including the Supreme Court, when substitute judges were needed. This idea led to her most innovative change. In the past, the practice had been to bring in on a temporary basis judges who had retired from the court. Bird wanted to continue to use re-tired judges, but she also assigned Municipal Court and Superior Court trial judges to sit for brief periods on the Courts of Appeal. She thought this practice would make for better judges. She felt she had become a better trial lawyer as a result of preparing appeals on her own cases. "It's good for the appellate judges to come into contact with the trial judges who are on the line every day, who see the impact, the practical impact, of what we do. . . . Some [appellate] judges have never been in the trial courts, either as lawyers or as judges. So it's very important for them to understand the perspective of someone at the trial level. Both sides gain an insight."

Bird was criticized immediately for this policy. She's so stupid, said some critics, that she wants to surround herself with equally inex-perienced people, trial court judges rather than experienced old hands. The testimonials from the lower court judges who have come "up" to the appellate courts have been so positive, however, that Bird thinks her approach has proven itself successful. Trial court judges have told her that they think the experience will make them less likely to make reversible errors.

Another Bird assignment policy has generated a savings and given more authority to presiding judges. She has greatly increased the use of blanket assignments. A blanket assignment from her authorizes a presiding judge in a given jurisdiction to use Municipal Court judges as Superior Court judges when the Superior Court docket is crowded. This is less expensive than having substitute judges sent from the outside. The increased use of the blanket policy increased the power of presiding judges to arrange personnel exchanges without getting in touch with her assignment staff in San Francisco. It also saved the taxpayers money—$250,000 during her first year as Chief Justice.

The idea for the increased use of blanket assignments came from the state's rural judges, many of whom preside in a one-judge county and often need to arrange exchanges when they must disqualify themselves from hearing a case because they know the litigants well. Bird once made a speech in which she thanked them for the idea. Soon afterward, she was taken to task in the press for insulting these rural judges by calling them the "cow county judges." A quick check would have informed the writer that the name she used is, in fact, their official one: the Cow County Judges Association. Far from being an insult, their name is a source of pride to them. The incident illustrates how easy it is for Bird to get in trouble with a careless press.

One of the two organized campaigns against her election in 1978, No-On-Bird, claimed that her use of trial judges on appellate assignments was a vast waste of money. The claim was false. A budget analyst for the legislature studied the budgets of the old and new systems and determined that the differential was negligible. It is believed that her new policy actually resulted in a savings because some trial judges are reversed less on technical errors after sitting temporarily on the appellate courts. Fewer retrials represent a savings.

The new Chief Justice was accused of assigning trial court judges to temporary spots on the appeals courts in order to build a political base. Judges would be grateful for the temporary elevation, went the speculation, and would become loyal to her. "That was nonsense," says Bird, and insists that her assignment policy is based on belief "in a democratic process with a small 'd'. I believe I can't as Chief Justice select out a few people and let them sit all the time."

Bird also wanted to move judges from lower court to higher court because she was concerned about the elitism within the judiciary. "I believed . . . that the judiciary was very fractured, [that] the judiciary did not look at itself as an organic whole. One of the ways to bring about unity was to get the people within the system to understand the rest of the system." Her musical chairs assignments would help that process. Even within the trial courts there were barriers between Municipal and Superior Court judges. As recently as a few years ago, the Superior Court judges in Los Angeles would not allow Municipal Court judges to eat in their cafeteria.

She broke the back of another seniority system, the appellate departments of the Superior Courts. "I anticipated there would be a loud reaction to this," she said. There was. Presiding judges complained and cries of "imperial chief justiceship" were heard. When Bird got to the Supreme Court, as part of learning the ropes, she went through a lot of old records. One of the things she discovered was that the same Superior Court judges tended to get assigned each year to the appellate departments of these courts. The three judges in each of the Superior Court appellate departments review all the appeals going out of their jurisdiction's Municipal Court. She discovered that in one jurisdiction one person had sat in the appellate division for thirteen years. In the past the power to appoint these people had been delegated by the Chief Justice to the presiding judge of each Superior Court. The first year she was Chief Justice she made the appointments herself. These appointments, she thought, should not be rewards for service but should go to judges with varying lengths of experience, and the makeup of the panel should change each year. For each panel she chose a judge of long experience, a judge of medium-length experience, and a new judge. She assigned a member of her staff to explain her plan to each presiding judge. However, some judges got their assignments from her before the presiding judge heard about her new system. One judge, a staunch supporter of Bird, was embarrassed to find out that he had been appointed to his court's appellate bench before his presiding judge was informed. After showing the presiding judges what she wanted, Bird wrote guidelines and asked the judges the next year to make the choices themselves, but according to democratic guidelines instead of according to seniority. Within two years the new system was working smoothly.

Another major change she made, one aimed indirectly at requiring Supreme Court justices to do more opinion-writing themselves, would not go so smoothly. Bird thought some justices relied too heavily on their law clerks and did too little basic work on their opinions. Some of the law clerks or research attorneys on the Supreme Court's central staff had been at the court longer than any justice and did most of the opinion-writing.

In a step that Bird says she now regrets, she wrote an article a few months after her arrival at the court, in the *American Bar Association Journal,* in which she advocated greater use of temporary law clerks instead of permanent research attorneys by appellate courts. She advocated a system closer to that used by the U.S. Supreme Court. This was perceived as an insult by Supreme Court staff attorneys, some of whom had spent their entire careers working for the Supreme Court. Bird thought then, as she still does, that it was important to have a mix of one-year law clerks and permanent staff. She thought the staff was too heavily weighted with permanent staff. She was concerned that the staff of permanent law clerks could, if relied on too heavily by the justices, become a shadow court.

She changed the functions of the court's central staff within her first weeks at the court. Each justice had a small staff of permanent research attorneys. But the chief justices of the past had used the central staff as their staff. In addition to preparing legal memorandums, they wrote opinions for the Chief Justice. When Bird first went to the court she received several calendar memorandums that had been written by the central staff describing criminal cases that would be argued at the hearing she would preside over her second week on the job. Bird reviewed the work and didn't like the quality of it. "I didn't agree with some of them," she told me. "Some of them I didn't feel were well written. We [she and her transition team] rewrote them. . . . I think that was like a slap in the face to the central staff . . . that I thought I was better than they were . . . I immediately . . . told the central staff . . . you will do no more opinion-writing. . . . Any opinion-writing for the Chief Justice will be done in my office." She told them their future responsibilities would be limited to writing memorandums for the justices' Wednesday conferences on State Bar matters and habeus issues and on criminal cases the justices were deciding whether to hear. That was still a lot of work, but it meant they would have no role in what most of them regarded as the most significant product of the work of the court, the individual justices' opinions. Some of them would later move to the staffs of individual justices so that they could once again write opinions.

Bird was critical of the work of the central staff, particularly that of Richard Morris, who had worked on former Chief Justice Wright's opinions before working on Bird's. Interestingly, Wright also made disparaging remarks to me about the work of Morris, who was introduced at Clark's farewell banquet in March 1981 as the father confessor of the court staff. But Wright never took steps to do anything about the problem. Bird, on the other hand, took immediate steps to remedy the situation. She hired her own staff of research attorneys, a mix of recent law-school graduates and experienced attorneys. She was accused of doing this because she was weak and could trust only her friends, yes-men and yes-women. The opposite is more likely. She has a strong, acute mind and sizes up talent perceptively. Instead of hiring yes-people, she hired bright and skillful people. She and they were soon producing well-researched and well-written opinions.

Bird also moved to reduce the number of unpublished opinions that came out of the Courts of Appeal and the number of "by the court" opinions issued by the Supreme Court without any justice's name signed to the opinion. Both of these mechanisms had been designed to help speed up the processing of cases. Even when she was a public defender, Bird recognized that the courts had a burdensome caseload. Nevertheless, she felt these two shortcuts kept justices from assuming public responsibility for their work. She wanted to find ways of eliminating case backlogs, ways that would not diminish court accountability.

A judge who admires Bird begged her to go more slowly even though he thought most of her changes were wise ones. "Rose, you have many years to make these changes," he said he told her. "Slow down." But that was not her style. Now, six years after she became Chief Justice, it is clear that her changes were not frivolous. Nor were they acts of someone trying to accumulate power for its own sake. Her new policies were well reasoned. There is little question that she believed, and probably correctly so, that the changes she initiated would improve the state courts and the way in which those courts serve the public. But she did not walk into a disaster area that required emergency measures. The courts of California had been functioning reasonably well.

So why the hurry? Bird's approach to administrative matters is to solve a perceived problem as quickly as possible after she has ascertained what the problem is and has consulted with others on how it needs to be solved. But some say her consultation did not involve thorough discussion of problems with those who were the causes of the problems.

Her fear that death was near was, Bird told me, part of her reason for initiating reforms so quickly. "I didn't know how much time I'd have," she said. In 1976, while Bird was still in Brown's cabinet, her right breast was removed because of cancer. She had her first recurrence in the fall of 1977, a few months after she came on the court, when a lump was removed. She felt well and was able to work long hours. Nevertheless, the prospect of death hovered and impelled her. In retrospect, she thinks that someone not driven by the prospect of death but who had the same goals for change in the court system would have probably taken five years to accomplish the changes she instituted within the first year on the job. "It would be a lot better that way," she told me. "You would see them [judges throughout the system] personally over a long period and build their trust in what you wanted to accomplish. Because I didn't know how much time I had, I moved quickly."

When Justice Clark once suggested to Bird that she could "dodge some political brickbats" if she would abandon her opinion in a particular case and join another justice's less controversial opinion, Bird said she told him that "I wasn't in the habit of dodging political brickbats." Later she testified: "From the time I came into this position I was regularly being hit by political brickbats, and I was simply used to it." Governor Brown's chief aide, Gray Davis, would tell me in 1980, "Rose is very nice, but she's not very political." Both Davis and Clark, probably for different reasons, were suggesting the same thing: be more clever, don't step on toes, don't rock the boat, make it easier on yourself. People who disliked her called her self-righteous. People who liked her looked at the same qualities and said she was highly principled. One judge who likes her told her only half in jest, "The trouble with you, Rose, is that you haven't learned to be a hypocrite."

Rose Bird is an extremely direct person. She will not play games in either important or unimportant matters. She says what she thinks, and she says it clearly. One of the problems with the institution she inherited was that though it did not participate in the compromises inherent in the other branches of government, it did sometimes express itself with indirection, imprecision, and elaborate confusion. She laughs at the trouble she had the first months she was at the court keeping a record of how a judge was voting. It is the Chief's job during the judges' private conferences to keep tabs on their votes on cases. Voting goes around the table by seniority. "It was like a minuet," she told me. "A justice would say, 'What a wonderful, carefully crafted memo you have done, Justice so-and-so. I found that especially your treatment of issue so-and-so was very thoughtfully done.' And he would go on for five minutes like that. I had trouble keeping the votes straight because I didn't realize that the person doing this basically disagreed with the entire memo. You soften the blow to the author . . . by telling him how beautifully it's written, how well it's crafted, but you end up saying you don't agree. . . . I was never used to that. I think it's a generational difference, and it's also a personality difference. If I don't agree with something or if I don't like something, I often take action, I'll tell you about it."

Her problem-solving approach contrasted most sharply with her predecessor's style in the way she handled suspected wrongdoing in the court. When asked, she said that had she come on the court and discovered that one of the justices was senile and completely unable to perform his duties, she would have immediately taken the matter to the Commission on Judicial Performance, the agency that didn't get the case of McComb until more than a decade after he became unable to function. What would she have done if she had been told a member of the court was giving information about pending cases to persons outside the court? She said she would have gone to the Commission on Judicial Performance and asked for an investigation. Perhaps those conclusions are easy to come to with the benefit of hindsight. But it was precisely this step that she took, and was much criticized for, when in November 1978 she wrote to the Commission and asked that there be an investigation of whether anyone on the court had improperly withheld decisions in order to assure her election victory.

In 1980 Governor Brown told a group of women leaders, some of whom had expressed concern about whether MediCal would continue to pay for abortions for poor women: "The real problem is Wiley Manuel and you should work on him." When Bird was told what he had said, she was outraged. A case concerning MediCal payment for abortions was then before the court. Presumably, Brown meant that because Manuel was a Catholic he might vote against state funding of abortions. Whatever he meant, any suggestion that a Supreme Court Justice should be lobbied is improper. Bird wrote to the Governor's office: "If this quote is accurate, it is frankly shocking. First, the issue is before this court. It has not even been argued so there is no way to know how any of the justices will vote. Second, the court is not the legislature in miniature to be pressured to bring about a desired result. I have spent the last 3½ years of my professional life fighting this type of pressure from the right wing. Do I now have to add the Governor of California to that list? I hope not. If the Governor did make those statements . . . they are at best inappropriate and at worst venal!"

Bird was direct, and so were those who opposed her. They would oppose her for many things she did, significant and insignificant. Perhaps it wasn't wise to be willing to take a beating with political brickbats. There was a truckload of them in the wings. The supply would last well beyond the 1978 election.

First there were the petty complaints. There were heavy drapes on the windows of the Chief Justice's chambers. Bird decided to remove them and replace them with narrow-slat Venetian blinds that would let in more light and save energy costs. Some court staff members were offended that she didn't like her office the way it had been. They were particularly upset when she wanted to move the table. The Chief Justice's office is a long room; it is both her working area and the place where the justices come for their weekly private conferences. They sit at a long table that fills one end of the room. Before she arrived at the court, Bird asked her aides to move the table. She wanted to arrange it in such a way that she could place a few chairs near her desk and be able to come from behind her desk and sit with people who came to meet with her. The protest was so strong, however, that she immediately asked that it be returned to its original position. Through the State's purchasing agency, she ordered new carpet for her office. When the carpet she had chosen from the list supplied her could not be found in California, the State ordered it from Georgia. Yet the story would be told later, privately and in the press, of how Bird had been so adamant about her choice of carpet that she demanded that the State get it wherever they could find it, "at whatever cost." Bird says that she never knew anything about a problem getting a carpet, and that she made no demands.

Some of the complaints against her were petty in the extreme. A few complained in behind-the-hand whispers that she did not even know how to dress well. Such complaints often were made at judges' meetings, though Bird herself was unaware of them. They complained about the colorful little bows she wore in her hair during the years she wore it in a bun. Fashionable dressing, of course, had never been an issue in the California judiciary before there was a woman chief justice. And the complaints usually came from judges who themselves would not be able to compete for any best-dressed lists.

A reporter called and wanted to know why she had had the taxpayers buy a new desk for her office. She had bought the desk herself, and given the old one to Justice Clark, who had admired it very much. That didn't get in the papers. A reporter called and wanted to know why she had had the taxpayers buy a refrigerator for her office. She had bought the tiny refrigerator herself for her own use and for that of her staff. No story appeared. A reporter called to find out why, after selling the court's limousine, she had had the state buy a brand new Ford Fairmount for her use. She had not ordered the car for herself. She had ordered it for Justice Clark. No story appeared about that either.

It seemed as though every time something new appeared in her office, a short time later the press would call to ask why she had purchased it. It became obvious that someone inside the court was giving detailed, though inaccurate, reports to the press about every item purchased. She had introduced "women's lib" into her office, one staff member told me in disgust. How so? On her desk, said my informant, was a coffee mug with "MS." written on it in big letters.

From the beginning, Bird received about 20 calls a day from the press. Most of them were about petty matters or from people asking what it felt like to be a woman chief justice. She calls them "do-you-roller-skate?" questions. Bird asked her executive assistant, Stephen Buehl, to return the calls. Reporters didn't like that. They wanted to talk to the Chief. They were disappointed, especially the reporters who had covered the court during Wright's time. He had been affable with them, often taking their calls himself. Wright, of course, not being the first female Chief Justice, did not get a hundred calls a week in his first months on the bench. Nor, affable as he was, did he supply reporters with confidential information.

Perhaps more troubling than the calls Bird's office got were the calls they did not get from reporters. At one point Bird had the locks changed on her office. Reporters wrote about it without asking why she changed them. A reporter from *The San Diego Union*, Margaret Warner, asked and was told. Unfortunately, her report never circulated beyond San Diego, and other papers keep repeating the change of locks as a sign of the Chief Justice's closed-door, if not paranoid, attitude. Actually, an unusual event had precipitated the changing of the locks. One Saturday night Bird and two members of her staff were still at work around 10 o'clock in her office. They were surprised when they heard a key turn in the door. They were even more surprised when the door opened up and in walked a man they all recognized as a Court of Appeal judge. He seemed a bit surprised himself. He stared at them briefly, offered no explanation for his presence, said, "Oh, I see you are working late," and left. As a judge who had matters pending before the Supreme Court, it was highly inappropriate for him to be going into a Supreme Court office where documents about his cases might be located. In any event, he had no business being there without an appointment. And it was difficult to find any benign explanation for his being there at that hour. The Chief inquired and found that one key opened every door in the Supreme Court. She ordered the locks on her office changed. Given the confidential nature of the documents in her office, her action seemed reasonable. When described without explanation, her act seemed paranoid.

Another time she ordered that the master key for the entire Supreme Court be changed. On the day in 1978 that the court took the tax-cutting Proposition 13 case, a case that was labeled "urgent" and that moved through the court with considerable speed because it affected every municipal and state agency in California, the master key to the court disappeared. A short time later a memo that had been written on the case by a member of the court's central staff was obtained by a reporter who regularly covered the court and given by her to a member of the staff of Attorney General Younger, a party to the lawsuit. The reporter provided the person with the names of the Supreme Court law clerks who were working on the case, with information on the judges' tentative votes, and with the name of the judge who would be writing the opinion. The person in the Attorney General's office was squeamish about what had happened and told Justice

Manuel. Naturally, Bird thought the combination of events—the disappearance of the master key and the giving of internal documents to the Attorney General—called for a new master key.

All the small things, the new carpet and getting rid of the drapes, became entwined in some staff members' minds with the few major changes. Initially hurt, staff members became angry. Bird admits now, "I didn't appreciate fully the institution from the inside, the interactions . . . how people have viewed their institution." The staff problems were the result of a complex mixture of personal emotion and professional pride and politics. Bird is right when she says that the bureaucracy in such a place can come to think that "it is the institution and that you [the judge] are the interloper. When you have people who have worked in an institution for thirty years, longer than any judge that's there, they feel that that institution is more theirs than anyone else's. It's human nature for them to feel that way."

Another important thing she didn't understand was that the institution was nearly sacred to some of the people who worked for the court. It was sacred not in the sense that justice is precious and is meted out here, but rather in the sense that the objects of the court were considered sacred. And it was sacred in the sense that justices were expected to be priests who protect and maintain the sacredness of the surroundings. And some of the staff members considered themselves acolytes who aided in the protection of the sacred objects.

Paul Ludlow, a Supreme Court bailiff who left in 1980 after a bitter public attack on Bird, who had refused to promote him, was near tears as he told me how Bird had destroyed the sacredness of the court: "The staff has always considered her chambers as a sanctuary deserving of the highest respect. . . . We have always considered the Chief's chambers off limits for other than official business. I was appalled the first time I saw members of Chief Justice Rose Bird's staff using her chambers to eat their lunch. There are seven leather chairs in there, and one day I happened to be going into her secretary's office just about lunch time, and I saw these four or five people on the Chief's staff eating their lunch at that conference table, sitting on those leather chairs. I liked to have blown my . . ." Ludlow is sad and furious as he tells the story. "Oh! I was just—" he searches for words strong enough to express his feelings. Finally: "It was sickening to think of it, it showed a lack of respect for the justices!

"What could I say? I wasn't about to say anything. [He would say a great deal two years later at a press conference.] But it really got to me. At the outset one of her attorneys had the audacity to change that conference table around to face north and south without the approval of the court. That table had been there for umpteen years in that position, and here you've got this little snotty-nosed attorney taking it upon himself to change that table around. Justice Mosk hit the ceiling. He said he wanted the table back the way it was. . . . And they changed it back. . . . I don't know what the point was, maybe to allow for better lighting while she was working in there. And, incidentally, under Wright nobody used his chambers to do their work, but some of Rose Bird's staff members used her chambers."

Ludlow remembers another event that saddened him deeply. "I was taking a group on a tour. I don't remember who they were, college students, or whatever. But at any rate, we were going into the courtroom, and I saw one of her law clerks sitting up there. He was sitting in Justice Manuel's chair at the bench. . . . Can you imagine that? This had come about because of her increasing her staff over what Wright had and thus the overcrowding and limited office space. . . . I saw him sitting there. He looked up and said something to the effect, 'I'm working now.' And I said, 'Well, I have to show these people this courtroom.' So I just ignored him. Boy, I was embarrassed."

Ludlow also was chagrined when the new Chief sold the court's limousine. ". . . It was good having the limousine. It shows some class and dignity. When you have four or five judges going to a banquet or dinner, it's good to show a little class and take them in a limousine. That's one of the things I like about President Reagan is that he's added a little class to the White House. Here we have Jerry Brown feeling that the little Plymouth is adequate. I take exception to that. . . . I'd say within six months after she came to the court she had one of her assistants take the limousine to Sacramento and put it on the auction. She uses her own car." Ludlow's voice contains both disappointment and contempt as he describes Bird's sale of the limousine.

Some of the people at the Supreme Court were like family to Ludlow. A retired army career man, former state police officer, and corrections officer, he had come to the court in 1970. As a bailiff he took pride in helping keep the place decorous, seeing that the justices' offices were well supplied, making repairs to furniture and equipment in the court's home offices and in circuit offices in Sacramento and Los Angeles. He had also developed some deep personal friendships at the court. "For three years I was not only Justice Peters' driver, but to a great extent I was a male nurse to him." Peters was the justice who had a progressive disease that crippled his body seriously but did not affect his mind. "It was 20 minutes to seven in the morning. I'll never forget it. I was the second person Mrs. Peters called to say he had died. . . . She asked me to be a pallbearer, which I considered a very high honor, considering the number of people that Justice Peters knew. And for me to be singled out to serve as a pallbearer along with people who were judges. I felt honored. It wasn't long after his death that Mrs. Peters and her daughter called me to her home. . . . She said, 'Paul, Janet and I have been discussing something that we know Ray would like for you to have,' and she handed me a little red leather case. In that case was Justice Peters' wristwatch." Ludlow leaves his kitchen, where we are talking, and comes back with the watch, a fine Swiss one. He is very proud of it.

"We got so close, almost like a father and son relationship, so close that he would tell me about the law. . . . I don't think it was so much because of my assistance to him, but I think it was because of our relationship that when he would go to dinner, I would quite often be invited to go with him and Mrs. Peters. . . . In spite of this close relationship I always respected him, not only because he was a man, but because of his position. And he respected me. And for that reason, when Justice Peters died, it was like my own father dying. It really got to me.

"It was like one big happy family at the court. There's nothing that any of us wouldn't have done for each other, gladly. But under Rose Bird the staff seemed to, well, that closeness seemed to fade, the harmony. That's the word, harmony, the harmony that existed under Wright seemed to fade under her."

Not everyone thought the pre-Bird days were perfect. But quite a few people did. They miss those days. Many of them speak of missing Chief Justice Wright.

Bird didn't understand the degree to which the court was family to some of the staff. She reflected on it four years after her arrival. "I think it's a matter of style. I'm not as gregarious as Wright was. Wright, I think, enjoyed going down the hallway, talking to each person. 'How are you? How are things?' And I think that's a very nice way to be. . . . I guess I'm more oriented to getting the work finished and achieving whatever I'm focused on at the moment. And I didn't have time to do it all. I guess also because it was so hostile here, maybe I withdrew more than I should have.

"I think in retrospect that if I had realized how close my analogy to the religious institution was to how people felt about this place, I would have understood much better that small things (taking down the drapes, selling the limousine, etc.) were tremendous symbols. Small changes meant a great deal and had a much greater impact than I had any concept of when I came into the system."

"Don Wright was a father to them," said one justice. "And they wanted Rose to be their mother, but she didn't take them into her arms." And it could be said that some of them responded like rejected children.

Bird did stay in her office most of the time, though she often visited justices in their chambers. In a move that didn't altogether please some members of the court, she made a special effort to befriend Justice Clark during the first year she was on the court. "I had heard that he and the previous Chief Justice didn't get along, that it had been a difficult situation for him for a long period. I sensed he had been made fun of, and I felt as Chief Justice I should reach out to everyone, including him." She appointed him court liaison with the Bar Association. Clark seemed grateful and surprised. He and all the other justices were given birthday parties by the Chief in her chambers and all staff members were invited. At the first party for Clark in 1977, she gave him a horseshoe, a nice good-luck charm for a rancher, she thought. And on Mosk's birthday there was an especially appropriate cake. He not only has a national reputation as a jurist, but is also an avid tennis player. So the Chief bought a cake decorated with an icing rendition of Mosk hitting a tennis ball. "At home on any court" was etched on the cake. Every New Year's there was a party in her office. It was true that she didn't like to be socializing in the halls as a matter of course, though she saw nothing wrong with it. She preferred to sit at her desk. She would meet with several staff people a day, but she met them in her office rather than in the corridors. Consequently, she was not seen with them; her socializing was not visible. Her style was to give occasional parties, most of them for the entire staff.

One thing that has never been reported is that the court staff was not unanimous in its dislike of Bird and her new policies. Some people were even enthusiastic about her arrival and the reforms she instituted. For some reason, reporters have not found these people, perhaps not even looked for them. One person who has worked at the court for many years said of his colleagues, "Who do these people think they are? She is the Chief Justice. I don't see anything wrong with what she's doing. And I don't see why she doesn't deserve my respect as much as Don Wright did. I get the feeling they just want to see her fail."

About a year after Bird became Chief Justice, she received an anonymous letter. It had been sent to the Bar Association and forwarded to her. The writer saw Bird as a hope for needed reform on the court staff. The writer, who identified him or herself as a Supreme Court employee, had written to the Bar asking for an investigation of attorneys who are paid to work full-time for the court but who conduct private law practices from their offices at the court. The writer said that practice had been a serious problem at the court for many years.

Apart from the question of being paid by the State during office hours, the problem with lawyers at the court having private practices is that any cases they work on could eventually be appealed to the court. Logically, they could be expected to have a strong bias in any such case. The writer of the anonymous letter reported that one lawyer at the court spent ninety percent of his workday conducting a private law practice at the court, not only preparing briefs, but having clients come to his office at the court. The writer said that although Chief Justice Wright disapproved of the man's practice, the Chief Justice didn't do anything about it. The writer reported that about 70 percent of the lawyers on the staff had some private law practice. The writer said that before Bird arrived at the court one staff lawyer's secretary was fired when she complained about doing work for him that was for his private practice rather than the Supreme Court.

The letter writer noted that when he or she worked fifteen years earlier for a private law firm in San Francisco, law clerks from the Supreme Court wrote briefs anonymously for the firm. "On appeal would the adversary party obtain justice?" asked the writer, adding that moonlighting by court staff attorneys, apart from being unethical, is also unfair to those other court attorneys who are forced to do not only their work but also that of the moonlighters.

"I am not an attorney, and I must remain anonymous for fear of retaliation," the letter writer said. "Bird probably doesn't even know me or recognize me. . . . Unfortunately, I only met her once . . . I am happy at what Bird is doing. She has changed the assignment of judges to including [sic] many minorities . . . and not allowing favoritism by constantly assigning retired judges, the same ones over and over again. Everyone, even before she was confirmed, decided she would be no good. She is strong and making changes. . . . She is working against a brick wall."

Bird was familiar with the basic problem the letter writer described, the moonlighting by staff attorneys. She had become aware of it soon after her arrival at the court. "When I saw it, I brought it up with the court, a request for a written rule that we limit outside employment. I haven't gotten it through here, but I have gotten it through every Court of Appeal." She found that some lawyers on the staff, in addition to conducting private law practices at the court, were grading State Bar examinations. They did it despite the fact that cases regarding the grading of the examinations were being litigated at the Supreme Court.

Bird issued a notice asking that no court personnel use the office phones for their personal business. That may seem petty, but it was prompted by an unusual discovery—that a court attaché was operating a blackjack counseling service from his desk at the court. His Supreme Court phone number was on his business card.

Some unnamed sources have been quoted in news stories as saying they wouldn't let their names be used publicly because they were afraid of retaliation from Bird. Interestingly, some on the staff who like her told me they have been afraid to let their names be used because they are afraid of retaliation from their colleagues. The press, unfortunately, apparently did not even look for these favorable anonymous sources and relied only on unfavorable ones.

One man who insisted on anonymity told me, "I was accused of being an informer—and just because I wasn't part of the hate campaign." He is both angry and sad as he describes the attitude toward Bird among some of his colleagues. "Sure," he says, "I was hoping someone on the court would get the job. After that was not the case, I felt she deserved my loyalty. But some said right away, 'Let's make it tough on her.' And they did."

Another member of the court staff told me of an extraordinarily unethical step taken by one supervisor. In one of the offices of the court where technical corrections on all justices' opinions are made, a supervisor gave at least one secretary specific orders not to correct any errors that appeared on opinions that came from Bird's office. The secretary told me the supervisor instructed her: "Don't correct any mistakes on Bird's papers. We don't want to do anything to help her. We want her to look foolish."

As the 1978 election approached, both natural and unnatural causes threatened Bird. There was the natural threat of her cancer. And there were the man-made threats. She was opposed from within the court and from outside the court. These two sources opposed her for different reasons. The forces who opposed her from the outside were the Law and Order Campaign Committee, by far the more active and vicious of the two, and No-On-Bird. The latter was an agriculture-based campaign organization headed by Mary Nimmo, the daughter of William Clark's friend Robert Nimmo, President Reagan's appointment as head of the Veterans Administration. It was Robert Nimmo who in July 1981 said on NBC's "Today" show that there was evidence that Agent Orange has caused nothing more serious in veterans exposed to it in Vietnam than teenage acne. Mary Nimmo herself would be appointed by the Reagan administration in 1981 to be Director of Public Relations for the United States Department of Commerce. Though her No-On-Bird campaign took pains to say it opposed Bird only because she was a poor administrator, in fact the public statements of both anti-Bird organizations opposed her on ideological grounds. Some of Justice Clark's closest friends were part of the Nimmo campaign organization.

Some people on the court staff also opposed her on ideological grounds, but that was not their basic complaint. They had been working with other liberals for years. These people were angry because she had disrupted their lives. As far as they were concerned, there had been too much change too fast. She had the nerve not only to change her own office, but to bring to the court her own small staff of attorneys and secretaries. In doing so, she was exercising the same prerogative that every justice on the court exercised. When she saw questionable practices, she moved quickly to change them. In another branch of the government or in corporate life, the steps she took as the new chief official likely would have been applauded as good management practices. But not in the village of the court.

It wasn't clear until 11 October 1978, slightly less than a month before the election, that these two forces—those outside the court and those inside—had come together to work for the defeat of the Chief Justice. On that day H. L. Richardson's Law and Order Campaign sent each member of the Supreme Court staff a self-addressed and stamped postcard and a letter asking them to indicate by an "X" whether they planned to vote yes or no on Bird on election day. Enclosed was a copy of an anonymous letter that had been sent to Richardson on 1 September on Supreme Court stationery. Underneath the name of the court, at the top of the letterhead, were these words: "Justices Chambers."

"As the letterhead indicates," began the letter to Richardson, "I am associated with the Supreme Court, and have been for some time. I strongly support your negative position on Rose Bird. I think I may have an idea for you. The enclosed roster represents a complete listing of Supreme Court personnel as of June '78. This includes all justices, their secretaries, attorneys, and law clerks, file clerks, librarians, and bailiffs. From my discussions with these 100-plus people, I now realize that *at least* [italics in original] 90 percent of them would vote to reject Bird." The letter suggested who should receive the letter and who should not receive it. Bird's staff and Court of Appeal justices should be omitted from the survey, presumably because they were expected to vote in favor of Bird and would skew the desired result: an overwhelming anti-Bird vote.

The letter closed: "If you need additional help, place a 'call Mom' personal ad in the *SF Chronicle* any Friday, using my psudonym [*sic*]: R. B. Hunter." Decoded, of course, it probably means Rose Bird Hunter.

Other members of the staff conducted their own Bird-hunting campaign. They told me they called relatives and friends throughout the state and asked them, in turn, to spread the word to vote no on Bird. Some of them told me they walked the streets of their neighborhoods in the Bay Area, went door to door urging a no vote on Bird. They were, of course, legitimately exercising their First Amendment rights.

But defeating a judge, particularly an appellate court judge, is not an easy thing. No appellate court judge had ever been rejected by California voters. And it didn't seem likely in 1978, despite the peculiar events leading up to the election. There had been accounts of petty complaints and inaccurate stories about Bird in the press, but there had been no hint of impropriety or injudicial performance on her part. Nevertheless, the efforts against her were significant. Not only did disgruntled staff members and the outside organized campaigns eventually mesh in their anti-Bird efforts; in addition, two justices became involved at the last minute, at least one of them apparently a willing party in the move to get rid of Bird.

One of Bird's lawyers during the 1979 investigation of the court, Jerome Falk, summed up the situation in the secret portion of the investigative hearings. Prior to the day before the election, he said, those who wanted to defeat her had "tried every political trick in the book, fair or foul . . . and it had not worked. . . . They tried the soft-on-crime issue, they tried the women's-emotionally-unstable issue, and a panoply of other pleas to the public. None of them looked, at that late date, like they were going to succeed." At the "eleventh hour and fifty-ninth minute," he said, they thought they had found the "only possible way" they could defeat her.

CHAPTER 5

"We're Not Playing Patty-Cake"

"We're not playing patty-cake. We're talking about the ideological direction of the court, and we've got to grab people's attention with tough talk."

—State Senator H. L. Richardson

It was the summer of 1978 and Republican Senator H. L. Richardson was talking tough to national political columnist Richard Reeves about his campaign to get Rose Bird off the California Supreme Court. At that time, Richardson was still hoping to raise a million dollars for his campaign against the Chief Justice.

A state senator since 1966, Richardson had been financing legislative races against liberal incumbents in the Assembly for nearly a decade. Just a year earlier he had raised $600,000 to defeat Governor Brown's veto of the Assembly's death penalty bill. The massive campaign was successful. The money came in handy, not only for the immediate campaign to get the death penalty bill passed. Richardson used it the next year to defeat those legislators who had voted against the override.

Clearly, Richardson was a force to be reckoned with. To be a liberal and come within his campaign sights was more like playing hara-kiri than playing patty-cake.

Senator Richardson is important to this story. He is, perhaps, important to the future of the judicial system, not only in California but in the nation. In the years since Ronald Reagan was Governor of California, Richardson has found a way to turn Reagan's anti-judiciary attacks into more than rhetoric. Richardson doesn't just lament liberal judges, he has created the means of removing them. The

New Right court watchers in Washington told me they view his work against the California courts as a model for what they will do to courts in other states and, more importantly, to the federal courts. Richardson was perfecting his attack on the courts in 1978.

Until 1978, Richardson and his campaign organizations had never ventured into judicial elections. They took their first step in 1978, the year that Rose Bird was on the ballot for approval. Richardson single-handedly changed the unwritten rules. Though the public has occasionally ousted a judge because of disagreement with his decisions, there has always been a generally accepted belief that it is important for the judiciary to be as independent as possible. Judges are not supposed to make their decisions according to the public's prejudices of the moment. This has meant that unless a judge acquired a reputation for being unfair or incompetent to perform, he or she could expect public acceptance.

Richardson made it clear in 1978 that he thought it was time to say goodbye to all that. He redefined judicial accountability. Along with Reagan and others in the New Right, he wanted judges to minimize the rights of defendants and maximize the number of convictions and the length of punishment. Richardson saw the courts as the last bastion of liberals. By 1978 he thought he could turn the tables on judges. He thought the pulse of the public by 1978 was so high about crime, that what had been considered impossible now could be done: throw a Supreme Court justice off the bench.

Who is this man who dared to accomplish what has never been accomplished, convince California voters to remove appellate court justices? He is a California combination of Jesse Helms and Richard Viguerie. Like them, his influence goes far beyond his home base, Arcadia, a small community of 47,000 people in southern California.

A maverick once shunned by California Republicans, Richardson is now a kingmaker. They used to avoid him like the plague. Now they show up at his press conferences and hope to receive his gilt by association with him. So, assured that now they need him more than he needs them, he laughs at them.

In his early years in politics, Richardson was called colorful, bizarre, extreme. Now he's called shrewd, though he still retains some of the early qualities. For instance, a few years ago he drove to Hangtown, a Gold Country town infamous as the scene of many hangings a century ago. Richardson was there to use a speech to a high-school class as the backdrop for a call for a return to public hanging of convicted criminals. He is a politician with a flair for his original occupation, advertising and public relations, where truth and myth often seem inseparable. Not all Republicans agree with Richardson's far-right politics. Sometimes he embarrasses them. Once, for instance, during a dispute on the Senate floor, he slugged another Republican, State Senator Milton Marks of San Francisco, in the mouth.

Richardson's politics put him slightly to the right of Attila the Hun, an assertion he would probably take as a compliment. But he can be as charming as Fred Astaire. He speaks with reporters in mind. He's the kind of interviewee who makes a reporter see his words in type as they are spoken.

The source of his significant power is the same as Viguerie's: computerized mailing lists. A former member of the John Birch Society, Richardson has founded a covey of organizations designed to further conservative causes. His fundraising groups include the Law and Order Campaign Committeee, the Free Market Political Action Committee, Gun Owners of California, and Gun Owners of America. Through his computer mail-order company, Computer Caging Corporation, Richardson raises money and mails campaign material to a continually growing mailing list. Numerous legislators have been defeated not by any grass-roots organization in their own district but by Richardson coming into their district and financing an opponent handpicked by him. Richardson's political machine, the computer, is effective not because of any loyal army of workers but because of contributions from thousands of fearful individual Californians, most of whom have never seen Richardson, have never voted for him, and have never heard him speak, but who believe he will help them keep their guns, get criminals off the street, and put prosecutors on the bench. With a push of the right buttons, for a fee, he can produce a massive list of people committed to a given New Right issue, people committed enough to give money. That's political power.

Richardson's tactics sometimes go beyond merely providing lists of known New Right donors. He also plays fast and loose with the truth. He got caught at it in 1981 when the State Senate was debating making Martin Luther King's birthday a state school holiday. Richardson was opposed to the idea. He distributed a five-page letter to the Senate and to the press in which he portrayed King as a Communist sympathizer. He wrote his colleagues that "many who have labored long and hard for equal rights see violence and hatred as the legacy of Martin Luther King Jr." Richardson then quoted in the letter a passage from King's book *Stride Toward Freedom:* "Almost anything, force, violence, murder, lying is a justifiable means toward the millennial end." "How can we honor anyone who would make such a statement?" Richardson implored his colleagues.

A short time later another senator, Nicholas Petris, a Democrat from Oakland, confronted the Senate with evidence that Richardson had been grossly devious. Richardson had lifted the King quote from this context: "Second, I strongly disagreed with Communism's ethical relativism. Since for the communist there is no divine government, no absolute moral order, there are no fixed amenable principles. Consequently, almost anything, force, violence, murder, lying, is a justifiable means toward the 'millennial' end. This type of relativism was abhorrent to me."

By 1980 Richardson felt powerful enough to tell a reporter: "I'm not strong enough to say who is going to be nominated for governor, but I'm sure as hell strong enough to say who won't be nominated." He had evidence of his power. "This is what we call our trophy room," he said as he guided a reporter to the office of one of his fundraising and lobbying organizations, Gun Owners of America. One wall is covered with photographs of defeated officeholders. Above the photographs is a black and white banner: "Taking the Anti-Gun Owners Out of Government." On display are people Richardson helped defeat—former State Senator Arlen F. Gregorio, former Congresswoman Yvonne Brathwaite Burke, and former U.S. Senator John V. Tunney. With contributions to his two gun owners' organizations, Richardson financed 24 candidates in the 1980 primary; 17 of them won. In the same primary he used money from his Law and Order Campaign Committee to finance candidates in 48 contested judicial, Assembly and Senate races. Thirty-one of Richardson's 48 candidates won. On another wall in his trophy room are some of the big-game winners he has supported: U.S. Senator S. I. Hayakawa, Lieutenant Governor Mike Curb, and President Ronald Reagan.

There was one person not on that wall that Richardson wanted very much to frame and put there: Chief Justice Rose Bird.

Until 1966 no campaign had ever been conducted against members of the Supreme Court. The campaigns of the state's appellate court judges had always been low-key. No one had ever been defeated. In fact, no appellate court judge ever received less than a 75 percent approval rating until 1966. That year the court had issued a decision that overturned a state law permitting discrimination in the sale and rental of housing. Southern Californians were outraged by the decision. A campaign against the three justices up for approval that year was organized and the "no" vote varied between 35 and 38 percent. Until 1978 that was the highest disapproval ever expressed in a Supreme Court election. The justice who received the highest no vote that year was Chief Justice Roger Traynor. Traynor had been Chief Justice since 1964 and had a national reputation as a brilliant and innovative jurist.

The 1978 campaign against Bird was crucial to Richardson. Given the fact that he wanted to get into the judge selection business in the same way that he already was in the legislator selection business, he had a lot riding on the election. Though it would become clear later that he had a lot of support in his effort to get rid of Bird—from inside the Supreme Court, from inside the State Attorney General's office, and from people now inside the White House—even some of his supporters thought he was politically foolish to take on a Supreme Court justice, even one whom he had been able to make into a symbol of all that was wrong with the judiciary. Why didn't he begin more modestly and focus only on lower court judges as he experimented with bringing his "tough talk" into the normally staid judicial elections? History should have told him that of all public officials, Supreme Court justices were the most difficult to defeat. They were nearly untouchable.

By late September 1978 his campaign against the Chief Justice was clearly faltering. "Efforts Lag in Drives to Oust Justice Bird" said a headline on a 17 October story by *Los Angeles Times* staff writer William Endicott. A *Times* poll taken in late October showed that though the outcome of the vote on Bird was in the hands of the undecided voters, there had been change in her favor since a poll taken in late September. On 2 November, five days before the election, Richardson told reporters he had raised only $200,000 of the million he had tried to raise for his campaign against Bird. By that time he had spent half the collected money on mailings to 500,000 southern California homes. Other money went for radio and television advertisements. He had produced and distributed television spots that were dramatic reenactments of rape and other crimes the ads claimed were endorsed or caused by judicial opinions written by Bird. Claims that the ads were unfair kept them off all but three stations.

Early on the morning of 7 November, anyone who had laughed at Richardson's gall in going after a Chief Justice was eating crow for breakfast. There in the morning papers and on all the radio and television news broadcasts was a story that would make people pause and think that day when they stood inside the voting booth and had to decide what to do about the line: "*Bird . . . Yes*_____ *No*_____" The story came from the front page of that morning's *Los Angeles Times*. The information in these first four paragraphs of the story would be repeated in papers and broadcast reports throughout the day:

> SACRAMENTO—The California Supreme Court has decided to overturn a 1975 law that requires prison terms for persons who use a gun during a violent crime, but has not made the decision public, well-placed court sources said Monday.
>
> The decision in *People vs. Tanner,* is certain to anger law enforcement officials around the state.
>
> The court sources said the decision was reached on a 4-3 vote, with

Chief Justice Rose Elizabeth Bird, whose name goes before voters today, among the majority.

The sources said that announcement of the decision is being delayed by Associate Justice Mathew O. Tobriner, who has been one of Ms. Bird's strong supporters against a well-organized campaign to win voter disapproval of her appointment to the court.

It was remarkable. By election day morning it looked as though Richardson might have the Chief Justice of the California Supreme Court on the edge of defeat. But perhaps even more remarkable was the fact that at the same time he had moved toward success in defeating her, he had also managed to bring into disrepute the integrity and honesty of the senior justice of the court, the widely respected Mathew O. Tobriner. Patty-cake? This man wasn't just going after the recent and somewhat controversial appointee, Bird. He had apparently decided to destroy, or help reporters destroy, a Supreme Court justice who had been on the court since 1962—the pride of the liberals. Liberal court-watchers would be saddened if Bird was defeated. But they would be grief-stricken by the damaging of Tobriner. Through the years, Tobriner's opinions may have angered some conservatives, but even by many of them he was considered a scholarly man of integrity. And to many liberals he was a mentor, even a hero.

When Richardson described to me a year later his contact with *Times* reporter Robert Fairbanks the day before the 1978 election, he said it was the first time he had been able to get a reporter to take seriously his accusations that the court was delaying decisions because of the elections. Richardson, or whoever had made it possible for the *Los Angeles Times* to get the information on which that story was based, had accomplished quite a coup. To get both Bird and Tobriner at the same time was a magnificent accomplishment, surely more than even the hard-playing Richardson could have hoped for, let alone planned, before election day. This one-two punch against the Supreme Court was like money in his long-term judicial campaign bank. Who could fail to be convinced that the judiciary of California was rotten to the core, and needed his reform, when the largest and most respected paper in the state on election day had written this devastating story about unethical political activity by perhaps both the Chief Justice and the senior member of the court?

Here was the state's court of last resort brought to its knees. One of the most respected newspapers, not only in the state but also in the country, had been confident enough of its sources to print a story that accused one of the justices of playing politics with court decisions. It was shocking news, especially to a public about to make a decision on the immediate political fortunes of the person on behalf of whom the alleged unethical activity—the delaying of a decision for political purposes—had taken place. Until now the average Californian might barely have recognized the names of appellate judges on the ballot; they weren't among the top ten newsmakers. But that day, 7 November 1978, Rose Bird was on every news report. It was hard to believe she was not aware of, if not a conspirator in, the wrongdoing. The *Times* had not even used the word "alleged"; readers would inevitably assume the reporters must have felt—must have *known*—their sources were certain of what they were talking about.

There was a crucial seventh paragraph in the *Times* story that seemed to add more veracity to the shocking news: "However, two other justices confirmed that individual decisions were signed some time ago by all members of the court. The justices could not explain why the outcome had not been announced."

Justices on the Supreme Court had talked with these reporters about the delay of a decision. Appellate judges usually speak only through their opinions. They aren't the kinds of sources who chat often with reporters, or have features written about themselves in *People Magazine* or the feature sections of newspapers, let alone chat about pending or completed judicial decisions. They usually refuse, as required by the judicial canons, to talk to anyone outside the court about a pending case. So it seemed quite significant that two justices had been willing to talk to reporters the day before election day, to confirm something about a pending case. That they were reported to have done so gave the impression that they had violated their normal silence to accomplish a greater good, to expose wrongdoing. That paragraph about the two "other justices" would be important in making the story seem believable. As the managing editor of the *Times* would tell me a year later, the presence of that paragraph in the story was central to the *Times* editors' decision to run the story.

Bird would win the election, but by a margin of only 1.7 percent. In other words, slightly more than 48 percent of the votes cast were against her. This made the anti-open-housing vote against the court in 1966 look mild by comparison.

Bird had won, but so had Richardson. He had won in several ways. Not only could he forever say Bird had *almost* lost. The election-day story's charges of unethical activity would place a heavy cloud over the court, a cloud that he could and would carry for years over every judge he chose to attack. Calls for an investigation of the court, even for impeachment hearings against Bird, began even as late voters were still on their way to the polls to vote in Bird. Spectacular grist for Richardson's mill. Two sensational news stories came out of California within three weeks of the election-day story about the Supreme Court: the killing of San Francisco's Mayor George Moscone and

Supervisor Harvey Milk by former Supervisor Dan White, and the deaths of more than nine hundred persons, most of them from the Bay Area, at the hands of former San Francisco pastor Jim Jones at Jonestown, Guyana. Despite the massive ongoing coverage of these two dramatic events, stories about wrongdoing at the Supreme Court continued to be on the front pages of California's newspapers. The national press came to write about the court, too. And rightly so, of course, for wrongdoing by such a widely respected and emulated court would naturally be a matter of national concern.

The ensuing stories added new details. First, there was a denial issued by Bird on election day: "There are *no completed cases* [italics hers] before this court where release has been delayed for political reasons or for any other reason extraneous to the decision-making process."

When *Times* reporter William Endicott called Tobriner late the afternoon before election day and asked him about the case, Tobriner, according to the story and according to Tobriner's testimony at the investigation the following summer, said: "I'm utterly sealed. My oath is not to disclose anything that goes on in this court. I can say nothing, absolutely zero, zero, zero."

In her one-page "Statement to the People of the State of California," issued too late on election day to affect voters, Bird strongly defended Tobriner. ". . . His refusal to answer any questions regarding a pending case is used to suggest that he is delaying release of that case until after the election. Nothing could be further from the truth. . . . Justice Tobriner's refusal to comment on a particular pending case was the only proper response. Canon 3(A) (6) of the Code of Judicial Conduct requires a judge to abstain from public comment about a pending or impending proceeding in any court. This principle applies not only to this court but also to courts throughout the land, including the United States Supreme Court.

"It is a curious coincidence that this story appears on the morning of the day when the voters are going to the polls. Those involved in the campaign against me, knowing full well that neither Justice Tobriner nor I may properly comment on any pending case, seek to exploit the fact that we honor that ethical standard.

"I will not permit Justice Tobriner's integrity to be maligned by those who seek momentary political advantage in their attacks against me. It is with a deep sense of sadness that I find it necessary to issue this statement today. However, I cannot stand by while an unprincipled attack is made on this court and one of its most distinguished members, Justice Mathew O. Tobriner."

The case that Tobriner was accused of delaying was not just any case. By 1978, when it looked as though the *Tanner* law might make history by removing a Chief Justice from office, the law had been associated with every attorney general's or governor's race for nearly a decade. Until Harold Tanner committed his crime in 1976, and so gave his name to it, the law was known only as the "use-a-gun-go-to-prison" law. During the 1970's, the bill was introduced in the legislature annually at the request of then Attorney General Evelle Younger. The Republican State Senator who kept introducing the bill for Younger, Fred Marler Jr., could not get the bill to go anywhere. It was defeated each time. But Marler's efforts were nonetheless rewarded. Ronald Reagan gave him a Superior Court judgeship before the future President became the former Governor.

The proposed law was still on Younger's mind in 1974 when he hoped he could succeed Reagan as Governor of California. He eventually dropped out of that race. But before he made that decision, he acquired a running mate: the "use-a-gun-go-to-prison" law was drafted as an initiative to run on the ballot during the primary race in the spring. It was called "Mandatory State Prison for Use of Gun." The initiative failed to get enough signatures to qualify for the ballot.

Ironically, it was under the new Jerry Brown administration that the law would be approved by the legislature. It was proposed by then Republican Senator George Deukmejian, a foe of the Governor. But Brown's office supported the bill and urged Assembly leaders to support it. The Governor spoke enthusiastically of the bill when he signed it. The new law required state prison terms when a gun was used in connection with certain crimes: murder, kidnapping, rape, robbery. But there was an important fact that neither politicians nor the press told the public: most people convicted of these crimes were already going to prison. In essence, the new law would affect only those for whom exceptions probably should be made. As one of Justice Clark's research attorneys, Maury Koblick, would testify at the 1979 investigation of the court, "It was a symbolic statute because most people who committed those enumerated felonies and used guns were going to prison already. It was more a popular statute than a statute that was to . . . put a large number of people into prison." As such, it was also a cruel way for legislators and law enforcement to gain popularity and votes.

"Use a gun, go to prison," said the billboards that Senator Deukmejian erected in urban parts of the state after the bill became law. They were paid for with money that included grants from the State Chamber of Commerce and the federal Law Enforcement Assistance Administration (LEAA). As you breezed down the freeway, the barrel of a gun took aim at you from the billboard. Beneath it was the bold message: "Use a gun, go to prison." Here was a law waiting to be tested. Harold Tanner didn't know it at the time, but at 3 o'clock on a July morning in 1976 he set in train a process that would eventually determine whether the law would stand up to the scrutiny of the state's highest court. In addition, his actions that day initiated the association of his name not only with the gun law but also with the supposed infamy of the State Supreme Court.

The case that married itself to the trial of the Supreme Court, *Tanner,* was almost as bizarre as the case against the court itself. Harold Tanner was 27 at the time he committed his crime. He worked for a private security firm that guards Seven-Eleven Stores. When the Seven-Eleven at East Palo Alto cancelled its contract with the firm, Harold Tanner hit upon an idea. He would stage a robbery at the store and, in doing so, would convince the store to renew its contract with the security firm. It was a pretty stupid idea.

At the time of the crime, Tanner was a clerk in a Seven-Eleven store in Hayward, a community across San Francisco Bay from East Palo Alto. He had no police record. His lawyer would later say that until the night of the robbery, "the most dangerous event of his life, other than serving in the Army, occurred when, as a teenager, he and his younger brother dressed up as Batman and Robin and climbed across rooftops to the delight of the neighborhood kids." But now, in the security business, Tanner was ambitious. In addition to working as a clerk for Seven-Eleven, he moonlighted for a private security firm that guarded several Seven-Eleven stores. This job required him to check employees' alertness by shoplifting minor items. He would return the goods and report to the store owners his evaluation of the store's security procedure. Tanner was apparently good at his work. He thought he would one day run the security firm.

But on his way to becoming Horatio Alger he went too far. When he learned that the East Palo Alto store had cancelled its contract with the firm, Tanner extended his employer's techniques from faked shoplifting to faked armed robbery. Tanner waited until a clerk he knew was on duty. He took an unloaded .22 pistol he believed to be inoperable, walked into the store and announced a holdup. According to the official record, the clerk said later that Tanner told him not to worry, that he would "understand later." Tanner told him to call the police, to play it straight, and to identify Tanner to the police. He left the store with $41, stopping to hold the door for an elderly woman customer who was coming in. He was arrested a few minutes later as he drove down the street. He protested that it was all a sham. "Sure, Harold," the arresting officer must have thought.

When Tanner went to trial, only the prosecutor would claim that he should go to prison. And even the prosecutor cited nothing in Tanner's background to justify imprisonment. It was the new law, the use-a-gun-go-to-prison law, that mandated it. Tanner must, the pros-

ecutor said, be sentenced to the five-to-life sentence the new law required. Even the sheriff disagreed with the prosecutor.

But a Reagan-appointed judge, Gerald Ragan of the San Mateo
County Superior Court, said no. He heard the facts of the case. He
heard the sheriff's detective recommend that for this individual
prison would be wrong; Tanner, the detective said, should serve a
short county jail term instead. The judge heard the probation officer
urge that Tanner should not go to prison but should instead serve six
months in jail and be required to undergo psychiatric treatment.

Because of other sentencing laws, to impose county jail rather than
a prison sentence a judge must place the defendant on probation. In
doing so, the judge makes a term in county jail a condition of the
probation. But the use-a-gun-go-to-prison law forbade probation
under any conditions if a gun was used in committing a robbery. As
Tanner's lawyer, Tom Nolan, put it, the only way that the judge could
avoid sentencing Tanner to a five-to-life sentence was by dismissing,
or striking, the charge that a gun was used. And this was the issue that
would later tear the Supreme Court apart. Did a judge retain that
power to strike despite the use-a-gun-go-to-prison law? When the case
was first decided by the Supreme Court, Justices Tobriner, Mosk and
Newman would claim that it was not necessary for the court to go to
the issue of whether the judge constitutionally had that power. They
claimed that because of another law still left on the books, a law that
provided for probation in exceptional cases, the judge could properly
decide to give probation. Justices Clark, Manuel, and Richardson disagreed. They claimed that the new statute forbade probation when a
gun was used and that the older statute did not mitigate the force of
the new statute. Bird agreed with the latter three justices that the
legislature had been clear in its intent to take away a judge's power to
grant probation, but she alone on the court spoke to the constitutional
issue, claiming that it was unconstitutional to remove a judge's power
to strike a prior finding.

Judge Ragan said from the bench that he thought the case was
"very, very rare . . . bizarre." He did not think Tanner should go to
prison. He struck out the gun-use charge, an act presumably easily
justified not only by Tanner's claim that he did not intend to rob but
also by the fact that Tanner's gun was unloaded and inoperable. With
the gun-use charge stricken, Tanner was eligible for probation, and
the new law no longer applied to him. The judge gave Tanner probation on condition that he serve a year in the county jail, that he
undergo psychiatric treatment, and that he not violate any laws for
five years. The Attorney General appealed Ragan's decision.

Appellate Court Judge Robert Kane, a judge who later would publicly call for Bird's removal, wrote the intermediate appellate opinion

saying that the judge could not strike the finding and must sentence Tanner to a prison term. When the case first came to the Supreme Court, Justice Clark recommended that the Supreme Court accept Kane's opinion and turn the case back to Judge Ragan for sentencing. Justice Tobriner opposed the Clark recommendation and a majority of the court joined him in voting to hear the case. The case was argued before the court in February 1978. The commission would later learn that in prosecutors' circles and publications a repetitious drumbeat — Tanner's-going-to-be-delayed-until-after-the-election — started as early as March, less than one month after the case was heard. That this drumbeat went beyond prosecutors' concern about the law to their concern about the 1978 election would not be clear for some time.

The election-day story was the first in an endless series of news stories that claimed Tobriner had delayed the Tanner decision. It became clear very soon that whoever those "high court sources" were, they were releasing confidential court information to reporters piecemeal. The information was often tantalizing, but none of it provided any confirmation of the original accusations.

On 15 November, a story claimed that the reason for the alleged delay of the *Tanner* decision, which was not officially released by the court until 22 December 1978, was that it contained a dissent by Justice William Clark that was sharply critical of the Chief Justice. The earliest stories had merely claimed that the decision had been delayed because it had overturned the use-a-gun-go-to-prison law. Now inside sources were saying it was more complicated than that; the dissenting opinion of Clark accused the Chief Justice of being inconsistent in her application of the law in two different cases in order to achieve the same end: victory for the defendants in both *Tanner* and *Caudillo,* the latter being a much-publicized rape case in which she had written a dissent that had attracted considerable controversial attention in the summer of 1978. The difficulty with this story about Clark's dissent, as well as some others, was that the "inside" sources were intentionally or unintentionally misrepresenting the Chief Justice's opinion in *Tanner* and were not providing reporters with any documentary evidence.

But a day later, 16 November, an original document was provided to the press by an inside source. Tobriner, it said, had asked his colleagues after election day to sign a statement saying the court had done nothing improper in its handling of *Tanner.* The interesting detail in this story was that one justice had refused to sign Tobriner's statement. A week later *The Washington Post* would report that the missing signature belonged to Justice Clark. He had refused to sign

Tobriner's statement that said "neither the final determination nor the filing of that decision has been delayed for political or any other improper reason." Clark told *Washington Post* reporter Lou Cannon that he had "decisive reasons" for not signing the statement Tobriner circulated. This was significant. Clark seemed to be saying he had reason to believe the decision may have been delayed for improper purposes. It would be many months before it would be known that there was sometimes a world of difference between what Clark actually knew and what he was willing to imply he knew. Cannon reported that Clark would not reveal his "decisive reasons" because he expected to have to testify under oath about the matter. Amid all the babble about whether yet other decisions were being delayed and all the news about why Bird and Tobriner probably would have wanted *Tanner* delayed, this remark by Clark was the first indication that the court might be investigated. On the same day, the California Chamber of Commerce, which had helped pay for the use-a-gun billboards, called for an investigation of the court.

Cannon's story appeared all over the country on Thanksgiving Day in papers that take the *Post*'s wire service. In the end its greatest significance would be that it suggested that yet another Supreme Court justice, Wiley Manuel, was involved in the unethical plot to delay a decision until after the election. Manuel was not named but the description made it clear he was being accused. Later stories would name him as an alleged participant in a scheme to delay.

The day after Cannon's story appeared, Bird wrote a letter to the chairman of the State's Commission on Judicial Performance, Court of Appeal Justice Bertram D. Janes, and requested that the Commission investigate "the charge that the Supreme Court improperly deferred announcing a decision in the *Tanner* case." At the same time she sent the letter, Bird issued a press release announcing she had asked for an investigation.

Her request for the investigation would itself become a source of controversy on several grounds. She had asked for it without consulting with the entire court. Some of the justices were enraged. Bird realizes her lack of consultation is a justifiable criticism. But at the time she wrote the letter, it was obvious that at least some of the accusations being made against the court were being made from within. It was obvious that documents that were released to establish false or half-truthful impressions probably were being released by a Supreme Court justice, for no one else had access to them. She thought it unlikely those people would want an investigation of the court.

As a citizen, despite the fact that she was the Chief Justice, Bird enjoyed the same privilege that any other citizen of California had:

she could request an investigation by the Commission. She was criticized for making the request public. Some even said that making the request public violated the rules that govern the Commission. The rules call for confidentiality of all papers filed with the Commission, but, in fact, the confidentiality is required of the Commission and its staff, not of the person filing the original request, according to Janes.

After promising that she would cooperate fully with any investigation by the Commission, Bird said in her letter to Janes: "It is my firm conviction that in this way the false allegations which have been made against this court and its justices can be fully and completely examined. If the charges were true, they would be grave. I know that they are not. But that is not enough. The people of California are also entitled to be assured their judges are conducting themselves properly. A full and fair examination of the charges by your Commission can clear the air, and thereby restore the public confidence in the judiciary which has been damaged by these false accusations."

Some people, including some members of the Judicial Council who would establish rules for how the hearing would be conducted, interpreted Bird's comment to Janes that she knew the charges were not true to be a demand by her that the Commission find there was no wrongdoing. Some thought it completely inappropriate for the Chief Justice to ask for an investigation of her own court, particularly without consulting her colleagues. When I talked with Janes in the summer of 1981, nearly two years after the extraordinary investigation had been completed, he reflected on how he had felt when he received the Chief's request. In the first place, it meant he would delay his retirement, not a pleasant thought to a man looking forward to returning to his home in the Sierra. He already had submitted some of the papers for his retirement from the bench in Sacramento. But such an investigation was a challenge he said he couldn't pass up. For six years he had been chairman of the Commission on Judicial Performance. He could not retire now and miss the biggest challenge of his career, an investigation of the Supreme Court as a whole. He withdrew his retirement papers. As a Court of Appeal judge in the state system, Janes had heard the same rumors about Bird that others had heard and accepted as truth—that she was inaccessible and not a good administrator. Nevertheless, he said he found it hard to condemn her request in the wholesale manner that many did. "She's at the head of the court and she had a problem festering there," said Janes. "She probably felt she had to act. . . . I think the Supreme Court is entitled to defend itself. I don't think it has to sit like a punching bag."

Another paragraph in Bird's letter to Janes would become quite controversial. She asked that if, "after investigation, the commission finds that circumstances warrant, it consider the issuance of a public report under the authority of Rule 902(b)(2), describing the Commission's factual findings and conclusions in sufficient detail to address all issues which have been raised."

What she was referring to was a rule that governed the operations of the Commission. The rule provided that any proceedings before the Commission were to be confidential, but that the Commisison could release information about its proceedings under certain circumstances. The rule Bird referred to described one of those circumstances, one that would cover the present investigation if a preliminary investigation of the court didn't lead to formal charges against any of the Supreme Court justices. The rule is: "If a judge is publicly associated with having engaged in serious reprehensible conduct or having committed a major offense, and after a preliminary investigation or a formal hearing it is determined there is no basis for further proceedings or recommendation of discipline, the Commission may issue a short explanatory statement."

In other words, Bird was suggesting that the Commission conduct its business as usual. First, there would be the private confidential investigation. Then, if at the end of that first stage, conducted in private as a grand jury investigation is, the Commission felt there was a basis for charges to be brought against a judge, it would proceed to a second stage. This stage would ordinarily consist of a closed hearing at which under-oath testimony would be heard from witnesses. The commissioners must decide at the conclusion of this second phase whether the evidence means that the charged justice should be: removed from the bench, publicly censured for his or her behavior, privately admonished, or cleared of wrongdoing. If the conclusion is that the judge should be either removed or censured, the Commission must file a copy of the transcript of the testimony taken in the case, plus a statement of its findings and conclusions with the clerk of the Supreme Court. At this point, the entire record of the investigation becomes public.

Rule 902(b)(2), referred to by Bird in her letter, provides for public disclosure of the results of an investigation of judges in the event that public attention was drawn to the accusation against a judge, but he or she was found innocent of wrongdoing at the end of stage one. Though the framers of the original rules governing investigations of judges had never anticipated that such an investigation might involve accusation against a Supreme Court justice, let alone every Supreme Court justice simultaneously—which is what ultimately happened as a result of the election day story—they had anticipated both the need for secrecy in the early stages of investigations and the need for public explanation of results of investigations that led to no charges. They also had provided for full disclosure of hearings and investigations that led to charges.

There are several reasons for confidential investigations of complaints against judges. The first is the same reason that has kept grand juries behind closed doors and that has kept most preliminary investigative bodies secret—initial investigations necessarily involve the pursuing of many threads of information, many of them utterly untrue. Many witnesses at this initial stage are found to be relying on either frivolous or malicious hearsay against the person they are accusing. Private investigations allow investigators to sift through both the undiscriminating as well as the discriminating witnesses to determine if there is cause for charges to be brought against the accused. The process can serve the best interests of all parties involved. If the only evidence against the person is based upon hearsay and innuendo, the investigators cannot show cause for bringing charges. If the evidence gathered in this initial confidential phase is valid then the case has a much greater chance of leading to charges.

Confidentiality at this stage is a means of preserving reputations that may be falsely maligned and of saving taxpayers' money from being spent on elaborate but unnecessary investigations. Another very important reason for it is that many witnesses, because they fear retaliation, will not come forward unless they can do so in secret. This gives investigators a chance to get information they will not get otherwise.

Those who established the rules of the Commission had another reason for thinking that it was important to provide confidentiality in the initial stages of an investigation of a judge. Judges are considered prestigious and powerful people, but they also probably have more enemies than any other group of people. By its very nature, their work creates enemies. In nearly every case they hear, one of the parties loses. And a number of those losing parties blame the judge. And some of the losers are willing to go quite far to get revenge. Consequently, many complaints officially filed against judges are found to be groundless complaints filed by disgruntled litigants.

But occasionally there is a case where the judge's questionable behavior is widely known before the complaints are filed, or, as in the 1978 accusations against the Supreme Court, where the press has publicized the accusations, so that a failure to report that a preliminary investigation found no wrongdoing would be disastrous to the investigated judge's reputation. He or she would be left twisting in the wind indefinitely. Hence the provision in the Commission's rules for publicizing conclusions in cases where complaints have been publicized.

Bird is blamed for precipitating the investigation by writing her letter to Janes. Janes told me, however, that the investigation would have taken place with or without the letter from Bird. In fact, the Commission had received several letters asking for an investigation before she sent hers. Actually, the Commission didn't need a letter from anyone; in the past, some of its investigations have been initiated by a story in a newspaper. The Commission's decision to investigate does not depend on a formal request being filed. The accusations that appeared on election day and were publicly repeated nearly daily thereafter, became even harsher and more condemnatory. They could not be ignored by the agency that had been set up in 1961 to investigate complaints against judges. With or without letters from Bird or anyone else, the Commission would have investigated the accusations. The only question was how. Resolving that question became a shrewd political game.

This question arose from several considerations. Because this investigation involved all the justices of the Supreme Court—in a collegial body where all were responsible for moving decisions, all would have to be questioned and investigated about accusations of delay—it would be unlike any other investigation conducted by the Commission. It was clear that the press interest would be enormous. The commissioners agreed with the Chief Justice that there must be a public report, but they did not agree that the existing rules provided for an adequate public report in the event that no basis for filing charges was found at the end of stage one, the investigative phase. They felt that the "short, explanatory statement" permitted under the existing rules would be an inadequate way to inform the public of the Commission's conclusions in that event. "It would be like a whitewash," Janes told me. The Commission was afraid that if it found no basis for charges and didn't release a substantial report on the reason for no charges, the Commission itself would be disgraced and accused of being a tool of the Supreme Court.

Richardson came very close to getting the voters of California to reject Bird on election day in 1978. He managed to create an impression of chaos, if not outright wrongdoing, in the Supreme Court. But the circus that erupted in esteemed judicial organizations as a result of his election-day success was at least as responsible as his campaign for sustaining the impression of chaos. Even the means of setting up the investigation were chaotic. When the esteemed Commission on Judicial Performance, the investigating agency, asked the esteemed Judicial Council, the rule-making body for the courts and affiliated bodies, for a rule change for this one investigation, it became clear that whatever the truth or falsity of the election-day accusations against the court, the path to discovering the truth would be paved with politics: the politics of the right, the politics of the legal establishment, the politics of sexism. Given how well each institution involved had performed before, what happened now as this historic investigation was prepared, was a disgrace.

It is two years since the end of the investigation. Justice Janes, now retired, is sitting at a picnic table on the front porch of his home a few miles outside Quincy, a beautiful village high in the Sierra. The records of the investigation are stored in his barn a few hundred feet away. He hasn't looked at them since the hearings ended in 1979. As we talk about the debacle that started when he and the other commissioners went to the Judicial Council and asked for a rule change, Janes hits the picnic table hard. "I used to slam my hand like that, and say that the prime thing we wanted was a public report. You know that's all the Commission ever asked. We didn't ask for any . . . this TV and radio and all this business. We didn't want that at all. All we wanted was the authority. . . . In view of the nature of the accusations, the fact that the Supreme Court was involved, we wanted to file a public report. We wanted to make public our findings and conclusions. . . . The word 'whitewash' was being used by the media, and by the legislature. [People were saying] 'Oh, hell, they'll just whitewash the courts.' And that's the thing we wanted to avoid."

The chances are pretty good that if the commission had conducted this investigation as usual—the first stage in private—and then issued the public statement it originally wanted to issue, the investigation of the justices of the California Supreme Court would have had a clear, satisfactory conclusion, one in which the public would have had a complete report on the nature of the evidence for or against the accused justices. To issue such a report, the commissioners would have had to interpret as a vague term the "short explanatory statement" specified in the rules. Short compared to what? Is a short statement one page, two pages? Well, ten pages is short compared to one hundred pages, but long compared to one page. And 250 pages would be short compared to the 3,000 pages of testimony taken during the investigation.

The Commission chose not to assume it had leeway to decide what "short" meant. Instead, it went to the Judicial Council, a 21-member body of judges, legislators, and representatives of the State Bar Board of Governors and the public. The Council makes rules and sets policy for courts and court-related agencies, such as Janes' Commission on Judicial Performance. The Commission asked the Council to relax the rules for just this one investigation, to permit it to issue a full report at the end of its investigation of the court. The normally staid and rational Council's reaction was panic. It was as though the Commission was throwing away the bath water, and as it did so, the Council yelled, "You forgot to throw away the baby!"

When the executive committee of the Judicial Council met on 9 January 1979 to consider the Commission's request for a rule change, one member, Orange County Superior Court Judge Bruce Sumner, told the committee that the Council should simply empower the Commission on Judicial Performance, for this one occasion, to be, in effect, a blue ribbon panel of ordinary citizens who just happened to be members also of the Commission. Now that, Justice Janes told me later, would have been a whitewash with a capital "W".

Three of the four members of the executive committee—all except Sumner—voted to recommend that the Council refuse to make a rule change and insist that the Commission proceed under the existing rules which already provided for public release of information. It was after Alameda County Superior Court Judge Spurgeon Avakian read the report making this recommendation that the Council started to panic. The Chief Justice's letter to Janes was interpreted in a variety of ways.

Though the meetings of the Council were open to press coverage and were covered, the public got no idea of the complexity of what was going on. A review of transcripts of the meetings reveals that the reporters present apparently had little understanding of the proceedings. And despite the fact that the Commission maintains a professional staff willing to explain its procedures to the press, the public had no way of knowing from press reports what the Commission's normal procedures were and how the Council drastically changed them for this one investigation. To the public it seemed simply a matter of whether the investigation would be open or closed. And that translated, of course, to: Will they open it and tell us the truth or will they close it and hide the truth?

Incredibly, the decision to publicly investigate the California Supreme Court justices was made by Judicial Council members who voted for it without realizing until later what they were voting for. The legislature was breathing down their necks. At one of the meetings of the Council, one of the legislature's representatives on the Council, Jack Fenton, challenged the judge members by saying, "You think your people are bad. You ought to see some of our crazies if they get started on this." It was a not-so-subtle threat about something they had been reading in recent stories: there were quite a few people in the legislature who wanted to hold impeachment hearings against one or more justices of the Supreme Court if the Commission on Judicial Performance didn't conduct an investigation. "There was extreme pressure from the legislature," said Sumner when I talked with him in 1981.

Sumner believes, as did at least one justice on the court, Stanley Mosk, that there should have been no investigation of the justices.

"The lesson for the future should be that a judicial decision can't be made the basis for an investigation because of its [the decision's] unpopularity," Sumner told me. "You're always going to find people saying that the judge has been paid off or made the decision because of some political reason. Along with the job of being a judge has to be a willingness to accept that type of criticism. . . . You just have to ride out the storm. The buck does stop here. . . . That criticism goes along with the job."

Sumner is right. Judges must be willing to ride out a storm when their decisions are criticized. But Sumner is also wrong. A judge should not expect to go uninvestigated when accusations of unethical conduct are made against him or her. And that was what was at stake here—the possibility of unethical conduct so serious that it could justify removal from the bench. For the public's sake and the court's sake, the wrongdoing needed to be investigated. To ignore it, as Sumner and Mosk wanted to do, would have been a political act as demeaning to the public and to the court as either unethical conduct or unfounded accusations of unethical conduct. When such accusations are made, the public clearly has a need to know—and a duty, through its constitutionally established body, the Commission on Judicial Performance, either to clear or to punish the accused.

Despite the fact that Sumner believed there should have been no investigation, he was one of the leaders of the move in the Council to hold a public investigation. What he got and what he wanted, however, were two very different things. He wanted the initial investigation to be private but stage two, the hearing that would follow the filing of charges found in stage one, to be public. What he got in the end was an open *initial* investigation.

Sumner had amazing things to say about what the Judicial Council did. It was clear, he said, that the special rule the Council adopted that required the Commission to conduct its initial investigation in public was unconstitutional. He nevertheless noted for the record that, because the Chief Justice "asked for it," the Council had no choice but to pass it, despite the fact that the Council knew it was unconstitutional. He said that if just one Supreme Court justice had said, "I don't think this should be done," the Council would not have required the public hearing. "Nobody on the court said, 'We disagree.' . . . Maybe we should have polled the members of the court to see if they agreed with the Chief Justice. But we assumed they were big kids, and if they didn't want this investigation they would have said so."

I expressed surprise to Sumner that the targets of the investigation—the justices of the court—would be regarded as rightfully having the power to shape, even halt, the investigation of themselves. I asked if I misunderstood him. No, he thought they should have been able to stop an investigation of themselves. I countered that "most citizens would have no say in who is going to investigate them" or whether they are going to be investigated. He reacted immediately and sharply: "We're not talking about citizens. We're talking about justices of the Supreme Court of the largest judicial system in the free world, three times bigger than the federal system. There's nothing bigger than the California court system!"

The Alice-in-Wonderland aura seemed to permeate every phase. As Chief Justice, Bird was chairperson of the Council, and Tobriner was vice-chairperson. Because the Council was making a decision about the rules of an investigation of them, the two justices removed themselves from the Council for these meetings. To those who believe in fairness and in the avoidance of even the appearance of conflict of interest, their action seemed logical. But to some on the Council, including Sumner, it seemed inappropriate and he said so at the meetings. She should have stayed on, he told me. She was playing politics by absenting herself from the process. Yet if she had stayed to participate in the decision, the same complaint of playing politics would surely—and with some justice—have been made. When I pointed out to Sumner that her letter did not ask for a public hearing but for a public report on the findings of the hearing, Sumner replied, "Ahhhh, very candidly, she was playing politics. She wanted, in my view, to appear to ask for a public investigation but not really ask for a public investigation." A short time earlier, he insisted that she had demanded a public investigation.

Later in the interview he told me, "It's her Council. . . . Without her leadership and without an indication from her we could only assume that she meant what she said. And when she said she wanted a public hearing, we proceeded to set up the machinery to allow that to happen." Sumner expressed regret at the damage the Council's action ultimately did to the court and to the Commission. I told him that I was willing to assume for the minute what I did not believe from the documentary evidence: that the Chief Justice specifically asked Janes to conduct a public hearing, something not authorized by the rules. If that were so, why didn't the Council do what it thought was proper rather than what it thought she wanted?

The painfully contorted illogicality of Sumner's response belatedly helped explain the political conundrum that shaped the investigation and that much later still haunted some of those who were investigated. Certain justice was not the goal in this case. Bafflement was.

"The Council," Sumner replied, "is just the lackey of the Chief Justice. . . . They [the justices by their silence] asked for it, and they got it. They didn't think it through. To me it's that simple. The Chief

Justice has imperial power, there's no comparable position in government."

"The Judicial Council is a check on that power, isn't it?" I asked Sumner.

"No."

"Why not?"

"They're all appointed by her," said Sumner. He was referring to the fact that 15 of the 21 members of the Council are appointed by the Chief Justice. However, the judges on this Council had been appointed not by Bird but by former Chief Justice Wright before he left office.

"You didn't have to vote the way you did, did you?" I asked Sumner.

"Yeah, that's right. . . . But that's what she wanted—a public hearing—so we let her do it. . . . We didn't think it was a good idea, but nobody asked us, they just told us."

I continued to be puzzled by his interpretation of Bird's letter, by his interpretation of the Commission's request to be able to issue a full report, and, perhaps most of all, by his claim that the Chief Justice, even when absent from the Council, has "imperial" power over it.

"Well, excuse the expression, but are you saying that the members of the Council are her rubberstamp?" I asked.

"Absolutely, it is," said Sumner.

"If you are in disagreement with her, you don't have to vote with her, do you?" I could tell Judge Sumner thought the question was silly. "I am naive?" I asked.

"You're naive." He explained that the Chief Justice doesn't appoint anybody except people who vote for what she wants. Finally, Sumner said, "Judges like to get promoted, and you don't want to be on the bad side of the Chief Justice."

"Are you saying that's part of what happened?" I asked.

"I think that's part of it, part of it."

"But a few of you weren't appointed to the Council by her" I reminded him.

"Most of us," he admitted, "weren't appointed by her. We were holdovers from Don Wright. Our terms were expiring [in a few days]."

So why, if they felt intimidated, couldn't they have been particularly courageous, stood their own ground, and done what they thought was right? If they believed, as Sumner suggested, that by their votes the Council was doing irreversible harm to both the Commission and the court, why didn't the Council refuse to take that harmful step? "If most of you were not appointed by her," I asked Sumner, "you were not 'her people.' But you're saying that because she's Chief Justice she has influence over your future careers?"

"Yes," said Judge Sumner. "The Judicial Council is a good deal like a presidential cabinet. . . . They want to stay . . . and she's very close to the Governor, and that's very well known [the Governor makes judicial appointments]." I gathered from the look on Sumner's face that, to put it politely, he was again wondering if I was a slow learner.

He paused. "This sounds very vicious," he said, "but you wanted to know what happened, and I'm trying to tell you."

The transcripts of the meetings of the Council and of its executive committee confirm that what went on was confusing at best, and more than likely—to use Sumner's word—vicious. All the people involved were intelligent and experienced both in their jobs and as members of the Council. For those reasons, their actions were an insult to themselves. They had to justify what they had done, inasmuch as their action went against not only what the Commission had asked them to do but also against the State Constitution. They would establish their justification by blaming the Chief Justice. Strangely, that same justification—"She made me do it!"—came from people who had made quite opposite assumptions about the Chief Justice's request for an investigation. Thus, some Judicial Council members said the Chief Justice had asked for an open investigation, and that they had voted to give her what she asked for, no matter that they believed the hearing should not be open. Others said she asked that there not be an open investigation, and so must have been trying to hide wrongdoing; these people said they voted for an open hearing in order to prevent her from obstructing justice. The Chief Justice could not, of course, have taken both positions. Most of these people were simply putting words in her mouth so she would appear to be a fool no matter what happened. Currying favor with her, as Sumner suggested, was probably the last thing on their minds. Not until the investigation could the public know whether or not she, like they, was playing politics with the judicial system.

So, in the midst of great confusion and political expediency, the Judicial Council gave birth to Rule 902.5 of the California Rules of Court. The rule required the Commission, in just this one case, to violate long-established rules of confidentiality and to hold a public hearing at the initial investigative stage. It was Seth Hufstedler, a prominent Los Angeles attorney and former president of the State Bar who was hired by the Commission as its special counsel for this investigation, who called the new rule a Rube Goldberg. The label was apt. Like the famous artist's contraptions, Rule 902.5 was unworkable. But a real Rube Goldberg is playful, it gets a laugh from the person who studies it and realizes its futility. Rule 902.5 didn't provoke laughs. It did provoke a few sheepish grins from those who recognized the devilishness of what they had done.

Justice Janes, the man who had delayed his retirement in order to preside as chairman of the Commission during the investigation, was astonished. He went to the Judicial Council meetings to plead for a modest rule change and felt consternation when the Council presented him with a monster rule change. Sensing Janes' reaction, a Council member said to him during the meeting, "Can you live with the rule?" Janes promptly responded, "No. . . . The complications are astronomical."

One of the complications was that the new rule meant that there would be virtually no due process during the investigation. In this one investigation, the due process guaranteed in all other investigations of judges—and of all citizens, for that matter—was removed. It was ironic, to say the least, that a court whose function is to guarantee due process lost that due process for itself. One commissioner who sat on the investigating panel angrily told me that the new rule "opened up tarring and feathering as an option to the Commission."

The Judicial Council had used the rhetoric of sunshine laws to force the Commission to hold an open investigation. The rhetoric was misplaced. It was as though the Judicial Council had assumed that the accused in this case did not need to be protected by the due process that initial confidential proceedings had guaranteed the subjects of all previous Commission investigations. "This doesn't come from court haters," said a judge member of the Judicial Council as he urged voting for an open investigation. The *Los Angeles Times,* said the judge, reported that the accusations "came from two justices." His comment implied that the sources, eventually to become witnesses, should be presumed to be pure as the driven snow because they were justices. The result of such thinking was, of course, not only unjust to the accused but also naive and elitist. For one thing, the Commission exists because judges, like other people, are not pure. But the assumption by the speaker was particularly ironic in view of the fact that the alleged misconduct about to be investigated was supposed to have been committed by one or more Supreme Court justices.

The Commission took another extraordinary step that caused removal of due process when it decided to admit legally inadmissable evidence during the hearing. This was done despite the fact that the Commission was supposed to be operating under a rule that explicitly requires: "At a hearing before the Commission or masters, *legal* evidence only shall be received. . . ." The result of suspending that rule was that the hearing was full of much hearsay, conjecture, speculation, and gossip that would have been inadmissible in courtrooms throughout the country. Such evidence was admitted even when it was irrelevant to the matters being investigated. Hufstedler told me later he thought the use of legally inadmissible evidence "was a very sad situation," but he felt it had to be done because the hearing was an investigative proceeding rather than a trial. Such proceedings, of course, are usually private and as such do not threaten due process. Even at its own closed hearings, the Commission faithfully obeys its rules not to hear legally inadmissible evidence.

The Commission took yet another unusual step depriving the Supreme Court justices of due process. Normally, the Commission appoints a panel of masters (judges who are not members of the Commission) to hear a case and then report their findings and conclusions to the Commission. But during this investigation of the justices of the state's highest court, it looked as though there would be *no* business as usual. The Commission decided that for this investigation the nine-member Commission would itself sit as a hearing panel to investigate the justices, and later, if it decided to file charges, would sit again as a panel of judges to hear testimony on the charges.

Stage instructions: enter Rube Goldberg II. With this decision, the Commission became all things to the accused. It would sit as prosecutor, as investigators, and as grand jurors. Then, if it decided in its capacity as grand jury to file charges, the same commissioners would doff their old hats and put on a series of new ones and sit as judge and as jury to hear testimony about the charges they earlier had decided to bring. This charade of justice would be laughable if the potential for miscarriage of justice to the accused, let alone to the system, were not so serious. In its later role as judge and jury the Commission would inevitably have a vested interest in not making itself look incompetent, if not silly, by dismissing charges it had deemed appropriate in its earlier wisdom when it sat as grand jury, prosecutor, and investigators.

If the reputation of the Supreme Court justices was on the line as preparations began for their investigation in 1979, so was the reputation of the investigating body, the Commission on Judicial Performance.

In legal circles throughout the country, this Commission had long been watched and imitated. Until Californians created it by referendum in 1960, there were few tools anywhere, short of impeachment, for admonishing or removing judges who engaged in unethical conduct or who refused to leave the bench despite inability to serve. By the time the Commission was taking on its biggest investigation, the justices of the Supreme Court, nearly every state had created a commission on the California model.

There was reason to admire and imitate the California commission. Before it was established, only two California judges had been removed from the bench since the state court system was established in 1850. They had been removed by impeachment many years ago.

By 1979 nearly 100 California judges had left the bench—some voluntarily, others involuntarily—because of the Commission's existence. The mere threat of investigation is a powerful tool of the Commission. In the Commission's first 20 years, 73 judges had resigned or retired while under investigation but before investigations and disciplinary recommendations had been concluded.

For those who fail to see the importance of confidential initial investigation of accusations, the Commission's annual report contains striking evidence of the necessity of that confidentiality. Most complaints do not lead to action against a judge because the Commission determines the complaint is inadequate or untruthful. During 1980, for instance, the Commission received and investigated complaints against 260 judges. In a judicial system with slightly more than 1,200 judges, complaints were filed against nearly 22 percent of them in one year. Of the 260 complaints, 195 were closed after initial review because, according to the Commission's report, the "allegations did not warrant further investigation or constitute misconduct . . ." Many complaints are filed with the Commission by litigants angry about a judge's decision in a case. In many, if not all, of these cases, reputations and careers would have been needlessly, and sometimes maliciously and falsely, ruined if the initial investigations had not been conducted confidentially. It was because of this clearly established pattern of falsely accusing judges, that many feared the forced abandonment of confidentiality during the 1979 investigation.

Because of the California Commission's role in influencing the cleansing of the judiciary everywhere, the question whether the Commission could successfully investigate the court scandal in 1979 was of special significance. If this model commission could not meet this challenge, who could be trusted to judge the judges?

Actually, as the stage was set for the 1979 investigation of the Supreme Court justices, there was great public optimism. The public, thanks to an uninformative—and perhaps genuinely uninformed—statewide press, had been given very little information about how the investigation would be conducted, and about how and why the rules had been changed. Coverage of the rule change by the Judicial Council had focused only on whether the investigation would be open or closed. An investigation would be closed, it was presumed by many, only if there was a desire to hide wrongdoing. And, conversely, only an open hearing would reveal wrongdoing. The public attitude was that something was wrong and that this investigation would reveal what it was. Once the wheels were set in motion, the truth would come tumbling out, and everybody would know whether the California Supreme Court was another revered American institution that would be exposed as having lost its integrity.

Whatever the answers in this investigation would be, it was assumed the answers would be clear. We the public would learn if any justices at the Supreme Court held a smoking gun that had been used in unethical activity. If they had, we would disarm that justice or justices, perhaps even remove one or more of them from the bench. We would do whatever was needed to restore this institution as the public's honest and respected arbiter of justice.

We would learn beyond the shadow of a doubt what had gone wrong. And we would right that wrong.

CHAPTER 6

It Was Not a Trial, but It Was

"There is no more pathetic sight than learned judges cringing in fear of an aggressive investigative commission, which is, in turn, pandering to an assaultive press. . . . The roast pig that they will get will not be worth the house burned down."—*California Supreme Court Justice Stanley Mosk in a speech before the American Bar Association convention in August of 1979 while he was still fighting in the courts to close the investigation of the Supreme Court justices.*

"Inside the auditorium at Golden Gate University, Supreme Court justices and their attorneys and staffs continued, for the fifth straight week, to treat each other like liars, backstabbers, and possible thieves."—*Bella Stumbo, who was sent to the hearings by* The Los Angeles Times *to do a color story during the hearings. This was her first paragraph.*

Golden Gate Law School was the setting for the historic investigation of the California Supreme Court. Golden Gate sits at the edge of San Francisco's gleaming business district. It is sleek and modern, with dark glass exterior. Inside, an auditorium, built like an amphitheater, looks down on a stage. At a long table on the stage sat members of the Commission on Judicial Performance. They faced a chair where men and women were led to be questioned, sometimes sharply and critically. The whole scene was brightly lit. Television cameras recorded it all. Press and spectators watched the proceedings. One Los Angeles television station carried every word of the open portion of the interrogation. All commercial stations in the state carried some footage on their evening news shows.

The Commission and its special counsel, Seth Hufstedler, went to great lengths to say it was not a trial. But for a population brought up on prime-time cops-and-robbers and courtroom television shows, it *was* a trial. And the people led to the interrogation chair were, therefore, the "defendants"—defendants who happened to be justices of the California Supreme Court. The accusations: one or more of you played politics with important court decisions; one or more of you broke the sacred rules of an appellate court by talking to the press about a pending case. But for much of the public, already conditioned by powerful newspapers and special-interest propaganda, the unstated accusation was: This is a corrupt and irresponsible court that is a threat to public safety. Senator Richardson's right-wing attackers could not have been more pleased if they had written the script and sponsored the television spectacular that was about to unfold.

There was a little truth and a lot of color in what both Justice Mosk and *Times* reporter Stumbo said about the event.

Mosk's statement, made in the middle of his own litigation to close the hearings, though protected by his First Amendment rights, struck some as arrogant. While it is important for investigations of judges, like the investigations of all other citizens, to include due process, it is gross arrogance to suggest that judges should not be investigated. The sight of judges being investigated is no more or less pathetic than the sight of other persons being investigated. Mosk went on in his speech to make it clear that he believed there should not be agencies to investigate judges, that periodic elections were the only appropriate way to get rid of scoundrels. Lack of due process might justifiably have been lamented by Mosk and all the other California Supreme Court justices, but to suggest that judges should not be investigated at all—that the judiciary is untouchable—is inappropriate in a democracy.

As for his reference to roast pig, it seems peculiarly ironic in retrospect, for Mosk helped assure—not by closing the hearings but by refusing to speak out on his own—that at least one justice would be publicly served up as a roast pig. It is hard to say which was more pathetic—the roast pig or Mosk's role as assistant cook.

Stumbo's colorful statement was closer to the truth than Mosk's but, like much of the colorful reporting that went on in this hearing, it was too generalized. Too many exciting forest stories never got down to the trees. Insignificant tidbits, small talk, or gossip dominated the press reports of the hearings and too much of the proceedings themselves. The original purpose of the hearings—to determine whether wrongdoing had occurred and, if it had, who was at fault—was lost.

Mosk was wrong when he claimed in papers filed in his lawsuit to close the hearings that the hearings themselves were conducted in a "circus" atmosphere. But it was true that some media coverage was circus-like. One San Francisco television station did an evening-news "special" on the hearings in which a reporter dressed as a sideshow barker dramatically urged people to come inside for the big one. In the next scene the same "reporter" was seen dressed as a big-time fight announcer intoning to his audience that "tonight we have in this corner Chief Justice Rose Bird, and in the other corner we have Justice William Clark. . . ." There followed snippets of actual television footage of testimony from each which were unimportant in themselves but which, intercut with the announcer's humorous comments, provided uninformative entertainment.

Even for a careful observer, the hearing was a difficult event to analyze. It was as though the maestro came out on the opening night of the symphony season and said, "You are about to hear a magnificent concert. But it isn't what you think it is. It is only a dress rehearsal. Welcome."

The introductory remarks promised significance: "This type of public commission hearing has never before occurred in California and perhaps never before anywhere else in this country," announced Commission Chairman Bertram Janes at the opening session of the hearing. "There has not been any such public proceeding before, nor, indeed, has there been any claim that any group of members of our Supreme Court has engaged in any conduct which was inappropriate before this time," said Special Counsel Seth Hufstedler in his opening remarks. The two people who led the investigation thus claimed historic importance for it.

But at the same time there was much caution about the legal significance of what was going on. "This is still an investigative proceeding. No charges have been filed against any justice at this time," said Janes the day the hearing opened. Exactly a month later, on 11 July, a lawyer for one of the justices would say to Janes and the other commissioners, "While this is, as it has often been stated, an investigatory proceeding . . . in the eyes of the public, your honor, and members of the commission, I think it is akin to a trial, because many persons among the public don't quite understand." In so many words, he was saying that the main players all knew that, although it was "just" an investigation, it might in fact turn out to be the only event, and as such was in some sense a "trial," its official status notwithstanding. Due process therefore seemed to require that any witness be questioned as carefully as he or she would be in any official trial. Whatever the proceedings were called, the lawyer was saying, they offered the only chance available to use due process to right wrongs.

Janes, with mild frustration, wasn't officially buying what he and the lawyer both knew was probably true, that this would be the only "trial." Janes went through it all again: "Let me explain briefly. We have our rules. We have our function[s] we are constantly required to perform . . . the rules adopted for this proceeding. How others see it is really—I don't want to say it's of no concern to us. The image of the commission as well as the image of the judiciary is of concern to everyone. But it cannot be converted into a trial by the statement or suggestion of counsel or even by the actions of the commission. It is still, for whatever meaning that term has to all of us, a preliminary hearing investigation."

But it was, in essence, a trial at which serious accusations would be made and denied. Technically, it could be compared most accurately to a grand jury investigation, but a grand jury investigation held in public. In public perception it was, inevitably, an event that would provide the first details that would make it possible to flesh out images of justices who, up to now, had spoken to the public only through their written opinions. Here on the stage of the auditorium at Golden Gate University Law School, five justices of the California Supreme Court would sit publicly, not in robes but in street clothes. They weren't learned cringers, to use Mosk's term, they were mere mortals. What they revealed about themselves and each other would remain for years the public's strongest image of the California Supreme Court. Decisions would come and go, but these hearings would stick with people. They would create a gnawing, if unspecified and uninformed, sense that something was wrong.

The "trial" began with the introduction of all major participants. The commissioners, in addition to Janes, were Hillel Chodos, 47, a Beverly Hills attorney who specializes in business litigation and trial and appellate work; Kathryn Gehrels, 72, a San Francisco lawyer who specializes in family law; Thomas Kongsgaard, 58, a Napa County Superior Court judge since 1959; Jerry Pacht, 59, a Los Angeles Superior Court judge since 1966 and a Municipal Court judge before that; Howard Schwartz, 47, an Oakland-Piedmont Municipal Court judge who has since become an Alameda County Superior Court judge; Margaret Ann Shaw, 59, a former teacher and then education consultant at the University of Southern California; and Thomas Willoughby, 46, consultant for the Assembly Resources, Land Use, and Energy Committee in Sacramento since 1976.

By law the Commission is composed of five judges, two lawyers, and two representatives of the general public. Willoughby and Shaw were the public representatives. The ninth member of the Commission, Court of Appeal Justice John T. Racanelli, removed himself early in the investigation because of his friendship with members of the Supreme Court. He did so, he said in a public statement, to avoid even the "appearance of impropriety." Eight members of the Commission would hear the evidence. But five members would have to agree on any decisions made. This would become significant later when the Commission lost two more members.

Five of the justices had hired lawyers to represent them during the investigation. They were introduced the first day: Harry Delizonna and Jerome B. Falk Jr. represented the Chief Justice; Gerald D. Marcus and Arthur T. Bridgett represented Justice Tobriner; Michael Traynor and Daniel Johnson Jr. represented Justice Manuel; J. Richard Johnston represented Justice Newman. Later, Justice Mosk would be represented by his son, Richard Mosk, and Edward Medvene. Justice Richardson had no lawyer. When Janes asked if any attorney was representing Justice Clark, one of Clark's research attorneys, Richard Morris, stood and said, "Justice Clark is not represented by counsel at this time. I am a staff member of Justice Clark's and I am here to observe these proceedings for him." And he did so throughout the proceeding. At least two of the other justices took second mortgages on their homes to pay their attorney's fees, which for some were more than $40,000, but Clark simply released his staff person to represent him, thereby assuring that Morris's services to him would be paid for by the taxpayers. Clark would testify that in the fall of 1978, after the controversial election-day story, his attorney on matters involving the investigation was none other than Edwin Meese, future White House counsel to President Reagan.

Hufstedler introduced the three lawyers from his Los Angeles firm who had worked as investigators with him on the case: Evelyn Balderman, Pierce O'Donnell, and Bertram Gindler. When witnesses were called Hufstedler or one of these lawyers from his staff would open each area of questioning. The questioning would be continued by members of the Commission. The two most active questioners on the Commission were Chodos and Willoughby. The two women, Gehrels and Shaw, seldom spoke.

Before any witnesses were called, Hufstedler made a lengthy opening statement and filed a background report with the Commission that included more than six hundred pieces of evidence. First, the issues to be investigated were set forth precisely by him:

"1. Was there any delay or irregularity in the handling of the *Tanner* case caused or instituted for any improper purpose?
"2. Was there any delay or irregularity in the handling of the *Fox* case or the *Levins* and *Hawkins* cases caused or instituted for the purpose of delaying the filing of the decision in either of these cases until after the date of the election of November 7, 1978?
"3. Did any justice improperly disclose confidential information about the *Fox* or *Tanner* case prior to the release of the decisions therein?"

The *Tanner* case was well known to the public, of course, by then. It was the case Tobriner had been accused of delaying because of the election. The *Tanner* decision was released on 22 December 1978, with a majority on the court holding that the trial judge had the discretion to strike the gun-use finding and grant the defendant probation. Then in January 1979 the court did an extraordinary thing: for the first time in 14 years it voted to rehear a case, the *Tanner* case. Mosk switched from Tobriner's opinion to Clark's dissent, creating a new majority and a new decision. He did so without explaining himself in an opinion. Given the significance of his vote, the absence of an explanation seemed strange. (In early 1982, Mosk voted in a case that dealt with a similar issue in the same way he had in the first *Tanner* case. This reversal, back to his original *Tanner* position, made it difficult not to assess his vote change in *Tanner* II as politically motivated to hurt the court.) That later *Tanner* opinion, which came to be called *Tanner* II, was filed during the early stages of the investigation of the court.

The cases that had been added to the investigation, *Fox, Levins,* and *Hawkins,* were not (and would never be) household words in California. The delay of *Tanner,* the accusation that had been made on election day, would remain the burning issue throughout the investigation. The hearings themselves would often be called the *Tanner* hearings. But Hufstedler explained that the other cases had been added because some news reporters had mentioned them, too, as possibly having been delayed. *Fox* was the decision, issued 15 December 1978, in which the court banned the city of Los Angeles from using tax money to light a cross at City Hall to observe Christmas and Easter. The *Hawkins* and *Levins* cases were companion cases, released by the court 9 November 1978, that guaranteed preliminary hearings to defendants indicted by a grand jury.

Hufstedler's speech to the Commission and to the television audience on the first day provided some background information about the court that, though legally accessible, was not generally known. Until his speech, few people, even in the legal community, understood how the court worked or how large its work load was. From Hufstedler's opening remarks and from later testimony, this statistical picture of the Supreme Court's work load emerged:

The court is asked to make decisions on more than 4,000 cases a year. It grants hearings on only 4 percent of those cases. The increase in petitions to the state Supreme Court has been dramatic, up from 1,292 in 1962 to 4,047 in 1976. During the first six months of 1978, the weekly average number of cases circulating in each justice's chamber was 163—including calendar (hearing) memorandum being written and reviewed, opinions being written, and written opinions that are circulating. The justices spend so much time preparing the memorandum recommending whether the court will hear cases it is being petitioned to hear, and preparing memorandum for each case to be heard at the monthly hearings, that for most of them only one day a week out of five is left for writing opinions. That explains why some of them work six days a week, plus evenings.

A crucial fact: from 1975 through 1978 there were approximately one hundred cases decided by the court that took as long or longer than *Tanner* from oral argument to the filing of decision; one case took 888 days.

The California Supreme Court's annual case load is 150 percent that of the U.S. Supreme Court. It probably has the largest case load of any appellate court in the United States. In the U.S. Supreme Court, each of the nine justices writes an average of 16½ opinions a year. At the California Supreme Court, each of the seven justices writes 23 opinions a year.

The record showed that the time from oral hearing of a case to release of the court's opinion in that case varies considerably. Sixty days is considered minimum. Two years is considered a long time. Five to seven months is the median time for an ordinary case. A case with four opinions, such as *Tanner* and *Fox*, takes longer than the average. During the period being investigated, the court had nine cases that had four opinions each. *Tanner* was in the middle, with four taking more time from hearing to decision, and four taking less time than *Tanner* from hearing to decision. *Fox* took the longest time: 14 months.

In 1977 the court had gone through unprecedented change. From March until July, when Newman was sworn in, the court had acquired three new justices, the most it had ever acquired in such a short time. None of them had had appellate court experience. Only one of them, Manuel, had ever been a judge before, and his experience was limited to one year on the Alameda County Superior Court. During 1977, the court issued only 99 decisions, considerably lower than the annual average of 160 from 1971 through 1978. But the new justices apparently caught on quickly. In 1978 they issued 160 decisions.

On the first day of the investigation, Hufstedler defined his own unique role as special counsel in this investigation: "This is not a prosecution. I am not a prosecuting attorney, nor am I a defense counsel, but indeed I am both. . . . I shall not be a prosecutor; I shall not be a defense counsel, but I shall seek to present all of the evidence which is relevant and to define that as well as we can." He was called "special counsel." But on more than one occasion, Hufstedler would slip and call himself "special prosecutor." Hufstedler was widely respected in legal circles and by the press. It was assumed by the Commission that if anyone could walk the tightrope required by being both firm prosecutor and staunch defender, Hufstedler could. He would have the confidence of the public. He was considered part of the inner circle of the state's legal establishment. His wife, Shirley Hufstedler, was appointed a federal judge by Lyndon Johnson in 1966 and U.S. Secretary of Education by President Carter. Seth Hufstedler's role was a difficult one, he said, a role neither the Commission nor any other government agency had ever asked anyone to fill. While the judge of evidence is supposed to be impartial, it is highly unusual for the gatherer of evidence to be impartial. Yet that was what he was supposed to be. His occasional reference to himself as special prosecutor certainly seemed to be an admission that he didn't always see himself as impartial.

By the time the hearing opened, Hufstedler said, he and the four lawyers working with him had spent two thousand hours collecting information. They had conducted 62 depositions under oath. They had interrogated all of the justices, almost the entire staff of the court, some former staff members, and many persons outside the court, including most of the professional staff of the criminal division in the State Attorney General's office. They had examined 1,300 pages of documentary materials, most of it from the records of the court and of individual justices.

In his opening remarks, Hufstedler spoke solemnly of the fact that the investigation might involve potential damage to the court. "We recognize the many risks that a proceeding such as this may cause. It may jeopardize the problems of the relationships of the court. . . . The commission, as I have indicated, has no choice. It must consider this matter and must resolve it." This statement encouraged the assumption, already widely held, that this public hearing would reveal and resolve any wrongdoing that had occurred.

But midway through Hufstedler's 69-page statement he made a crucial point. The search would not be quite what the public expected. He and his staff had already ascertained that the official records made it clear that no case was actually signed and ready to be filed by election day. Technically, there was no question—decisions had not been officially completed, signed and okayed by all justices, and then delayed. "So," said special counsel, "the question in these proceedings is not were they all signed up . . . and not filed. *The question is why weren't they signed up earlier?*"

This statement, which was hardly, if at all, noted by the press, indicated that the hearing was going to be a complex process. The questions wouldn't just be "Did you do it?" or, "Didn't you do it?" but also, "Why did you do it?" or "Why didn't you do it?" or "Will you please prove that you never beat your wife?" For example, during

Tobriner's testimony, he was asked by Hufstedler what the Chief Justice had told him about whether she had asked Justice Manuel to write a separate dissent in the *Tanner* case. Tobriner responded, "She at no time told me she suggested to Justice Manuel he should write a dissent." Then Hufstedler asked him, "Did she tell you she had not made such a suggestion?"

Here in this open hearing that would have fewer rules of evidence than a secret grand jury, there apparently was not even an expectation of finding a smoking gun. Perhaps it was all going to hinge on whether each individual justice could make the commissioners—and the public—believe that he or she privately had never wanted, or tried, to delay one of these decisions. On the first day testimony was heard, Chairman Janes said, "We will hear all evidence which might suggest that there was an infringement of any of the rules which govern the conduct of judges. And we must hear all of the evidence which would indicate that there was no such infringement."

It thus appeared that this "trial" was going to require the potential defendants—the seven justices of the California Supreme Court—to prove that they were not guilty. It is a fundamental principle of American law that one is innocent until proven guilty. But in this instance, because it was a preliminary investigation or public grand jury, the justices would be presumed guilty until proven innocent.

What was happening was extraordinary. Undoubtedly, any appellate court in the country would have prevented a state from investigating an ordinary citizen in this way. It also was extraordinary because of the public climate in which the "trial" was held. Many people assume that, however much they may disagree with the opinions of the Supreme Court justices, these justices are honest people. But equal in power to that assumption at the time of the investigation was another assumption: that accusations would not be made in a news story in the large and respected *Los Angeles Times* unless they were true. Indeed, despite literally hundreds of stories having been written and broadcast by other news media in the months since the election, the original accusations were still reported as having validity. No story had appeared saying the story had been disproven. The fall of Richard Nixon at the hands of *The Washington Post* in 1974 had given investigative reporting considerable credibility. And this election-day story seemed to have sources more credible than the *Post*'s Deep Throat, whose identity has remained unknown. The *Times* story was based, at least in part, on the word of two Supreme Court justices whose identity was assumed (and would later be confirmed)—hardly your average disgruntled government employee or shadowy Deep Throat.

CHAPTER 7

The Trial Begins

The first witness was Frank Richardson, the only justice on the court never to have been tainted by any hint of wrongdoing in the events leading to the investigation. Special Counsel Hufstedler had wanted to start with Tobriner, who was under the darkest cloud. But Commission Chairman Janes insisted that his former colleague and fishing buddy, Richardson, should run the race first.

Richardson was Governor Reagan's last appointment to the California Supreme Court. The Governor reportedly had chosen him only after the man he replaced, Justice Louis Burke, said he wanted to retire but wanted to be assured ahead of time that the Governor would appoint a qualified person. The action by Burke was said to be a direct result of the general frustration on the court with Reagan's appointment of the unqualified Clark. Richardson and Janes had both been appointed by Reagan to the Court of Appeal in Sacramento. While there Janes and Richardson became friends. He is not related to Senator H. L. Richardson.

When the testimony finally began there were many questions that had been generated by six months of news stories. It was assumed these basic questions would be answered during the course of testimony:

• Tobriner—Did he delay the *Tanner* decision? Will he say he did? Will anybody else say they think he did? If he did, will he explain why he did it? Did he do it to protect the Chief Justice at the polls? Was he asked by anybody else, on or off the court, to delay the decision? Did he ask anybody else to take steps that would delay it?

• Bird—Did she want the *Tanner* opinion, or any other opinion, delayed until after the election? Did she directly or indirectly ask Tobriner to delay it? Did he ever tell her he was delaying it, whatever her wishes about it were? Did she ask Wiley Manuel to write a dissent in order to assure the delay of the *Tanner* case? Did she write her concurring opinion in *Tanner* not out of conviction but out of a desire to add a new element that would effectively delay it? Did she write a lengthy concurring opinion in the *Fox* case in order to delay that case?

• Manuel—Did anyone suggest to him that he should write a separate dissent in order to protect the Chief Justice? Did anyone suggest to him that he should write a separate dissent in *Tanner* in order to delay the case until after the election? Did he, on his own, decide that he would write the separate dissent in order to prevent the case from coming out before the election?

• Newman—Did he take any steps to delay the *Fox* opinion? Did he delay reacting to the Chief Justice's long concurring opinion in the *Fox* case in order to prevent the case from being released before the election? Had anyone told him they wanted to see the case delayed until after the election?

• Clark—Did he leak confidential information to the press before or after the election? Did he know that any other justice had delayed an opinion or had asked someone else to delay an opinion? Why had he refused to sign Justice Tobriner's statement claiming that the *Tanner* case had been handled normally? Why did he tell the press he had "decisive" reasons for not signing it? Had he released Justice Tobriner's statement to the press? Had anyone on his staff leaked confidential information to the press? Did he take any steps himself to delay the *Tanner* decision?

• Mosk—Did he leak confidential information to the press before or after the election? Did he know that any other justice had delayed an opinion or had asked someone else to delay an opinion? Had anyone on his staff leaked confidential information to the press? Did he want adversely to affect the Chief Justice's chances at the polls?

• Richardson—None of the news stories that appeared before the investigation indicated there was much to ask Richardson. He was the only justice on the court presumed to be completely innocent. That would remain true throughout the proceeding. The Commission and its counsel used his presence as a witness primarily to get more information about court procedures on the record. From him and others they would learn the path a developing decision takes from beginning to end.

When a case has been scheduled for oral argument before the Supreme Court, it is assigned to a particular justice who will write a memorandum on the issues in the case. Copies of the memorandum are distributed to each justice in advance of this hearing, and any justice may write an additional memorandum on the case. After oral argument, when cases are argued by opposing lawyers, the justices return to the Chief Justice's chambers and vote on each case they have heard. If the position taken by the justice who wrote the memorandum in a given case is adopted by the majority, that justice is likely to be assigned by the Chief Justice to write the majority opinion. All votes taken at this conference—in fact, all votes throughout the opinion-writing process—are tentative and can change at any time. What was originally a majority opinion can become a minority opinion, and vice versa. Speaking of the power of the opinion-writing, as opposed to the preliminary voting when the case is discussed at conference, U.S. Supreme Court Justice Byron R. White once said, "Votes change in the writing perhaps more often than in conference."

The majority author at the California Supreme Court receives "the box" upon being assigned the case. The box, labelled with the name of the case, contains the trial transcript, and all other records of the case, including the Court of Appeal record, and all briefs filed by the litigants. When the majority author completes the majority opinion, it is placed in the box and sent to the court Secretary's office, the transfer point each time the box moves from one justice to another. If the Secretary's office has been told that a member of the minority wants to write a dissenting opinion the box is sent to that person next. The completed dissenting opinion is sent back to the majority-opinion author. This is done because the majority author might want to change the majority opinion in light of the disssent. The majority writer might, for instance, want to speak to a new issue raised in the dissent, or might feel the majority opinion has been mischaracterized in the dissenting opinion and want to respond to that. All justices receive duplicate copies of opinions as they are prepared, but most do not work on a case until the box, containing the entire record of a case, comes to their office.

Each time a change is made in any opinion, the process begins again. All signatures become moot, the entire file goes back to square one, to the majority author, and travels down the line again to get new signatures from everyone. This is why the fact that at one time a case may have had the signatures of all seven justices on one opinion is meaningless for the purposes of judging whether it was then near completion. It is also the reason why a case like *Tanner,* which had multiple opinions—a majority opinion, a concurring opinion, and two dissenting opinions (one of them Clark's, rewritten three times)—can take several months to reach completion. The decision is not completed until all seven justices have signed off on the last revision. The box stops here.

There were constant references to "the box" during the investigation, conjuring up an image of the court being a quiet place where the main activity in the somber hallways is the occasional movement of couriers carrying oversized shoeboxes from one justice's chambers to another's.

Aside from the utilitarian function of Richardson's testimony, in that it provided a description of the court's operation, what was most interesting about it was that he made it clear he thought there had been no wrongdoing by anyone. The justice recalled that there was discussion in the court's weekly conferences about the status of *Tanner* in mid-October after public accusations of delay in the case were made by the Republican gubernatorial candidate, Attorney General Evelle Younger. "The question of the status of the *Tanner* case was mentioned," he said. He could not recall who had mentioned it. But others, including Justice Clark, would testify that it was Clark who brought it up at two October conferences.

"Do you remember whether or not anyone asked whether or not the case had been delayed or was being held up in any way?" Richardson was asked. ". . . The question, as I recall it, related to where is it and what's happening to it. . . . I did not then feel nor do I feel now that there was anyone trying to hold it up."

Later, Hufstedler would say, "I'm asking now if you have any additional knowledge or information indicating that it [*Tanner*] was not delayed . . ."

Richardson: "I have no information or knowledge that the case was delayed, and I have no information it was not delayed. I don't—I do not, I do not know any reason, I have no knowledge or information or reason to suggest to me now or then that the case was improperly delayed or delayed intentionally or otherwise." Tobriner had circulated his majority opinion in the *Tanner* case 25 days after the oral hearing in the case. That, said Richardson, was "really quite prompt." He said the average time taken for the preparation and first circulation of majority opinions is 60 to 90 days. If so, his testimony provided convincing evidence that at least in the earliest stages of the case there was no action by Tobriner to delay it.

"There were changes and variances in the opinions," Richardson said. "There were changes in votes, but this happens with considerable frequency and there's nothing to my mind and my knowledge or information about it which would spotlight *Tanner* as receiving differential treatment."

It was clear from Richardson's testimony that he was not quick to accuse, that he would not be looking for wrongdoing among the justices: "I value my colleagues very highly. They are a group of able, hardworking people, And I have never felt in this case or any other that I should push an individual who is working on a case because I don't want to point a finger. I have my faults and they're numerous. This is a sensitive area to a justice."

But it also became clear that this mild-mannered man who didn't point a finger could not be pushed around. Commissioner Chodos often played the role of bully in the questioning of the witnesses. Sometimes he did it effectively, eliciting information that might not otherwise have come out. He tried the technique unsuccessfully with Richardson. "Would it be fair to say," he asked Richardson, "that at least as far as you observed in October, at the time this Younger article came to public attention, that the case had been decided, that is to say, that the seven justices had all assumed positions on the issue which, as far as you were aware, they were going to adhere to?"

Richardson: "I can't say that, Mr. Chodos, because really there are situations in which at the last moment, there will be a change of theory or theme. I had thought, I had in my mind that the case is generally resolved, but I couldn't have said it with suffiicient certainty to say the case is decided, ladies and gentlemen, let's file it. That's not the way things go."

Chodos: "I understand that, Justice Richardson, and there is always the theoretical possibility in any indication."

Richardson: "More than theoretical. It's real."

He said it had not occurred to him that the *Tanner* case had political overtones until Younger made his accusations. Then, for the first time, he saw the case as politically sensitive, not in terms of its content but in terms of its timing.

Justice Tobriner would claim that he never saw the *Tanner* case as having meaning in connection with the election. Many observers, including some Commission members, would question the credibility of that claim. But he was adamant about it. He was talking about his reaction on 11 September, when he first read a green sheet in which Clark notified the court that the Chief Justice's staff had said his comments in his *Tanner* dissent about the Chief's *Caudillo* opinion were "politically motivated." Tobriner testified: "I never thought it had anything to do with an election. Politically motivated could mean that it perhaps was something that was for political connotations, other than an election. I didn't give it any thought, to tell you the truth. I just looked at it and passed it on and said, 'This is another one of those things.'"

Commissioner Willoughby asked him exactly what the term "politically motivated" meant to him when he saw it on Clark's memo. "Is it politically motivated in the sense that this is a personal dig or is it in some larger sense? . . . Do you have any recollection of your reaction to that term?" Willoughby asked.

Tobriner: "I didn't take it seriously, Mr. Willoughby. I just felt that was perhaps a conflict among the staffs. Perhaps it had been written by Justice Clark's staff. I didn't know how Justice Clark handles matters with his staff, and I didn't concern myself about this. I did not think that was an important matter at all, because we have had accusations made back and forth, even by justices, that sometimes are politically motivated. It's nothing unusual in a collegial court where there are seven members that some kind of claims are going to be made by one justice against another."

Hufstedler asked Tobriner, "By September 21, had it occurred to you at all, had it crossed your mind into your consciousness that if the *Tanner* case was in fact filed before the election it might have any impact of any kind upon the re-election of the Chief Justice?"

Tobriner: "It had not crossed my mind that the *Tanner* case would have any effect. I did not consider . . . the *Tanner* case an unusual case that had any particular special political significance, but I may add that many cases in our court—in fact, almost all cases—do have political consequences."

Hufstedler: "Let me move that inquiry up to the day before the election, the 6th of November. Up until that time had the thought ever crossed your mind, entered your conscious mind, that if the *Tanner* case was released before the election it might have some impact on the Chief Justice's re-election?"

Tobriner: "It had not."

Chodos reminded Justice Tobriner that when *Tanner* was brought up at conference in October, Younger's accusations that *Tanner* was being delayed for political purposes already had been made in the press. "Are you telling us, Justice Tobriner," said Chodos, "that at that conference when the issue of *Tanner* was discussed that there was no discussion that called to mind the connection or possible connection between *Tanner* and the Chief Justice's confirmation campaign?"

Tobriner: "Let me answer that. . . . Mr. Younger made the accusation . . . that the court was withholding a determination of the constitutionality of the death penalty, and likewise, holding up not only the *Tanner* case but other cases. . . . I knew that was untrue, and, indeed, Mr. Younger recanted that statement. He took it back a few days later. So . . . I did not consider the Younger references to be of any significance because they were not correct. . . . The *Tanner* case was not in my possession at that time. That had already been transferred to Justice Manuel. I paid little heed to what was said about the *Tanner* case at that point."

Chodos: "So the fact that the Younger statement was inaccurate or even that it had been retracted would not necessarily mean to you that it could not have some impact on the election, isn't that right?"

Tobriner: "I must not quite agree with that, Mr. Chodos. The statement made by a candidate that is recanted by the candidate can be more disadvantageous to the candidate than had he not said it in the first place. I think that's what happened here."

Inexplicably—and inaccurately—Hufstedler then announced that though Younger had recanted on his accusation that there were death penalty cases that had been delayed, he had never recanted his accusation that the *Tanner* case had been held up. That was wrong. Younger first said he was "certain" *Tanner* was being delayed. The next day, when he explicitly denied his earlier claim about the death penalty, he said he was still right about *Tanner*. Later that same day, he said he was not "certain," and that he had meant to raise a "question" about *Tanner* rather than make a "charge."

Many people thought Tobriner's expressed lack of concern about whether the *Tanner* case could affect the election was not credible. Hufstedler would come back to it again. "I want again to ask you the question: At any time before November 6th when you began your work on the revision of the *Tanner* opinion did you believe that the *Tanner* case was politically sensitive for the court?"

Tobriner: "I didn't really think it was politically sensitive, but I suppose that Justice Clark's suggestions made me realize it might have been a little bit more so, but I can't remember really thinking about that very much. . . . That occurred to me, of course, after the election."

Hufstedler: "Did it occur to you before November 6th that the *Tanner* case might increase or cause tension between Justice Clark and the Chief Justice?"

Tobriner: "That's possible."

Perhaps the most important information in Tobriner's testimony came in a description of a 21 September conversation with Clark. On that day, according to testimony of both Clark and Tobriner, Clark had come to Tobriner's office and told him he had a problem with the Chief Justice. He briefly discussed the *Caudillo* footnote. Clark made the same suggestion to Tobriner that he would make to the Chief Justice in mid-October: *that she could delay filing the* Tanner *decision until after the election if she thought his (Clark's) dissent was politically motivated.*

"What did you make of all of that?" asked Commissioner Willoughby.

Tobriner: "As I have told you, I thought that it was a reference that was not possible to carry out. And I told him that, that it was wrong to do that."

Willoughby: "I understand that you are saying it's wrong to delay. But I am saying do you recall what your understanding was of the situation he was trying to describe to you about *Caudillo* and its relationship to the election?"

Tobriner: "Obviously, Justice Clark thought it might affect the election, from what he said to me. I didn't necessarily share that opinion. It seemed to me that the case of *Tanner* was not that important with respect to the election. I didn't connect the two, particularly, although he did."

Court watchers assumed that because Tobriner was the only justice on the court who befriended Bird when she came to the court, they might have discussed together each new development in the campaign against her in the months before election day. The testimony of both of them painted a different picture. They talked occasionally, but she did not keep him informed about newspaper articles that appeared in publications out of San Francisco about her election or comments that were being made about the possible connection between particular cases and her election. Assuming that Tobriner told the truth when he testified under oath, he didn't even tell the Chief Justice about his disturbing 2 September conversation with Clark.

It *had* disturbed him, this suggestion by Clark that the Chief Justice could delay the release of a decision until after the election. He testified he thought delay for political purposes would be wrong. He took what was for him an unusual step. When Clark left his office that day, Tobriner called in one of his research attorneys, Hal Cohen, and told him what Clark had said. Cohen said he didn't believe Clark could be serious. Tobriner said he didn't know. Bird had apparently not told Tobriner about the conversations that had taken place between herself and Clark and between their staffs prior to Tobriner's 21 September conversation with Clark, conversations both Bird and Clark and their staffs would describe to the Commission.

"I didn't know exactly what had taken place between Chief Justice Bird and Justice Clark," he testified. He was asked if he told the Chief Justice about Clark's conversation with him before the election. "I did not," said Tobriner. "I didn't feel it was up to me to create any more tension on this question between the two of them. . . . I did not [tell her] until later, my reason being I didn't want to add any more fuel to the problem that already apparently existed."

Cohen later testified that on election day he accompanied Tobriner to the Chief Justice's office for a meeting with her and members of her staff. Bird and Tobriner then, for the first time, told each other that Clark had suggested separately to each of them that the *Tanner* decision could be delayed until after the election. "I remember," Cohen told the Commission, "that one of the justices said it—that they had had a prior conversation with Justice Clark in which Justice Clark had made the statement that [he would have] no objection [to] having the case held up until after the election. One of the justices said it, and then the other one . . . said, 'That's funny,' or 'That's strange, I have had a similar conversation.'"

Tobriner described the same election-day meeting. "We were very much disturbed about the press reports that I had held up the *Tanner* case and that it could have been released if I had not held it up. I was terrifically upset . . . I was, as I say, very upset that these allegations should have been made that I was holding up the *Tanner* case. I told them how absolutely untrue it was. She knew that anyhow. . . . We speculated on how this could have possibly happened. . . . We wondered who were the sources used by the news media. . . . Somewhere along the course of that conversation, the Chief Justice told me that Justice Clark had also had a conversation with her about holding the *Tanner* case beyond the election. . . . She stated that he had said as much to her and that, indeed, notes had been taken of that conversation by Steve Buehl [Bird's executive assistant]. . . . She described to me that he suggested that the opinion could be held up until after the election. . . . She said [to Clark] 'That's impossible. We can't do that.' We discussed why Justice Clark should have ever made those suggestions and what was behind it. . . . I suggested perhaps I should make sure that all the members of the court agreed there had been no improper withholding of the *Tanner* case because of the election and perhaps I should work up a statement whereby that was set forth. . . . That's what precipitated the writing of the statement." He was speaking of the 9 November statement which he asked each justice to sign, and which Clark refused to sign and urged Richardson and Mosk not to sign either. The statement, which said the case had been handled normally, would later be released to the press by unnamed sources, along with the information that one justice had refused to sign it.

Hufstedler knew from Clark's deposition that he would testify that Tobriner had told him in November 1978 that if he refused to sign Tobriner's statement he would be investigated by the Commission on Judicial Performance. In anticipation of that testimony, Hufstedler asked Tobriner if he had said that "in words, substance, or effect."

"I did not," said Tobriner. "I emphasize I did not."

"What else did you talk about?" Hufstedler asked, still inquiring about the election-day meeting of Tobriner and the Chief Justice with their staffs.

Tobriner was a somewhat stooped man. Some news accounts described him as "frail and bent" when he walked to the witness stand the first day of his testimony—an accurate enough description as far as first appearances go. When Tobriner spoke, however, any impression of frailness disappeared. He usually talked with intensity and excitement, giving spectators the feeling that he was full of vitality. His voice was direct and spirited as he answered questions day after day, knowing that some in the audience were having trouble believing that he had not thought about whether the *Tanner* case would have an impact on the election. Not until Hufstedler asked, "What else did you talk about?" did it become clear what impact the accusation of improper conduct had had upon Tobriner. Then the depth of his sadness poured out.

"The effect of this upon the court, how disastrous this was to the court. Indeed, how disastrous it was to my own reputation, to my own integrity. I expressed myself in strong terms that after seventeen years on the court that I should be accused of holding a case up, to me, was disastrous, was a tragedy. At least in my life."

"All right," said Hufstedler, "what other subjects did you discuss?"

"What could we do to correct it, how we could possibly correct the matter. We didn't realize—we didn't figure out any way to do that. The damage had been done."

Chodos accused Tobriner of thinking the accusations were a tragedy only because his name was associated with them. Tobriner replied that he did view it as a personal tragedy but also as a tragedy for the court. Chodos asked Tobriner why he did not avert the "tragedy" by convening the court in early October, after his meeting with Clark, and by urging that the court quickly publish the *Tanner* opinion in order to eliminate any accusations. "That would have been an available procedure, would it not?"

Tobriner responded that "the possibility that you are speaking about, I don't think occurred to anybody on the court. . . . There were many cases that were referred to in these articles that you have mentioned, particularly the Younger thing. . . . How could we convene our court and say we have got to hurry, we have got to pass on these cases expeditiously and more quickly than we could other cases in order to satisfy the newspapers that we were doing that? We cannot run our court on the beck and call of the newspaper writers who say that some cases are not coming out as fast as they should." One commissioner, Judge Pacht, asked, "You draw a distinction between a charge made by a candidate for governor and a charge made that two justices of the Supreme Court have talked about a case which is still in progress?" "I certainly do," replied Tobriner. (The reference was to the fact that two justices had been credited with partially confirming the election-day story.)

When Bird took the stand a few days later, Chodos asked her the same questions. "Did you ever discuss the likelihood that in view of these accusations, if *Fox* and *Tanner* were not actually filed before the election it was inevitable that some newspaper would come out with a 'See, we told you so' article after the election?"

Bird: "I don't know. . . . Of course on election day, once we saw . . . the line-up of votes, we knew that it would be almost impossible for anyone on the outside to believe that in fact it wasn't ready to go. That part of the statement in the press—the line-up of votes—was accurate."

"But given the circumstances," said Chodos, "didn't it occur to you . . . that it was almost inevitable that this accusation would be repeated after the election and that it would be a traumatic experience for the court which could be avoided simply by taking these two cases out of the pile and getting the three-page dissents done early . . . and getting it filed?"

Bird: "I think I was aware of the fact that these accusations would probably not go away. Once they're made, they're almost impossible to disprove. My own feeling, and it is a very strong one, is that once you start the process of moving cases based on what happens on the outside, you end up with a product that perhaps is different as a result of that pressure. And if we are to be the institution among the tripartite system that is above the politics of the moment and above the pressure points of the moment, then we can't do that."

Chodos: ". . . Is it not a fact that if you just sat all seven justices down and did away with this formal rotation of the box . . . and said, 'Look, we've got this election coming up. The newspapers are screaming like barking dogs . . . and the only way we can quiet the newspapers is to get this opinion filed. Let's all sign it today and file it tomorrow.' That could all have been done in a matter of a few hours, a couple of days?"

Bird: "I'm not certain that's accurate, Mr. Chodos. And second, I'm not certain that it is a good precedent to have a candidate for governor determine what cases are going to come out of our court at what point."

It was an amazing suggestion, this one from Chodos. This court spends time discussing and writing memorandum on over four thousand cases a year, 3 percent of which it then hears and writes decisions on. That it should be willing to take these cases out of line, in order to save its own hide from newspaper criticism, seemed a preposterous way of setting court priorities. If Chodos' suggestion were followed to its logical conclusion, only those litigants most able to catch the news media's attention would get speedy decisions.

Chodos suggested to Tobriner that he should have gone to Justice Manuel between 21 September and 24 October and tried to hasten Manuel's work on *Tanner* because of what Younger said in mid-

October. "He didn't spend the whole time from 21 September until 24 October working on nothing but his dissent in *Tanner,* obviously. You are satisfied that that's true, aren't you?" Chodos asked. The question seemed particularly irrelevant a few days later when testimony would reveal that Justice Clark was, in fact, during that time asking Justice Manuel to delay writing his dissent. And because of an event yet to come, the public would never hear how Justice Manuel would testify on this subject.

But now Justice Tobriner said to Chodos, "I surely don't know what the picture was with Justice Manuel. I realize my own picture is very rough trying to handle all these cases, and he may very well face what I face, which was he had other matters to attend to. . . . So I surely will not for one moment suggest that Justice Manuel was delaying the case."

Again, Chodos asked, "Did it not occur to you that in order to avoid the appearance of this very impropriety . . . that perhaps *Tanner* could be taken first and other boxes later so as to hasten the publication of *Tanner?*"

"The answer is no," said Tobriner. "If you are suggesting I should go to Justice Manuel and have him hasten his dissent as you suggest, that is not my function. I don't think that's proper to do it. I think each justice has his right and duty, indeed, to write his own opinion and carefully present his position. And the fact that Mr. Younger has made some cracks about not getting out death penalty cases and other cases seemed to me . . . did not create an appearance of impropriety. And surely what Justice Clark said to me was my private information, not to be divulged to anyone. Except it happens we must do it here under these circumstances. But that was a private conversation."

Tobriner was questioned about his reaction to a memorandum sent 20 December, two days before *Tanner* was filed and released, by Justice Clark to the Chief Justice with copies to all other justices. The memo began: "In conscience, it must be clear to all on the court that the *Tanner* case was signed up and ready for filing well in advance of November. The question appears to be why it was not filed." Tobriner said that at the conference held the day the Clark memo was received, he told Clark he was "astonished at several of the allegations or indirect charges contained in that memo." He said he told Clark in front of all the justices that he couldn't understand how Clark could write such a memorandum "in view of what you told me on November 28th." The two had met that day, along with Cohen, in Tobriner's office. Clark had told Tobriner then that he knew of no impropriety in the handling of *Tanner.* Tobriner testified that at the 20 December conference, Clark had said, "I am not claiming anything was irregular about the *Tanner* case. I don't want you to be upset about it and I don't mean to make any personal attack on you." Tobriner said Clark didn't respond to his claim that the memo was contrary to what Clark had said 28 November, but Clark now said in conference that Tobriner should not take his memo seriously. Tobriner testified, "I said, 'Why did you write the memo?' He didn't answer."

Richard Morris, Clark's research attorney, came to see Tobriner the day after the conference at which Tobriner had tried to decipher the meaning of Clark's memorandum. Tobriner said Morris told him that "Justice Clark did not want me to think that he had suggested that there was any improper handling of the *Tanner* case. . . . He said he had told Jack Frankel [the full-time counsel to the Commission] that the *Tanner* case was handled in normal fashion and it took no longer time than usual. . . . He reiterated that Justice Clark could not find anything wrong with the handling of the case."

Commissioner Willoughby asked Tobriner, "If he indicated to you that it [Clark's memorandum] wasn't meant to disparage you or attack your motives or anything like that, did he indicate what the reference in the memo of the 20th was intended to mean?"

Tobriner: "I asked him, why was this in here then, this 'in conscience' statement. And he gave me no answer except to say he had no belief that the *Tanner* case had been mishandled or handled irregularly; that neither Justice Clark or Mr. Morris felt it had been handled in an improper fashion. I couldn't understand why it was put in there. I kept asking him, and he said, 'Don't misunderstand, we didn't mean to impugn you.'"

"Was it your view," Chodos asked Justice Tobriner, "that Justice Clark and Mr. Morris were playing games with you about this position?"

Tobriner: "Mr. Chodos, you are expressing exactly my doubts. I didn't know and I don't know to this moment what this is all about. I can't understand contradictory statements like this, and I asked Mr. Morris to try to explain. I have never had an explanation. That's why I can't give you one, either."

Hufstedler placed a newspaper story on a board, and on a screen in the front of the auditorium appeared the enlarged first paragraph of the *Los Angeles Times* election-day story:

> SACRAMENTO—The California Supreme Court has decided to overturn a 1975 law that requires prison terms for persons who use a gun during a violent crime, but has not made the decision public, well-placed court sources said Monday.

"Now, I gather from the testimony you have given us," said Hufstedler, "you violently disagree with that statement that the *Tanner* case had been decided and was being held up at that point?"

Tobriner: "That's an understatement."

Hufstedler asked him for his understanding of the judicial canons about comments by the court to reporters.

Tobriner: "I think the implication of the canons is that you should never disclose anything that goes on with respect to a pending case, and obviously would more emphatically prohibit a breach of the confidence which was a false statement with respect to the pending case."

Near the end of Tobriner's time on the stand, Special Counsel Hufstedler carefully asked him a series of basic questions.

Hufstedler: "Did you take any step deliberately to delay the proceeding of the *Tanner* case?"

Tobriner: "I did not."

Hufstedler: "Did you take any step to hold up the *Tanner* case in connection with any political consideration?"

Tobriner: "I did not, emphatically."

Hufstedler: "Did you take any step at any time during the *Tanner* case to aid the Chief Justice's chance of re-election?"

Tobriner: "I did not."

Hufstedler: "Did you ask Justice Manuel to write a separate dissent to help slow down the processing of the *Tanner* case?"

Tobriner: "I did not, emphatically."

Hufstedler: "Or, did you ask him to write a separate dissent for any purpose?"

Tobriner: "I did not. I never discussed it with Justice Manuel prior to the time that he wrote his dissent."

Hufstedler: "Do you know of anyone else who asked Justice Manuel to write a separate dissent?"

Tobriner: "I do not."

Hufstedler: "Did the *Caudillo* case citation in the Clark dissent delay the processing of *Tanner* in any way?"

Tobriner: "It did not delay the process in any way."

Before Tobriner left the stand on his fourth and final day as witness, Chodos had one more question. He reminded Tobriner that earlier in his testimony he had referred to the election-day story as a "tragedy" for both himself and the court. Now Chodos asked, "Justice Tobriner, is it your view that the tragedy was not that the court should be accused of delaying cases or that one justice, say Justice Clark, should bring up such an idea or should pass memos suggesting that *Tanner* is being improperly withheld, but that the tragedy is that it should get out in the press? Not that it should happen, but that it should be publicly revealed and distributed?"

It was a devastating question, a grand finale to four days of questioning of the senior justice of the court, the man who from the beginning had been the one accused of the basic wrongdoing being examined: delaying *Tanner* in order to protect the Chief Justice on election day. It was a taunt: Look, wouldn't it be perfectly fine if this had happened but never been revealed? Isn't that what you really think, Your Honor?

Tobriner responded with a fervent denial. "Mr. Chodos, I think it would be a tragedy for the court to hold a case back for election. I also think it is a worse—well, a similar—tragedy for the press falsely to represent that that occurred. I put it on both grounds. I say it would be a tragedy for the court—to reemphasize it—to deliberately hold back a decision because of an election. But I think it is doubly tragic for the press to falsely tell the people, the public. that that occurred when it did not occur. That brings about disrepute for the court."

"Further questions?" asked Commission Chairman Janes. There were none. "Very well. . . . You would be on call if your presence were required. Meantime, we will let you get back to work." Justice Tobriner rose from the witness chair, stepped off the stage, and walked down the aisle of the auditorium. A few spectators, and then a few more, broke into applause. He shyly nodded appreciation.

If Tobriner isolated himself from the knowledge of what was being said in the outside world about the court's timing of opinions, Bird lived in nearly constant knowledge of it. Press calls poured into her office asking about whether *Tanner* was being delayed. Stephen Buehl, Bird's executive assistant, seemed to spend all day some days talking to reporters who were calling with these questions. He said he answered all their calls—until election day. He thinks there were so many that day that he briefly gave up responding to all the calls. But in late October most, if not all, of the press calls were stimulated by Younger's charges in mid-October. Though Younger retracted his charges, reporters kept asking about them. This probably happened largely because Younger, after his retractions, when speaking in a different region of the state, accompanied by some news reporters, would make his charges again but with weaker verbs. Good reporters followed up his charges each time with questions to the Supreme Court. During the weeks immediately before the election, Senator H. L. Richardson also was holding press conferences every few days announcing that Supreme Court decisions were being delayed. Sometimes his press conferences resulted in stories, but these stories also included Buehl's denials, his statements that the records had been checked and that there were no completed decisions being held up, no decisions being delayed because of the election.

When I asked Richardson several months later exactly what he knew about the delays he was publicly accusing the court of in the fall of 1978, he told me: "When it came to *Tanner,* or any other decisions, my judgment, very honestly, was a subjective judgment based on how Bird and Tobriner acted in the past. I never had any specific knowledge. I made a projection on her past behavior. I knew she was against the death penalty and that she'd probably be against *Tanner.* I made a projection. I wanted the press to pursue it."

The subjective political projections being made publicly by Richardson and Younger kept the Chief Justice's phones ringing for about three weeks before the election. Other justices apparently did not get these calls, except for Clark, who testified he had gotten at least one inquiry about whether the court was delaying cases prior to the day before election day. Bird did not tell the rest of the court about the barrage of calls until the 25 October conference. It was then that Clark asked when *Tanner* was going to come out. He had asked that at the previous week's conference. But he had also privately told the Chief Justice about two weeks before that she could delay *Tanner.* Perhaps it was because of these conflicting messages from Clark—in private he said: "You could delay it"; in judicial conference he said, "Why isn't it coming out?"—that Bird made what she referred to in her testimony as a "sarcastic" comment at the 25 October conference—"something to the effect that I thought it strange that the only two cases [*Tanner* and *Fox*] that the newspapers were specifically raising were two cases in which there was a dissent by a particular judge [Clark] on the court. . . . It was, as I look back," she told the Commission, "perhaps poor judgment on my part to have made a sarcastic reference."

On the stand, Bird seemed to be a person at home with herself, willing in public, as she is in private, to point to her own weaknesses. She has done so in less formal public circumstances than the hearing. Introducing herself at a meeting of the Sacramento County Bar Association in 1980, she said, "for those of you who don't know me, my name is Rose Bird. I am the individual who gave merit selection of judges a bad name."

Testifying before the Commission, in addition to evoking her "sarcasm" towards Clark, she also described herself as treating him "coolly but correctly" after becoming frustrated over his public criticism of the court. She would be much criticized later for this seemingly unimportant behavior. Clark would describe it too, sometimes inaccurately, witness the tale about his secretary being prevented from getting Bird's old carpet. His staff, he said, wondered if this was a sign that the Chief Justice was angry at him. He testified he was alarmed for his staff. Given the missing ingredients of his testimony, such as the fact that during the same period the Chief had the State purchase a car for Clark's use, his telling a public investigator's hearing about a scrap of carpet wanted by 15 people besides his secretary seemed like bizarre distortion—far worse than her cool but correct behavior. His comments about the carpet were inevitably linked by reporters to the much earlier stories in which staff members had described Bird changing the locks on doors and changing judicial appointment procedures. It is well known that executives, male and female, exhibit a wide array of managerial styles—wide enough, certainly, to include occasional sarcasm, or treating people correctly but coolly as opposed to openly and warmly.

Bird had been aware in July of speculation about delay in *Tanner* in news columns written by Clark's friend George Nicholson (then executive director of the state District Attorneys' Association, later an assistant attorney general under Deukmejian, and in 1982, with strong financial support from kingmaker H. L. Richardson, the unsuccessful Republican candidate for State Attorney General). In September, Clark's friend Edwin Meese joined in the speculation. The Chief Justice was also aware that some of the correspondence from the "No-On-Bird Committee" run by Mary Nimmo claimed the court was delaying decisions. A letter of 15 August sent by the No-On-Bird group to national corporations began: "We don't have to tell you that Rose Bird is no friend of agriculture. Her record as Agriculture Secretary, in drafting of the ALRA and meddling in farm labor, is abundantly clear." The letter was sent to corporations around the nation that had given money the previous year to a successful fight against Proposition 14, a farm labor referendum in California. They were asked for money now for the campaign to remove Rose Bird from the Supreme Court. The letter stated baldly that "cases are being stalled until after November for purely political reasons."

Bird had plenty of reason in the fall of 1978 to believe that events beyond her control were designed to pull her into a quagmire. Her behavior toward Clark and his toward her would later be described to me by some commissioners as a "childish quarrel." It is surprising that the behavior in question is not viewed in a more serious light. Bird knew that there were echoes of Clark's personal comments throughout the campaign literature against her. She knew that his friends were writing newspaper columns saying that the *Tanner* case was likely to be delayed until after the election, and were doing so without evidence. And, according to the testimony, no one else on the court mentioned, or even thought of, delaying the case except Clark. In view of what she knew in the fall of 1978, it must have been easy for her to think that the actions he took, beginning with his *Caudillo* footnote, had something to do with trying to guarantee that the predictions of her enemies—his friends—outside the court would come true.

Bird testified that her question about whether Clark's 15 August dissent was "politically motivated" arose because she was certain his legal argument in the dissent—that she had been inconsistent as between *Caudillo* and *Tanner*—was erroneous. Consequently, she thought there must be another reason for his making this charge against her. The research attorney she asked to consult with Clark's staff reached the same conclusion she reached: that Clark's staff had no adequate legal explanation of why the citation was in his dissent. She said that at first she didn't think of the offensive footnote in terms of the upcoming election, but just that "it was done to personally embarrass me. . . . I thought it was done not to personally embarrass me within the court, but to demean me in the eyes of the public."

She testified that a number of embarrassing incidents had occurred in the recent past. Clark had spoken with Court of Appeal judges about the logjam of cases at the Supreme Court, complaining about her failure to administer effectively. His complaint was made soon after three new justices had joined the court. In September 1978 Clark made a public speech on the subject at the State Bar convention. He claimed then that the Supreme Court should be required to meet the 90-day rule, a rule that required the Courts of Appeal to file cases within 90 days after oral argument. The law technically did apply to the Supreme Court, but because the court had usually found it necessary to take much longer to decide its cases, it had evaded the issue for nearly the entire life of the law by not declaring cases officially submitted until a decision was ready to be filed and released. This meant the clock did not start running on the 90 days until the decision was about to be released. Rose Bird did not invent this evading device. It had been invented out of necessity by one of her most respected predecessors, Chief Justice Phil S. Gibson. As though taking a cue from Clark's public speeches on the matter, Senator Richardson's Law and Order Campaign Committee filed a lawsuit against the court in 1978 and claimed the court was violating the 90-day law and that the justices should not receive their salaries. A Superior Court judge ruled in favor of Richardson and in 1979 cut off the justices' salaries. Attorney General Younger, the appropriate official to represent the Supreme Court's interests in the case, instead wrote a letter to Richardson warmly endorsing his case against the court, his client. Given the fact that anyone familiar with the court's workings cannot help but conclude that it would be impossible for the court to finish most cases within 90 days after oral argument, this was clearly a harassment suit, one that dovetailed nicely with the current anti-court atmosphere. The case was eventually dropped, but not before the public's suspicions about wrongdoing at the high court had significantly deepened.

Earlier in 1978, Bird testified, Clark brought public embarrassment to her in another incident. He disqualified himself from sitting on a particular case and was replaced by a temporary judge, so Bird put out a routine press release naming the judge in question. Clark instructed her staff to remove his name from the release, so as not to say which justice the temporary judge was replacing. Newspaper articles then reported that Bird was arrogant for not revealing who was being replaced in the case. "An editorial came out in *The San Francisco Chronicle*," she told the Commission, "speaking in terms of their hope that it was my inexperience and not my callousness toward the public generally that caused me not to give out the information. . . . I informed him of the editorial in the *Chronicle*, that it had been critical. I did not ask him to correct the record. I assumed that he would, as a gentleman, correct it. It did not happen . . . I had hoped that he would simply pick up the telephone, call the editor and correct the record. Just for the future . . . I did not expect any kind of retraction from the newspaper. . . . I simply felt that it was unfair to leave the impression that it was due to my callousness and . . . inexperience that we had not given out his name. . . ."

Bird testified that her original intention in confronting Clark about the claim in his *Tanner* dissent that she was being inconsistent was to "call him on what he was doing this time. . . . I had not called him previously on the other occasions." She thought she would nip this embarrassing situation—the attack made against her in his *Tanner* dissent—by trying to correct it before it became public. To say her direct approach this time—asking the question, "Is it politically motivated?"—brought about an effect opposite to the one she said she intended is to put it mildly.

Bird said she continued to think of the problem between herself and Clark about the *Tanner* case as another attempt to personally embarrass her. Only later, she said, did she "begin to see a pattern might be there as to why this was done."

"At what point did you perceive such a pattern?" asked Hufstedler.

Bird: "When Mr. Younger began charging the court with delaying this case."

Hufstedler: "And at that point did you believe then that there may have been some connection between the [Clark's] *Caudillo* citation and your upcoming election?"

Bird: "I think the possibility crossed my mind."

Chodos asked the Chief Justice if she did not infer that "in view of his [Clark's] offer [that he would withdraw his *Caudillo* reference if she would withdraw her constitutional argument] and in view of the fact that this course was theoretically available to you, that he really was, that he really believed in good faith, however foolishly, that *Caudillo* was relevant and he . . . wasn't going out of his way to embarrass you?"

Bird: "It may have been possible that that was his intent. I had difficulty appreciating that intent since what he was asking me to do was the very thing that he was criticizing me for in the footnote"—i.e., being inconsistent in her statement of legal philosophy. "My problem with his suggestion was that I simply intellectually could not sign the lead opinion. I didn't agree with it."

In the third week of November 1978 Bird prepared a description of the court's procedures. It described how a decision worked its way from oral hearing to filing. One justice, she testified, objected to the memorandum being released to the public. That was Justice Clark. He told her it "would be a mistake to release it because it would simply raise the issue [of delay] once again in the public's minds and cause some more stories." This was strange, given the fact that at almost the same time he was urging her to be silent he was giving an interview to a reporter in which he became the first person to say there would be an investigation of the court over delay of decisions. He himself was generating stories, raising the issue again.

At the meeting Bird and Clark had in October, on the day Younger's accusations of delay appeared, Bird testified, as would Clark later, that it was he who brought up the possibility of delaying the *Tanner* decision until after the election. She also must have thought she needed to point out to Clark that her dissent in *Tanner* had not been intended to produce delay of the decision, for she told him then that her dissent had "nothing to do with holding up cases." Notes taken by Buehl during that meeting report that she told Clark, "If I wanted to do that, we wouldn't have gotten out Proposition 13 or busing, or I would have joined you and Richardson in *Caudillo* because I knew my decision was going to put me out on a limb." Busing and Proposition 13 were recent cases in which Bird had taken unpopular positions. She alone dissented in September 1978 from the court's opinion upholding the very popular tax-cutting proposition. She thought one portion of the new law violated the equal protection clause of the United States Constitution because it would cause unequal taxation of identical properties.

William Clark would be the next witness after Bird. As he waited in the wings, she was asked by a commissioner, "Is it fair to state that he [Clark] suggested that the court might delay the filing of the decision until after the election in order to demonstrate that it was not responding to pressure from [Attorney] General Younger?"

Bird: "That was my understanding."

"And up to that time, or for that matter, at any time during *Tanner,* was there any other justice or person, other than Justice Clark, who suggested that the filing of the *Tanner* case be delayed until after the election?"

Bird: "No."

Rose Elizabeth Bird, Chief Justice of the California Supreme Court, 1977—

National Security Advisor William P. Clark, a justice of the California Supreme Court from 1973 to 1981.

Mathew O. Tobriner, a justice of the California Supreme
Court, 1962–1982.

Wiley Manuel, a justice of the California Supreme Court,
1977–1981.

Stanley Mosk, a justice of the California Supreme Court, 1964–

Donald Wright, Chief Justice of the California Supreme Court from 1970 to 1977, swears in Ronald Reagan to his second term as Governor of California in 1971.

CHAPTER 8

Justice Clark, the Lone Public Accuser

Of all the justices heard by the public, only William Clark was an accuser. Indeed, of *all* witnesses heard in public, only Justice Clark was an accuser. Near the end of his testimony he claimed that another justice, Stanley Mosk, was also an accuser. But the public would never learn—during or after the hearings—if Mosk was in fact an accuser. The public would have only Clark's word for it.

Clark testified that the *Tanner* decision could have and should have been filed before the election. The month after the election he wrote a memorandum to the court that said: "In conscience it must be clear to all on the court that the *Tanner* case was signed up and ready for filing well in advance of November." The question, he told his fellow justices then, was why was it not filed.

The tallest member of the court, Clark spoke extremely slowly at times. He was diffident and genial in manner most of the time. His face occasionally looked like that of a puzzled schoolboy. He was a difficult witness to understand. It was like watching a magician who does tricks of now-you-see-it and now-you-don't. A comment by him would lead you to think, "Ah, now we're going to hear what makes him think there was wrongdoing." But, when he was asked to explain his claims, it would turn out he could not produce any substantiation. On the one hand, he suspected *Tanner* had been handled improperly; on the other hand, he told them he knew of no impropriety by any judge in the handling of it or any other case.

137

In five days of testimony he produced much damaging innuendo and few, if any, supporting facts. He alone made damaging accusations. But he said he felt no responsibility to verify whether these public accusations were true. Indeed, he told the Commission he had *never* examined the official records—which were available to him—or done any checking before or after he made his accusations to determine if they were true. Though he sounded charming and genial, the content of what he said was at times, to put it mildly, bizarre. Because his accusations were so serious, just as those made in *The Los Angeles Times* on election day were, they had to be examined. The reputations of justices, and the reputation of the court itself, were at stake.

After swearing to tell the truth, each justice was asked to summarize his or her formal education. This was probably a moment that Justice Clark longed to have behind him. He said he had no college degree and no law-school degree. In a somewhat self-effacing manner, he described his departure from Loyola Law School in Los Angeles. "In my third year, the dean, Father Donovan, approached me and suggested that I consider some other profession. So I did not graduate from Loyola." He then explained that he studied the law on his own and eventually, on the second try, passed the State Bar exam.

If Father Donovan had been alive and watching the hearing of the Commission on Judicial Performance on television in 1979, he probably would have felt vindicated in his early assessment of Clark. He probably would have been truly shocked a few years later to know that the student he had asked to leave law school had become one of the highest officials in the White House and was being considered for appointment to the U.S. Supreme Court.

At one point in Clark's testimony, Hufstedler restated to Justice Clark the distinctions Chief Justice Bird had drawn between the issues in the *Tanner* and *Caudillo* cases. Hufstedler explained that the Chief maintained that in *Caudillo* the basic issue was whether the judge could increase a sentence once it was determined the defendant was going to go to prison, but in *Tanner* the issue was whether the judge had the authority to strike a finding, which in this case would have meant that he could strike the gun-use charge, and grant probation rather than require the convicted person to go to prison. After Hufstedler finished his summary of the issue, he asked Justice Clark if he believed the difference explained by the Chief was an important issue in the cases.

Justice Clark replied that Bird's testimony at the hearing was the first time he had heard her explanation of why the two cases were different. "And I frankly didn't understand it," he said of her testimony and of what Hufstedler had just explained. It was strange he would say he had not heard her explanation before, for she had testified about talking to him about it at the very time it was in dispute. Her law clerks had testified about describing it to his law clerks. Clark himself had testified as to what she had told him, the same explanation, in essence, that she gave at the hearing. He obviously had heard what she said, but, as he admitted on the stand, he had never understood it.

Furthermore, he testified, "I must admit I didn't spend much time in contemplation of that. But—so I am unable to answer your question." It was an amazing comment, given the fact that the disagreement over the distinction between the two cases had been central to the conflict between Bird and Clark and, apparently, believed by him to be central to the reason for the *Tanner* decision allegedly being delayed until after the election.

The Chief Justice testified that neither she nor her staff ever got an explanation from Clark or his staff as to why he thought his controversial reference to her *Caudillo* opinion was an appropriate legal citation in *Tanner*. And Clark admitted that he had not wanted to discuss that with her, despite the fact that it was central to the controversy between them. Instead of explaining to her why he used it, he testified he was only interested in talking to her about why she thought he was "politically motivated."

When the Commission first asked Clark to explain why he included the *Caudillo* citation in his dissent in the *Tanner* case, Justice Clark asked permission to answer by showing the Commission a large chart he had prepared the night before. On this visual aid, he illustrated that by 30 May 1978, the day the *Tanner* box went to the Chief Justice after the opinions had been signed by the other six justices, all of those six justices had agreed that the use-a-gun-go-to-prison statute was constitutional. The bold lines and columns of the chart were impressive, easily grasped. But there was a problem. The information on the chart was wrong. By that date three justices, those signing Tobriner's majority opinion, had explicitly said they were not dealing with the constitutionality of the law. And the two who joined Clark's early dissent, had dealt with constitutionality only by implication.

When Clark completed his explanation of the chart, Special Counsel Hufstedler, sounding more like a patient teacher than an investigator, asked Justice Clark if there wasn't a rule of jurisprudence that "says in effect that if you can dispose of a matter by some means other than constitutional grounds that you should avoid the constitutional grounds?" Justice Clark agreed, but his voice indicated he was perplexed.

Hufstedler explained that in the majority opinion, Justice Tobriner had stated that because the legislature had not eliminated a previous

statute that gave trial judges the right to strike a finding, the legislature did not, in the *Tanner* statute now before the court, remove a trial
judge's power to strike a finding. In essence, the majority was saying
that the legislature had created an ambiguous situation by having
these two conflicting statutes on the books. Because the majority assumed the new statute had not eliminated a trial judge's power to
strike a finding of gun use, the majority didn't need to deal with
whether the new statute was constitutional. Having explained that
rationale to Justice Clark, Hufstedler then read to him directly from
the majority opinion: "We need not reach the constitutional issue. . . ."

"Do I read that correctly?" he asked his witness. "Is that not a
statement that the three judges signing this [majority opinion] did not
make the constitutional determination in the *Tanner* case. . . ?"

"Obviously, that's a synopsis," Clark responded in self-protective
understatement. He said he did not remember what the majority
opinion had said on this major point that just minutes before he had
been boldly, but erroneously, illustrating for the Commission, the
reporters, and the television audience. He said he would have to re-
read the majority opinion. Then he added, "I don't know that the six
votes up here [a reference to the now unhelpful chart] as against
three makes that much difference."

This elaborately illustrated error, lack of memory, or deliberate
distortion—whatever it was—did not, of course, point to any wrongdoing. But, putting the most benign interpretation on it—that he
really didn't understand the opinions central to the investigation—his
error illustrated his problems as a judge. He seemed to have difficulty
dealing with the simplest legal concepts and even in remembering
major details about court opinions. By the time he testified, the case
he was discussing had become, because of this investigation, the most
controversial case ever decided by the California Supreme Court.

In his effort to discredit the Chief Justice and make her appear
inconsistent in the two cases, *Caudillo* and *Tanner*, Justice Clark had
apparently forgotten a previous dissenting opinion he had written
about a judge's authority to strike a finding. In *Tanner* he maintained
in his dissenting opinion and throughout the investigation that there
was no constitutional authority for a judge to strike, or remove, a
finding established in court. What no one, including Justice Clark,
remembered then was that in *Foss,* a case decided by the court five
years earlier, Clark had maintained precisely the opposite. He wrote
then that a trial judge has an "inherent" power to strike a finding.
This means that Clark was guilty in his *Tanner* dissent of precisely the
inconsistency he had evoked in criticizing the Chief Justice. He
seemed to have trouble not only understanding legal concepts but
also remembering concepts he himself had articulated earlier. Others

would speculate that this lack of memory about even his own work might result from the fact that he himself had little to do with writing his opinions, particularly in his early years on the court, and that aides wrote most of his work. If true, his problem was a vivid illustration of Bird's concern that judges can become too dependent on their law clerks.

Another illustration seems to confirm that Clark had little to do with his own decisions, except to point his research attorneys in a policy direction. Clark issued opinions in two land-use cases that dealt with the same issue. But he dealt with them so differently, and without explanation, that, as one law professor concluded, "he couldn't possibly have written them." He apparently didn't remember what his earlier opinion had said. And that was apparently also true when he dealt in *Tanner* with whether a judge has the power to strike a finding.

Clark was the only justice to testify that he had even suspected that the *Tanner* opinion had been delayed. The strong December memo to his fellow justices, declaring that it was clear *Tanner* had been delayed, was damning. Presumably, he would have written it only after careful thought and research of the readily available records on how *Tanner* moved through the court. By the time the memo was written, it had been announced that there would be an official investigation of the justices regarding the very claims he was making in the memo. The commissioners tried during the 1979 hearing to learn the basis of his assertion. These exchanges illustrate the difficulty of their task:

QUESTION: Is it your feeling that despite the filing of a separate dissent on October 24th, that the opinion could have been filed before election day [7 November]?

CLARK: When I wrote that [the memo] I was not looking at any particular phase or date. I did not look at the chronology.

QUESTION: The thing that puzzles me, Justice Clark. . . . The statement in your memo is that the case "was signed up and ready for filing well in advance of November." Did you mean days or weeks or couple of months, or did you mean it was perhaps ready for filing the first of October?

CLARK: As I have said, I have no time frame on it.

QUESTION: You stated that this is your belief now . . . I don't really understand what facts you summoned or marshaled to support your belief in light of the fact that it was technically—we all know that all the signatures hadn't been obtained. Could you tell me what things . . . you now see that led you to conclude that *Tanner* was ready for filing "well in advance of November"?

CLARK: I have marshaled no facts. . . . I still believe in what I wrote on 20 December 1978.

QUESTION: . . . *Tanner* was not all wrapped up prior to October 10. Is that a fair statement?

CLARK: Yes, I think it is.

QUESTION: It was not ready for filing?

CLARK: Yes.

QUESTION: Would you say then it's also a correct statement that probably *Tanner* was not ready for filing until Justice Manuel had had a reasonable period to write [his 24 October dissent]?

CLARK: Yes.

QUESTION: What puzzles me, we start whittling away at the days and weeks of October, it doesn't seem to me that at that point you . . . arrive at the point well in advance of November where you say the opinion was ready for filing.

CLARK: I think your assumption is a good one.

QUESTION: Well, are you saying then that the term "well in advance of November," as used in your memo, was an overstatement?

CLARK: I don't think so.

QUESTION: . . . I can't reconcile in my own mind . . . that what I have just discussed here is accurate and correct and that your statement that the opinion was ready for filing "well in advance" is also correct. Can you reconcile those two?

CLARK: No, I don't attempt to. I understand your concern.

QUESTION: I just am trying to understand what you really meant when you said the opinion was ready for filing "well in advance" of the November election. . . . Are you saying it was just a matter of two or three weeks?

CLARK: No. I wrote what I wrote, and felt that way then and, as I said, I feel no differently today.

QUESTION: Justice Clark, are you saying not that it was ready to file, but that it could and should have been ready to file well in advance of November?

CLARK: Yes.

QUESTION: Was it your—is it your—are you telling us that . . . these changes and the discussions and the possible reconciliations [in the months before the election] all related to cosmetic aspects . . . instead of the substantive aspects? Is that your position?

CLARK: It is.

Within the next hour of testimony:

CLARK: The cosmetology, I think, occurred between election and filing. I didn't feel that . . . cosmetic activity occurred prior to the election.

QUESTION: You think the case should have moved faster and . . . there are no specific reasons for that view that you have in mind now?

CLARK: I don't think so.

QUESTION: Where should it have moved faster? . . . What was wrong with the process as you observed it?

CLARK: I have not considered the question before today. . . . [Witness is shown exhibit that shows chronology of how *Tanner* case moved through the court.] I am unable to suggest on which day or days the case might have been filed.

QUESTION: With regard to your memorandum, "In conscience it must be clear to all on the court that the *Tanner* case was signed up and ready for filing well in advance of November," were you using that then in the sense of under your court rules . . . that that process had been completed? Or were you using it in some other sense?

CLARK: In the technical sense that you have alluded to in your past two questions, my statement is probably incorrect.

QUESTION: In what respect is it correct, Justice Clark?

CLARK: . . . That it could and should have been filed.

Given the fact that he was the only accuser, Clark didn't provide the Commission with much evidence. His answers caused cruel mischief, but they neither acquitted nor convicted. As a commissioner would tell me two years later, "He just left Tobriner spinning in the wind." Before Clark left the witness stand, he would put a tight spin on the rope.

In September 1978 Edwin Meese and two other lawyers—George Nicholson, then the executive director of the California District Attorneys Association, and William Janes, an official in Attorney General Younger's office—wrote an article about the State Supreme Court in an anniversary edition of *The Los Angeles Daily Journal,* a paper of legal news with a statewide circulation. The article, which became significant in the investigation because Clark had been given an advance copy to review, was critical of the court. Most important, it predicted that the *Tanner* decision would not be released until after the election because, it said, the majority opinion was likely to be a political liability for some justices who would be on the November ballot. Clark said he talked with his friend Meese about the article before publication but insisted he did not talk with him about the *Tanner* case.

Clark praised the article when he testified but said he dismissed the writers' prediction that *Tanner* would not get out until after the election. "I felt . . . the speculation in this article, particularly about *Tanner,* would not be what we might call inside information. . . . The very opposite is suggested." An insider, he said, "would have believed, as I think I did then, that *Tanner* would be filed before the election. . . . At that point I truly felt that *Tanner* would be filed soon. . . . An insider on our court would, if he were to speculate to lawyers like this—and I am not suggesting that occurred—would have to say it should be filed any time."

One of the commissioners asked it it wasn't true that by a few weeks before the article appeared the likelihood of *Tanner* being filed quickly had lapsed because of the controversy that had been stirred over his claim that the Chief Justice was inconsistent in *Caudillo* and *Tanner*. "I don't think so," replied Clark, "I think what occurred thereafter could not have been anticipated."

An insider, he said, would know that all seven justices would have signed off on an opinion by that time and that the case could be expected to be filed soon. His repeated reference to the fact that seven signatures meant a decision was ready to be filed soon was surprising. While he may have been able on election eve to fool a reporter who was unfamiliar with the court and apparently convince him that seven signatures at any time meant an opinion was completed, it was peculiar that he would have thought that he could mislead the members of the Commission. By this time in the investigation they were well schooled in how the court works and knew that the existence of seven signatures on an opinion at any one time is relatively useless as a measure of whether a decision is ready to be filed. Nevertheless, he persisted in making the reference many times in his five days of testimony.

Clark's testimony should have raised the question of whether it was he—rather than Tobriner, Bird, Manuel, or anyone else—who had taken steps to delay *Tanner* until after the election. In order to make the Meese-Nicholson-Richardson campaign strategy work, of course, it was necessary for *Tanner* not to be issued before the election. Surely even the most mildly suspicious person would wonder if Clark's own repeated revisions of his dissent, each of which required time-consuming recirculation of the entire *Tanner* box to each justice, and his suggestions to Bird and Tobriner that the Chief Justice delay the case until after the election, were not, in fact, part of the larger anti-Bird campaign strategy.

Contrary to Clark's claim, any informed and honest court insider at the time Meese and his co-authors submitted their still-unpublished article to Clark, and certainly by the time it was published, would have known that this decision had quite a few hurdles yet—that it would be safe, and politically valuable, from their viewpoint—to predict that it *would not* get out before the election because it *could not* get out by then. By that time, late August–early September, insiders close to Clark knew that a storm was brewing. His staff had been predicting the decision would not get out before the election. They knew the existence of seven signatures at an earlier time certainly was irrelevant now, that new opinions in the case were being generated, and that each one required each of the seven justices to review all the materials again and to sign off again.

Clark revised his original dissent twice in August. The first time he added six pages to speak to the constitutional issue raised in the Chief Justice's concurring opinion. It was this revision that first included the reference to her *Caudillo* opinion. The second time, he revised it in order to expand his criticism of her after she and her staff had asked if his *Caudillo* reference was "politically motivated." His comments about her alleged inconsistency were tangential, not necessary, as he admitted, to the legal points in his dissent. Commissioner Chodos asked him if he hadn't, "in effect, postponed the filing of *Tanner* by exercising your prerogative . . . to comment acerbically . . . on the concurring opinion?" Clark disagreed. By that time in the proceedings, the word "delay" was not a reference to the normal slow pace that the processing of many decisions takes; rather, it was a pejorative term that referred to a willful attempt to keep the decision from coming out by election day—it referred to the wrongdoing the Commission was trying to prove or disprove. Clark now said he did not consider his two (eventually three) revisions a delay. "If there was a delay, it was created by the unanticipated reaction to the cite of one case." This was a misleading comment, directed at the Chief Justice's reaction to his citation critical of her. Though she had asked him if his action was politically motivated, and had tried to explain to him and his staff the differences in the two cases, she didn't even have the *Tanner* box from 11 July until after the election. She was taking no action on the case, and there is no testimony or other evidence that during this time she was suggesting anyone else should take any action that would delay it.

Clark implied several times in his testimony that Justice Manuel wrote his separate dissent only to defend the Chief. He even said at one time that Manuel was "forced" to write his dissent. That was similar to a charge made by a nameless source in the Thanksgiving Day 1979 *Washington Post* news story for which Clark was the only named source, a charge that the decision had been effectively delayed by either Tobriner or Bird asking another justice to write a separate dissent. But, questioned closely by a commissioner, Clark said he meant Manuel was "forced" by circumstances, and that he (Clark) never heard that anyone had asked Manuel to write a dissent. On the other hand, Clark only fueled suspicions when he said that two members of Manuel's staff had told Clark they thought his criticism of the Chief Justice in his dissent was appropriate, and that they had urged him not to drop that reference. Clark said that, in all his conversations with Manuel in September and October of 1978, Manuel had never discussed the merits of Clark's *Caudillo* citation with him. Clark suggested that Manuel wrote a separate dissent, if not because he was asked, then because he wanted to be polite to the Chief and not because he disagreed with Clark.

Manuel told quite a different story. His testimony repudiated Clark's. Unfortunately because he testified in private after the hearings were closed by court order, the public never had a chance to hear his explanation of his decision to write a separate dissent. Manuel said that the first of the conversations that he and Clark had about *Tanner* was initiated by him for the very purpose of telling Clark he didn't think his reference to *Caudillo* was legally appropriate.

"It was late in the afternoon," Manuel testified in the private session. "I believe it was around the 27th or so of September [a week after Clark had inexplicably asked Justice Tobriner to transfer the *Tanner* box to Justice Manuel]. . . . I happened to be talking to my clerk, Barbara Spencer . . . talking to her about the *Tanner* case. . . . He [Clark] came over to the door and we said, 'Hi.' I said, 'By the way, may I see you?' . . . We left Barbara Spencer and went either to my chambers or Justice Clark's chambers. I indicated to him at that time that I was beginning to go over his opinion and I was having some difficulty with the matter, particularly the reference to *Caudillo*." In dramatic contradiction with Clark's testimony, Manuel said, "I indicated to him that it didn't seem to me that his reference was proper [as a legal point] . . . because I believed that he was using the *Caudillo* reference to prove too much.

"I told him I thought it's one thing to talk about the power of the legislature to enhance a penalty, but I thought it was another thing to indicate that what was said in *Caudillo* also covered the many restrictions on that power."

Manuel's testimony that he didn't want to sign the later Clark dissent was supported by the sworn testimony of another witness, Jane Brady, a lawyer on the central staff of the court for many years. She said Manuel had told her on two occasions that he did not want to sign the Clark dissent, that he didn't think the *Caudillo* reference was fair.

In the closed hearing, Justice Manuel told the commissioners that Clark offered no rationale for his use of the *Caudillo* reference, didn't discuss it at all—just as he had not discussed it with the Chief Justice. According to Manuel, when he complained to Clark about the dissent, Clark only responded that he "would think about it and get back to me. And then he left."

Manuel said he had very strong feelings on the matter. He considered both Clark and Bird to be his friends. Nevertheless, he testified that he considered Clark's reference to the Chief's *Caudillo* opinion not only legally inappropriate but "considered this just part of a running series of attacks on the Chief and the court." Later, Justice Newman, in his secret testimony, would describe Clark's *Caudillo* reference in his dissent as a "joke in bad taste."

Manuel thought it was worse than a joke. "I didn't think the . . . citation was appropriate. . . . I could not sign an opinion where my signature would indicate an endorsement of the use of it. . . . I feel to this day that the *Caudillo* reference wasn't a proper one." He said he didn't believe the Chief Justice was inconsistent, but if there had been an inconsistency, "this wasn't an appropriate way to do it [point it out]." Manuel said he had had misgivings months earlier about signing Clark's harsh original dissent, even before it contained the attack on the Chief Justice. He had told Clark earlier that he was signing his first dissent on condition that Clark would eventually tone down the language of the first paragraph. Clark had accused the majority of using "judicial fiat" and had written that "in no other instance has the majority so flagrantly disregarded legislative prerogative and the separation of powers doctrine as in this case."

Manuel was asked by the Commission if he would have refused to sign the harsh Clark dissent if he had agreed with the legal point being made in the section he regarded as offensive. Manuel said that both legal inappropriateness and intemperate language had motivated him not to sign Clark's dissent, but that he could imagine refusing to sign an opinion over only the issue of intemperate language. "So . . . you understand my position, I can remember when we went through the Jesse Carter period on this court. . . . I never thought very highly of that. And I thought it scandalized the court to have justices using language that I thought was somewhat intemperate. Frankly, I would not encourage that kind of tactic. . . . I would hate to see us return . . . to the Jesse Carter days."

For anyone who knew the reputation of the late Jesse Carter in his later years, the remark meant that Manuel must have been extremely upset with Clark's combative language in the *Tanner* dissent. Jesse Carter was a justice on the California Supreme Court from 1939 to 1959. As a reporter put it in a story about Justice Carter's threats to shoot Marin County officials in 1958: "He has gained a national reputation for colorful language in his frequent dissenting opinions." That, apparently, was an understatement.

When water from the justice's private fish and irrigation pond flooded homes that year, the Marin County Board of Supervisors voted to drain the water from the pond. Carter met with reporters at his home and told them, "I'll shoot the first S.O.B. who sets foot on my property." To demonstrate he wasn't using hyperbole, he opened a closet door and showed them a .35 automatic rifle, a .30-06 automatic rifle, a .300 magnum rifle, a .25 automatic rifle, a .30 caliber carbine, a 12-gauge shotgun, and a 20-gauge rifle. The supervisors' action, he told reporters, was "an un-American procedure. It is just like Nazi Germany or Soviet Russia." As a young attorney general in the late 1950's, Manuel was familiar with Carter's sometimes vindictive approach. Now that Manuel was on the court, he said, he was determined not to encourage such an approach.

Manuel told the Commission that Clark came back to his office the day after Manuel asked him to reconsider the appropriateness of his *Caudillo* dissent. "He said he thought about it and couldn't make a change," Manuel testified. "He didn't give a reason for his conclusion."

In addition to differing on whether Manuel had ever told Clark he disagreed with his *Caudillo* reference, Manuel and Clark's sworn testimony differed on another significant point. Each testified they had had three conversations with each other in September and October about the *Caudillo* reference in Clark's dissent. Both testified that Clark had told Manuel to delay writing a new dissent, that it might be unnecessary if Clark could resolve his conflict with the Chief Justice. Clark said he went to Manuel's office after his mid-October conversation with the Chief Justice and said, "Wiley, I have struck out," and indicated to Manuel that he should go ahead with his work on *Tanner*. But Manuel testified that Clark *never* came back. He said that, though Clark had told him to wait for word from him on whether to write, he in fact never let him know whether he had resolved his differences with the Chief Justice.

After the election, newspaper reports based on information from a nameless source, believed to be Clark, accused Manuel of delaying the decision at the request of Tobriner or Bird between 21 September and 24 October, the day Manuel circulated his dissent.

The charge was astonishing. It was Clark who, according to his own testimony and Justice Tobriner's testimony, asked Tobriner on 21 September to forward the *Tanner* box to Manuel for action. At one point Clark even said he thought he himself took the box from Tobriner's office to the court Secretary's office and asked that it be transferred to Manuel. Both Clark and Manuel testified that Manuel had never asked for the box; Manuel said he was surprised when it arrived, and Clark said he had just assumed Manuel would want it. He never explained why he assumed that.

After assuring that the box would get into Manuel's hands, Clark then, according to both his and Manuel's testimony, urged Manuel, during the first 19 of the 33 days that he held the box, to delay writing an opinion. Manuel said that when Clark didn't get back to him about whether his controversy with the Chief Justice had been settled, his own sense of urgency impelled him to rush ahead with his dissent, despite other pressing matters in his office. This was corroborated by another witness, court central staff attorney Brady, who testified that one of Manuel's law clerks asked her in mid-October to review a draft of Manuel's proposed dissent: "She told me that he [Manuel] was quite anxious that it be circulated as soon as possible so the cases wouldn't be held up." He was in such a hurry, she said, that his law clerk "declined any suggested modifications."

"No, never," Manuel said when asked if Bird, Tobriner, or anyone else had asked him to write a separate dissent in *Tanner*. Perhaps he was merely "encouraged" by them? "No," said Manuel.

Manuel said he was shocked when he read *The Los Angeles Times* on the morning of 11 October 1978. On that day a story quoted Evelle Younger, the Attorney General and then the Republican gubernatorial candidate, saying he was "certain" the *Tanner* case had already been decided by the court but was being withheld until after the November election because it might be politically damaging to justices up for approval by the voters on election day. (Younger retracted his accusations the next day.)

As of that morning, Manuel was still obliging Justice Clark's request that he not work on *Tanner* pending Clark's resolution of the dispute between himself and the Chief Justice. After he read the story, Manuel said, he walked down the hall to see the Chief Justice. "I was disturbed by the article," he told the Commission in secret session. He said he told her he was upset. "The article had accused us of delaying *Tanner,* and, as far as I knew, there were no delays. And I felt particularly concerned because I now had the box. . . . As far as I knew there was nothing amiss. . . . The case was being handled in the usual fashion."

Evelle Younger had been Manuel's boss before Manuel left the Attorney General's office in 1976 to go on the Superior Court, where he served a year before being appointed to the Supreme Court. The person who was making this public accusation at the time Manuel had the box was "a person that I had worked with, and I believe who respected me as a professional lawyer while I was in the office. . . . Because of that I felt very personally concerned. If it had been the District Attorney of Mono [County], it wouldn't have hit me quite the same way. It just bothered me that now I had the box and I had a hot potato. . . . And my respect for him is that I couldn't imagine his making the statement just out of the blue. . . . I don't think he is given to giving irrational or insane statements. I felt that somebody, maybe on his political staff, had said this. . . . I felt very concerned. . . . I didn't think there was any truth in the accusation."

Later, said Manuel in his secret testimony, he was aggravated further by the fact that some of his former colleagues in the Attorney General's office took the unethical step of talking to him about Younger's charges about a pending case. "A few of the deputies in the office, more or less in a kind of teasing way, indicated, 'Ah, hah, you guys are holding up something.' And I expressed my real annoyance, I guess anger, even though they were friends of mine." One of them was Deputy Attorney General John Klee. "Klee has a way of needling you. He was telling me what was in the newspaper and saying, 'Why don't you guys decide this case?' I told him, 'His information is wrong, and I don't know why Younger is saying this. . . . How can the Attorney General make those kinds of statements? . . . He is totally wrong.' "

The Chief Justice also was irritated that day by Younger's accusations. She suggested to Manuel that someone inside the court might be responsible for the candidate's comments. Manuel said she told him not to feel pressured. Clark also met with the Chief Justice that day. He said she told him about the Younger story. Clark testified that his response when she told him about the story was, "Oh, did Younger call Wiley?" It was a strange, perhaps mean, question, given the fact that any justice's talking to Younger, or to anybody else outside the court, about pending cases, would be considered improper. But it seemed especially strange for Clark to imply such a thing. Even according to his own testimony, he still had not given Manuel the promised go-ahead. According to Manuel, as we have noted, that go-ahead was never given. According to Clark, he gave it later on the day Younger's accusations appeared in print, after he met with the Chief Justice.

Younger had made two major claims at political rallies on 9 and 10 October: that the Supreme Court was withholding decisions on death penalty cases and that it had completed but was withholding the *Tanner* decision, all until after the election. These decisions would be "politically embarrassing" for the court, said Younger. He insisted he was "certain" that the *Tanner* case was being withheld, and added, "I am aware of the seriousness of the charges I am making." In a deposition given under oath a year later he told Commission investigators that reporters had quoted him accurately.

But the day the *Times'* first story appeared, Younger publicly retracted his original charges. Court records and an assistant attorney general in Younger's office had revealed in the meantime that no death penalty case was even before the court. That day Younger told reporters that he had been wrong on the death penalty case, but at first said he was still right about the *Tanner* case. But as he talked that day, he changed even that claim. Earlier he had said he was "certain" the *Tanner* case was being delayed; later in the day he said he was stating "more of a question than a charge." A *Times* story the next day reported his retractions about both the death penalty case and the *Tanner* case.

In the three and one-half weeks between this embarrassing episode and the 7 November election, Younger occasionally repeated his charge that *Tanner* had been decided and was being delayed, despite his mid-October retraction. When I interviewed Younger in the summer of 1981, he said he had felt free to continue to make the charge about *Tanner* "because Rose Bird never denied it." That was not true. In the same 12 October story in which Younger reversed himself on the nonexistent death penalty cases and the *Tanner* case, Bird, through her executive assistant, Stephen Buehl, said publicly that Younger's charges of delay were unfounded. "There are no cases, no opinions, in the court where all the justices have reached their final decisions that have not been announced," Buehl told the press. (Until the *Times'* election-day story, earlier press stories on the delay issue had duly reported Bird's checks on the record and denials of delay.)

"I used some careless language," Younger told me in 1981. "Certainly, in the course of a campaign—" His voice dropped off and he paused as he looked out over downtown Los Angeles. Then he completed the thought, selecting his words carefully. "Well, I know I did—you say things that, on reflection, were not as accurate as they should've been."

Nevertheless, Younger said he still believed in 1981 that decisions were delayed by the court for political purposes in 1978, "but obviously I could not prove it." He said that at the time he made the public accusation about *Tanner* being delayed, "I felt my information was strong." I asked him his source. "It came from members of my staff who talked to people on the Supreme Court staff." He then made an observation that many who oppose the court make, and, like others, he seemed to say it with glee rather than disappointment: "I guess we'll never know what really happened, the public will never know."

When he gave a sworn deposition, never publicly revealed, to the Commission's investigators in 1979, Younger told them his source of information about the delay was Herbert Ellingwood, who in 1978 was a special assistant attorney general in Younger's Sacramento office. Ellingwood had moved to Younger's staff from Governor Reagan's staff. When Reagan became President, Ellingwood became his deputy counsel at the White House.

By the time all the testimony, public and private, had been given, the Commission was still chasing leads that went nowhere. At that point in the closed sessions, Special Counsel Hufstedler and his staff read portions of depositions of people who had been deposed but had not testified before the Commission. The Commission heard Younger's first.

Under oath, he said he decided that what Ellingwood had told him about *Tanner* was "of legitimate political comment" and called Ellingwood and said, " 'I intend to use this . . . so I want to know if you regard your source of information as reliable. Bear in mind that I don't want to be unfair or embarrass myself. Is your source reliable?' And he answered in the affirmative. . . . He probably wouldn't tell me if I said, 'Who's your source?' So I didn't ask. I assumed it was some person on the court."

It was logical for Younger to make that assumption, for he probably realized that his longtime aide Ellingwood was a close friend of Justice Clark. But as the State's top law-enforcement officer he should also have realized that it would have been highly improper for his aide and a Supreme Court justice to be discussing a case pending before the court, particularly a case like *Tanner* in which the Attorney General was a party. No such concerns seemed to torment Younger. Instead, he seemed to be glad that he could assume his aide got the information about *Tanner* from a justice of the court.

"No justice on the Supreme Court or appellate court told me. . . . No member of the [court] staff talked to me about it," Ellingwood said in his never-revealed sworn deposition to the Commission. It is clear that Ellingwood was pivotal to Younger's making the public accusation that *Tanner* was being delayed for political purposes. If Ellingwood's sworn deposition is truthful, he spread this damaging accusation with no knowledge of whether it was true.

"The basis [for the accusation]," Ellingwood said under oath, "was the accumulated conversation from all the people to whom I'd talked. . . . I believed then and I believe now that the Supreme Court withheld decisions for political purposes. That is, pending the election. . . . And that's what I told Mr. Younger." It was "an accumulation of a lot of conversations and speculation and reading of reports, that sort of thing." It was, in short, gossip. Ellingwood said he also based his opinion on "nineteen years of political experience." Political experience is a curious basis for an assistant to the Attorney General to use in order to "confirm" accusations so serious that they could have led to the removal of judges from the high court—judges whom Ellingwood, presumably, would like to have seen removed.

Ellingwood was described to me by former Chief Justice Wright as a right-wing ideologue who did not care about judicial fairness. His political experience had been acquired at Governor Reagan's knee: as Legal Affairs Secretary to the Governor from the last years of his Sacramento administration on, Ellingwood was responsible for picking the Governor's judicial appointees. He held this office the whole time that Clark was making his rapid ascent from a position as the Governor's Chief of Staff, via Superior Court and State Court of Appeal judgeships, to the California Supreme Court. (When Reagan became President, Clark and Ellingwood found themselves working together again—as top presidential aides.)

The investigators asked Ellingwood who the participants were in the conversations where he learned about alleged court delays. "Well, within the Attorney General's office, everywhere you go." The rumors began in March of 1978, he said. It didn't make sense that such rumors could have been believed in March, unless they were being said by someone who had the power to delay the case. The public hearing in the case had been held only a month earlier, and no one could intelligently complain within a month that the case was late. No case would even be out of the hands of the majority opinion writer, the first person who works on it, by that time.

"It was common conversation in the hallways, whether it was the legislative hallways or the court hallways, whether it was in San Francisco or here [Sacramento]. So it's an accumulation of all that talk."

Still trying to find evidence of even hearsay from somebody who claimed to know something about the delays, the investigator asked Ellingwood what knowledge the people he talked with had. He responded: "Nobody with whom I talked inside the office or outside the office gave me their source." It seemed a startling admission for a prosecutor, and one who had played such a key role in spreading the information.

Although Ellingwood said no one on the Supreme Court or its staff talked with him about *Tanner,* he said he did talk with Justice Clark, whom he described as a personal friend, that fall. He said he asked Justice Clark to let him know when the *Tanner* decision was due to come out, but he said Clark never let him know.

Because of the significance of Younger's statements during the campaign, the Commission's investigators told the panel they had done "an intensive investigation" of the Attorney General's office. They interviewed 15 people, most of them under oath. These witnesses constituted nearly all the high officials in the criminal division of the Attorney General's staff throughout the state.

Each of them, in separate interviews, the Commission was told, agreed on these three important points: "A, I have no source within the court from which I obtained any information about a pending case before it was handed down. B, I don't know of anybody else in the Attorney General's office who did either. C, I never heard anybody say that they did."

The intensive investigation of the Attorney General's office, never revealed to the public, added up to this significant finding: evidence of massive gossip and no knowledge among the State's highest law-enforcement officials about the delaying of Supreme Court decisions. Also, it showed a willingness among them, including the Attorney General himself, to be publicly malicious with gossip that, if true, could have led to the removal of justices from the bench. It was strange behavior for prosecutors whose work is supposed to be based on verifiable evidence. They seemed not to mind if they destroyed the reputation of the State's highest court with mere gossip. It may even have been their intent, given the pervasiveness of the rumor they spread so widely and so freely and so soon after the hearing in the case.

The investigation of the Attorney General's office turned up an ironic piece of information. On 28 September 1978, the head of the criminal division prepared a long list of cases that the office thought had been pending too long before the Supreme Court. The list was prepared as the basis for a letter the staff wanted the Attorney General to write complaining about the delays. Interestingly, *Tanner* was *not* on the original list. It was added later, but not until a week after Younger had made both his public accusation and his retraction.

An examination of the testimony and evidence presented to the Commission shows that nearly all conversation about delaying the decision until after the election emanated from one place: Justice Clark's office. From July on, according to testimony from his staff, the *Tanner* case was always spoken of in his office in terms of whether it would get out before or after the election. Why that crucial time-frame? Why not before September? before the New Year? Who suggested the election as an important time-frame? What was the reason for Clark's election deadline for the case? What was the reason for his friends on the outside having this same deadline for the case? These questions were not asked at the hearing.

Even if one assumes that all the other justices and their staff members lied under oath and only Clark and his staff told the truth, the testimony still shows that the possibility of the *Tanner* decision being delayed for election purposes was being discussed in Clark's office perpetually beginning in July and continuing until the election. A Clark staff member said it was discussed by Clark at formal meetings with his law clerks between four and ten times from the end of August until the election. Assuming that all witnesses who testified about the delay testified truthfully, the only justice who ever suggested the case could or should be delayed until the election was Clark.

Speaking of how he felt about the timing of the case, on 21 September 1978, Clark referred to himself, as he sometimes did, in the third person: "At that time, Clark couldn't care less whether the opinion called *People* v. *Tanner* was filed before or after election day." It was on 21 September that Clark met with Tobriner and asked him to pass the *Tanner* box to Manuel. "Did you ever come to care about that before election day?" Clark was asked. "I don't think so."

However, Clark's activity before and after 21 September, according to the testimony of himself, his staff, and others, shows that he hardly could have cared more whether the *Tanner* decision was going to be filed before election day, 7 November. The testimony shows him eager in late August and early September to know what was happening in the case, presumably interested in seeing the case completed. After 9 September, he became even more eager, asking his staff what they could do to move the case. But in late September, he took steps that had the effect of guaranteeing that the decision would *not* be ready for filing on election day—urging Manuel to delay his work on the case and simultaneously telling Tobriner and Bird it could be delayed. It is logical to conclude that the early strategy of opponents of Bird was to hasten the issuance of the *Tanner* decision so it could be used against her in the election. But, when it seemed it might not be completed before the election, the strategy apparently shifted in order to guarantee that it would not be ready by election day. That would permit opponents to accuse the court of improper delay—in the end, a far more sensational and damaging charge than accusing her in the months before the election of being soft on criminals.

Talk about delay of the case until after the election began in Clark's chambers in July while Clark was still in Europe. Maury Koblick, one of Clark's research attorneys, testified that as soon as he saw the concurring opinion when it was circulated in mid-July he thought her opinion would do "quite a bit of harm to her election campaign unless the opinion was not issued before the election." At first the remarks about delay were a joke. Koblick described himself and Richard Morris, Clark's senior research attorney, and members of Richardson's staff and the central staff of the court, standing around in the hallway joking about *Tanner:* "Why are you rushing the work on *Tanner*? It's not going to be filed until after the election."

Morris, in Clark's absence, had withdrawn Clark's dissent as soon as he saw the Chief's opinion in mid-July, because he knew Clark would want to change it. The text of the confidential portion of the testimony revealed that at the same time as Clark's staff and others were joking in the hallway outside Clark's office about the delay of the *Tanner* decision, similar comments were being made, but not humorously, in the corridors of the criminal division of the State Attorney General's office, a party to the *Tanner* suit.

When Clark returned from Europe, he learned what had happened to the *Tanner* case in his absence. Morris told him that the Chief had been unfairly criticized for her opinion in the *Caudillo* case. He told him about the scathing and carelessly reported story in July in a statewide magazine, *New West*, about her *Caudillo* opinion. Morris said he told Clark that her *Caudillo* opinion had unfairly become an issue in the campaign to defeat the Chief Justice in November. Knowing all this, Clark decided that when he revised his *Tanner* dissent he would include a footnote that would draw attention to her *Caudillo* opinion. Whatever his intention, judicial dissent or political act, the result was perfect campaign fodder for those working against Bird. In essence, he was making precisely the claim they made, that Bird bent over backwards—bending the law one way in *Caudillo* and another way in *Tanner*—in order to have both cases result to the benefit of the criminal defendants.

In a disingenuous observation to the Commission, Clark said that he didn't think anyone in the campaign against Bird would be interested in his footnote; perhaps only six law professors would note it, and they wouldn't do so, he said, until six months later. Clark is an accomplished artist with the press. He knew that if Bird's opinion in *Caudillo* had already become an important issue in the campaign, an attack by him in an opinion released between then and the election would be to the anti-Bird campaign what a can of gasoline is to a campfire. Reporters often don't read court opinions carefully, but they would certainly notice an attack by Clark on the Chief Justice about a rape case that by July had become a key weapon in the campaign against her—even if the attack was in a footnote.

Clark told the Commission that the purpose of the footnote in his first revised dissent was to attract the Chief's attention, not the attention of her fellow justices, let alone the press and the electorate. If it was his intention to let her know judicially and judiciously that she was inconsistent and should reconsider her opinion, he could have done what other justices testified they had done in the past when trying to convince a colleague to change his or her mind—he could have written an internal memo to her. The writing of the footnote may not have been dishonorable—Clark really may have not understood whether what he said was legally appropriate. Rather, it is his explanation that it was a private communication between him and the Chief Justice that is disingenuous. If there was any doubt about that, his next step eliminated that doubt. Within ten days of circulating his first revised dissent, he withdrew it and revised it yet again. This was done after members of the Chief Justice's staff, at her direction, had met with Morris and asked if the footnote was politically motivated and told Morris that the Chief thought the footnote was legally inappropriate. This time Clark made sure that all within the court would know about the struggle between himself and the Chief. To his second revised dissent, he attached a green memo. In it he said the Chief Justice had requested that the *Caudillo* footnote be deleted because it was "inapposite and 'politically motivated.' I reject both the request and the unfortunate reasoning . . . I now expand the discussion of *Caudillo* to show that it is clearly apposite, moving it from footnote to body." By that time, according to both Clark and Bird's testimony, she and he had talked about his reference to *Caudillo* and she had specifically told him she was not asking him to remove it.

Clark was asked by the Commission if he thought, at the time he decided to expand the attack on the Chief in his second revised dissent, that the case would be useful to voters if it was filed before the election. "I don't think so," said Clark ambiguously. "I realize that that was probably the Chief's concern," he said less ambiguously, pointing the finger again. It was one of several times when he cleverly implied he thought the Chief wanted the decision delayed because of the election.

From 25 August through the first nine days of September, according to Koblick, Clark was asking his research attorneys what was happening with *Tanner*. At one point he suggested that one of them should ask Hal Cohen, one of Tobriner's law clerks, what was happening with *Tanner*. Because Tobriner had written the majority opinion in the case, each time there was a new or revised dissent written, the box would return to the original writer, Tobriner, and begin the round for signature approval again. That nothing had happened when it was returned by Clark to Tobriner on 25 August was not surprising. Tobriner had been on vacation for the month of August. And the first week of September he, like Clark, was at the court's monthly hearing every day, not in his office working on opinions. And Cohen was on vacation in September.

But Koblick testified that he didn't think Clark had a sense of urgency about getting *Tanner* completed until about 10 or 15 September. "Around about there, all of a sudden he was saying, 'What can we do to move it along?'" The staff told him they thought that because the matter was in the hands of the lead opinion writer there was nothing they could do, but perhaps Clark could bring up the matter at weekly conference. According to Clark he did so—but not until a month later.

At about the same time, mid-September, that Clark was telling his staff that *Tanner* needed to be moved along, he spoke at a public session of the State Bar convention in San Francisco. During the same meeting, an unnamed Supreme Court justice, believed to be Clark, told a reporter for a small legal publication that *Tanner* could be expected to be released within a week. The published remark would produce expectation and disappointment in a small audience, but was unrealistic. Given the multiple opinions that already existed in *Tanner* by that time, not to mention the inevitable additional changes that would still be made, including some in Clark's re-re-revised dissent, it was impossible to believe in mid-September that *Tanner* would be released in a week.

About a week after Clark had expressed strong urgency to his staff about the need to get the *Tanner* decision completed, he had his 21 September meeting with Justice Tobriner. Just days earlier he had been asking his staff to find out what Tobriner was doing with *Tanner*. By his own description, he didn't want to discuss the case with Tobriner. He said that when Tobriner said, "Bill, *Caudillo* doesn't belong in your opinion, and I agree with Rose in that regard," Clark told Tobriner, "Matt, that is not the question at this moment." He said he told Tobriner he had come to talk to him about a personal problem, about the "treatment" Bird was giving him and his staff. Asked by the Commission to explain the "treatment," Clark said the Chief Justice had snubbed one of his law clerks in the elevator one day, and that she had snubbed him when he walked into the weekly Wednesday conference. Clark said his secretary had been offended when she did not receive a promised piece of old carpet when the Chief Justice recarpeted her office in 1977. Clark felt the secretary had not received the carpet because the Chief Justice was retaliating against him. "This may sound petty now," Clark told the Commission, "but it seemed rather important to us at the time."

Clark said he discouraged Tobriner from talking about the *Tanner* decision, but did tell him that if the Chief Justice removed the reason for his dissent—if she would abandon her opinion that the *Tanner* law was unconstitutional and sign either Tobriner or Clark's opinion— Clark would remove the attack about her inconsistency. But, more surprising, according to both Clark and Tobriner's testimony, Clark then told Tobriner that if the Chief Justice thought his dissent was politically motivated she could solve the problem by delaying the opinion until after the election. Both Clark and Bird testified that he also made the same suggestion to her in mid-October. She testified that she thought his suggestion was "a little game" he was playing. Her feeling that a game was going on was not dispelled when Clark, during the next two weekly conferences, wanted to know what was happening with *Tanner*.

Clark offered a peculiar explanation of why he told the Chief she could withhold the opinion until after the election if she thought his dissent was politically motivated. He said he was not urging her to do it, but wanted to "demonstrate" to her that she had the power to withhold or file it and that he did not have the power to do either. The Chief Justice signs the submittal order that releases a completed decision, once all parts of it are signed by each justice. But each justice has the power to delay any opinion interminably by simply not signing off on any portion of it. By the time he was having this October conversation with the Chief Justice, Clark had been effectively delaying the opinion himself, as he himself and Manuel would testify. When asked at the hearing if he thought the holding up of an opinion for political purposes was "unethical, reprehensible, and improper," Clark said yes. He then was asked if he regarded such delay in those terms when he suggested it to the Chief Justice, and Clark said, "I don't think I thought of it . . . I did not think of ethics at all."

Before Clark left Justice Tobriner's chambers on 21 September, he asked Tobriner to send the *Tanner* box to Justice Manuel. For the next 19 days, he urged Manuel to hold off taking any action on the *Tanner* case until he resolved his dispute with the Chief Justice. In early October, according to the testimony of a Clark staff member, during the time he was telling Manuel not to complete his work on *Tanner,* Clark expressed "resignation" to his staff that *Tanner* "wouldn't get out before the election and there was nothing that could be done about it."

One of Clark's law clerks testified that it was "unusual" for Clark to show such intense interest in a case. "Certainly he did not exhibit that interest frequently," said Koblick.

The most crucial piece of testimony in the public portion of the investigation came on the third day of Justice Clark's testimony. By that time, Justices Richardson, Tobriner, and Bird had all testified and so had numerous members of the court staff. Though there had been scintillating moments, there had been no evidence yet that anyone knew, or even believed, that the principal accusation being pursued—that Justice Tobriner had delayed the *Tanner* decision until after the election and had done so to help assure Bird's confirmation by the voters—had any truth to it. The Commission was still pursuing bubbles, most of them blown into the air by Clark. Most of what he said would dissolve when he was pushed to explain the basis for his accusations.

At last, however, there came a startling piece of information, a new trail to pursue. It was the kind of testimony that produces screaming headlines and causes broadcast journalists to speak in exclamation points. It wasn't clear evidence of wrongdoing. But it pointed to potential evidence that another justice, Stanley Mosk, shared Clark's belief that wrongdoing might have occurred and that Mosk might actually know of some evidence that decisions were delayed. As such, the following testimony from Clark was the most important piece of testimony yet given in the long hearing: "At the time of the January [1979] calendar [hearing] in Los Angeles," Clark told the Commission, "Justice Mosk . . . said, 'Bill, before election day I told Matt that it was obvious that cases were being held for filing after election, and I told him that it was obvious and if it were later revealed he would have to pay the consequences.'"

Clark added weight to this startling testimony by saying that he had reviewed the entire conversation, as Mosk had related it in January, with Mosk just the week before his testimony in preparation for Clark's appearance before the Commission. "I said, 'Stan, you remember what you told me concerning what you had told Justice Tobriner before the election,' and I said, 'I may have to testify to that, and I want to be sure what you told me.'" The witness said he then repeated to Mosk what he had told him in January, and Mosk responded: "'Yes, Bill, that is correct. In fact, I had two such discussions with Justice Tobriner.'"

That Stanley Mosk might have said such a thing to Tobriner was important. He had special relationships with the three major parties—Tobriner, Bird and Clark. Until Bird joined the court, Mosk and Clark were not close colleagues. In fact, one justice recalls that Mosk "had only disdain for Clark before Rose Bird came on the court." Mosk and Tobriner had been friends for many years. Both were liberals who had been appointed to the high court by Pat Brown, Tobriner in 1962 and Mosk in 1964. Mosk's son, Richard, had been Tobriner's law clerk and later named a child after Tobriner. A warm friendship had continued between Richard Mosk and Tobriner. Through the years Tobriner and Stanley Mosk habitually signed each other's majority opinions. They were of like mind on many matters.

The relationship between the two justices became stormy after Bird was appointed. Many people, including Tobriner and Wright, had thought Mosk the logical person to become the next Chief Justice in 1977. Mosk thought so too. There were published reports as early as 1960, when he was in his first term as State Attorney General, that his real ambition was to become Chief Justice of the California Supreme Court. Many admirers on and off the bench expected him to be appointed in 1977. But Jerry Brown wanted to appoint a younger person. Not only was Mosk upset at not being made Chief Justice himself; he was upset that the choice was Rose Bird. A member of the court staff remembers that Mosk was "beside himself" the day her appointment was announced. "He told me, 'You don't take an intern in a hospital and make him chief of surgery.'" Tobriner told me that as soon as Bird was approved, Mosk "complained to me bitterly about it. . . . Months later he told me that I should have voted against her, that I should have known that she was not suited for this position."

Mosk had been a consummate politician all his life. In his 20's, he worked as executive secretary to Governor Culbert Olson. The Governor's last official act before leaving office in 1943 was to appoint Mosk to the Superior Court in Los Angeles. At 32, he was the youngest judge in the state. In March 1945 he left the bench to serve in the Army Transportation Corps. It was a short tour of duty, and six months later he was out of the Army and back on the bench. The then Chief Justice of the State Supreme Court made a special request for Mosk to be discharged from the Army and returned to the bench because of the crowded Los Angeles court schedules.

In 1958 Mosk re-entered politics. He sought the Democratic nomination for Attorney General that spring, won the primary, and went on to win the post in November. He caused a stir by not resigning from the bench until he had won the election. Running in his judicial robes, said the Los Angeles Bar Association, was in violation of the canons of judicial ethics. The Association passed resolutions strongly critical of Mosk. A poll of state judges showed that 62.5 percent of them strongly disapproved of an incumbent judge running for a partisan political office, and 67.3 percent strongly disapproved of him using his judicial title in a partisan political campaign.

In 1960, when Governor Pat Brown wanted to run for President, Mosk was his hand-picked candidate to be California's Democratic national committeeman. In 1964, while still Attorney General, Mosk himself had national political ambitions. He was one of three persons who wanted to run in the Democratic primary for the Senate seat being vacated by ailing Senator Clair Engle. Brown forced Mosk out of the primary in March and supported State Controller Alan Cranston. (Cranston lost the primary that year and was first elected to the Senate in 1968.)

Mosk's political enemies then successfully forced him out of the campaign by threatening to make public claims that he had social contacts with people who his enemies alleged were part of organized crime or had ties to organized crime. In September 1981 the National Foundation to Fight Political Corruption, a right-wing organization with John Feliz, the executive director of Richardson's Law and Order Campaign Committee, on its board, held simultaneous press conferences in Los Angeles and Sacramento to revive that old accusation against Mosk and to call for an investigation. All the major news media in the state covered the press conferences and received news releases accompanied by documents that purported to be Los Angeles Police Department files on Mosk. No newspaper or wire service in the state ran a word about the press conferences. It was unclear whether they felt the information was libelous or whether they responded to pressure from Mosk and people close to him not to run the story. Such pressure was applied, however. Mosk's son, Richard, was reported to have called major news media urging them not to run any stories about the claims made about his father. (Upon learning about this book, Richard Mosk placed such a call to me, asking me to agree not to report the claims made against his father.) In any event, the absence of any mention of the press conferences contrasts sharply with the way the press handled stories about other members of the court in November 1978—stories for which reporters said Mosk was a source.

During the 1964 senate race, Mosk denied that Pat Brown had promised him the next seat on the State Supreme Court as a consolation prize for getting out of the race. Brown did not deny it, and by September 1964, when the next vacancy on the court occurred, Mosk was in place at the court.

Ten years later, in 1974, there would be a brief flurry about whether Mosk was unethically involved in politics from the bench. A politician called for Mosk to resign from the court because he was allegedly making partisan political contributions while sitting on the court. The attack was based on a report that Mosk had maintained a campaign fund that dated back to his 1962 campaign for re-election as Attorney General and since then made political contributions from it. Jerry Brown, Secretary of State in 1974, announced that Mosk had violated no law. But Brown, then running for his first term as Governor, added that his office was responsible only for seeing that public officials make their financial filings, and "any question of impropriety in those filings is investigated by the Attorney General." The Attorney General at the time, Evelle Younger, never investigated the matter. Mosk has been successful in keeping any of the insinuations of wrongdoing by him from becoming public issues. But allegations against him have been investigated at least twice by the Commission on Judicial Performance.

At the same time, Mosk has been one of the most publicly respected members of the court. As both judge and politician, he is known as an urbane and charming host. In 1961, it was Mosk and his wife who gave a reception in Washington for the 500 Californians who went to President Kennedy's inauguration. In 1981 the exclusive luncheon he gave for his new friend William Clark when Clark left the court to become Deputy Secretary of State attracted much attention in the San Francisco society columns.

Among his admirers are many well-known people, including federal judges. Mosk has said he likes to have his beliefs equated with those of U.S. Supreme Court Justices William Douglas and William Brennan. He is a man who has always been proud of the pre-eminent position of the California Supreme Court and of his own role in its greatness. It is because of his longstanding repute that people pay special notice when Mosk denigrates his own court, as he did in public in March 1981 when he spoke to a group of law students in San Diego and asked rhetorically, "Is the best of the California Supreme Court in its past? Has the prestige of the [Chief Justice Phillip S.] Gibson Court, the [Chief Justice Roger J.] Traynor Court and the [Chief Justice Donald R.] Wright Court—the Golden Age—been reduced to a mere devalued-currency age? Have the lowered expectations advocated by Jerry Brown had their impact on the California judiciary?"

Until the week before the 1978 election, Mosk's attitude toward Bird was not generally known except at the court and among those who knew him well in legal circles and had heard his private sniping remarks about her. But the Friday before the election his attitude became public knowledge. Newspapers reported then that he had refused the Appellate Judge of the Year Award from the California Trial Lawyers Association (CTLA). The Association had earlier voted to support Bird's confirmation at the polls. In a letter to the CTLA's Board of Governors, the president of the Association reported that Mosk told him "we had no business getting involved in the Rose Bird campaign or coming out in support of her without knowing all the facts." After the initial stories appeared, Mosk issued a confusing press release. It said, "I wrote no letter to CTLA and did not authorize anyone to write one on my behalf." It was confusing because there had never been a claim that he had written a letter. He also said in his news release, "I did not indicate to CTLA or to any other group how I intend to vote on any issue next Tuesday." Two days after the election, the justices learned what the public would learn later—that Stanley Mosk was one of two justices who had spoken with *Los Angeles Times* reporters the night before the election when the reporters were trying to find out if a decision had been improperly delayed by Tobriner.

Clark's testimony that Mosk had privately accused Tobriner of delaying decisions until after the election was, of course, crucial. Clark, as the lone accuser, had made numerous damning statements during his testimony. But nothing that he said had any basis, even in hearsay, let alone in direct knowledge. But now he was claiming that this widely respected longtime member of the court, Stanley Mosk, had told him that he had actually directly accused Tobriner of delaying decisions.

Not only was this testimony by Clark crucial. It was also totally unexpected, even by the Commission's investigators. Clark and Mosk, like the other justices and their staff members, had been interviewed and deposed under oath, some of them several times. Little that was said in public by any witness was a surprise to the investigators. Until this point in the hearing, only this statement by Clark was both new and important. It was, in fact, startling. Hufstedler reminded Clark that during the times when he was deposed "you did not tell me about this conversation" and asked him why he had not. "One, I wasn't asked," replied Clark. Strangely, though the information was central to the investigation, he said, "I didn't feel like I should volunteer it. I have been greatly troubled over it."

Clark's reluctance to volunteer this crucial piece of information was inexplicable. By the time of the hearing in the summer of 1979, Clark himself had been frequently suggesting, both privately and publicly, that cases had been held up on purpose because of the election. He had refused to offer the Commission any basis for his belief. In fact, it seemed he had no basis for any of his accusations. He seemed to be speculating. But now, on the last day of his testimony, he revealed that he learned two months after the election that Mosk not only shared his belief but also had had a face-to-face confrontation with Justice Tobriner, the man accused of causing the delay of *Tanner,* and accused him of improperly delaying the case. Mosk, according to Clark, believed that Tobriner was responsible for delaying more than one case for election purposes. This was a bombshell. No one—no Commission investigators and no reporters—had heretofore discovered that this conversation had taken place between Mosk and Tobriner.

Hufstedler's ensuing questions brought forth a demeanor and emotions in Clark that seemed to reveal a man who knew fully the weight of what he had just said. He gave listeners the impression that he had been fretting about what he should do with this significant information for as many months as he had held it in his mind. He knew he had just revealed the most significant clue the Commission had yet been given. One got the impression he would sleep easier that night, having gotten this until-now-hidden clue off his chest.

"Well, did you not tell me about it because of some conscious determination that you felt you would rather not testify about that subject?" asked Hufstedler.

CLARK: Probably in part. Even to the point, I think I have done a pretty successful job of, shall we say, storing it somewhere other than up front.

"It was not a subject you wanted to testify about, is that what you are telling me?"

CLARK: Frankly, that's it.

"[Were] you hoping that the conversation with Justice Mosk that you have told us about would not become the subject matter of testimony here?"

CLARK: Deep down [I hoped] I wouldn't be the first one asked about it. If I can be honest with you, I kind of hoped that it would go away, and if it didn't go away, that it would not be asked of Clark, Clark not having been a part of the conversation referred to, and Clark not having been asked. . . . (He was asked if Mosk had told him what made it "obvious" that cases "were being delayed 'til after the election.")

CLARK: "No."

The witness was asked if, upon learning Justice Mosk's important accusation about Justice Tobriner, he asked Mosk about the fact that he (Mosk) had signed in November a statement claiming that as of the election the *Tanner* case had not been "delayed for a political or any other improper reason." Clark said he had not. At another point in his testimony, Clark said that he had gotten the impression from Mosk that he had signed the statement "reluctantly." That, too, seemed to add credence to what he now reported Mosk had told him.

"Did you pursue at all any question of Justice Mosk as to why he had not mentioned that to you earlier when you and he had discussed delays in the *Tanner* and *Fox* cases?" A judge on the Commission asked.

CLARK: "No. Quite frankly, judge, I don't think I wanted to hear any more."

The Commission certainly wanted to hear more. Until the moment Clark said Mosk had told him that he personally had accused Tobriner of withholding decisions until after the election, the only thing that seemed significant about Mosk's forthcoming testimony was what he would say about conversations with reporters the night before the election. But Clark's testimony cast a whole new light on Mosk's testimony. It made Mosk appear potentially as the Commission's single most important witness. What would he say he said to Tobriner? What was his basis for accusing Tobriner? What did Mosk know? And what would he say Tobriner said to him when he accused him to his face of delaying decisions? The Clark testimony about Mosk raised many questions that, if answered, could move the investigation off dead center. Only Mosk could answer the questions.

It looked as though Mosk might hold the key to the investigation and the key to the reputations of those justices who had now been under the cloud of public accusation for ten months. Local news-papers called Mosk the "most respected" member of the court. This was a witness who would be taken seriously.

But there was a critical problem. Shortly before Clark made his revelation about Mosk, it had been publicly announced that Mosk would not testify in public. He intended to file a lawsuit, which he did the day after Clark's sensational testimony. In his suit Mosk claimed the hearings were unconstitutional because they were public, and that he could not be compelled to testify in public.

After Clark testified about the Mosk conversation with Tobriner, Gerald Marcus, Tobriner's lawyer, rose and announced gravely: "I can't consider anything of greater importance than what has just hap-pened to a man of the integrity and honor of Justice Tobriner." Marcus seemed stunned. ". . . We now seriously see a possibility that the person who would be best able to testify directly may or may not be present."

CHAPTER 9

Justice Mosk Gags the Commission

Stanley Mosk went to court 6 July 1979, and asked that the hearings be closed. It was unconstitutional, he claimed, to hold an open investigation of the court. His suit would not be settled until October 18, more than three months later. If the hearings themselves were confusing, the series of court entanglements that occurred along the way to getting a conclusion in Mosk's suit were chaotic. Some people considered them humiliating to the Commission and to some of the justices. Ultimately, they would be disastrous to the public's right to know and to the officially uncharged but publicly accused justices.

If Mosk moved to close the hearings because of the feeling he expressed during his litigation to a meeting of the American Bar Association—"There is no more pathethic sight than learned judges cringing in fear of an aggressive investigative commission"—then his lawsuit was an avoidance of accountability. But if he filed it because he believed the open hearings were unconstitutional, then his lawsuit was not only appropriate, but praiseworthy.

It is the timing of his suit that raises uncomfortable questions. He filed it just as it became clear that he would have crucial information to tell the Commission. It was filed after the Commission was approximately 80 percent through with its investigation. Many would criticize Mosk for the lateness in filing the suit. These critics argue that all the justices knew from the beginning they would be subpoenaed to testify before the Commission. If he didn't believe the hearings should be open, why didn't he file his lawsuit before the hearings began? If it was the principle of constitutionality of the open process, rather than just his own hide, that he cared about, why didn't he file the suit before the hearings began and try to assure that the entire hearing would be confidential?

In point of fact, however, criticism of Mosk on such grounds is unjustified. He was out of the country in January 1979 when the Judicial Council adopted the new rule that required the Commission to hold a public hearing. Upon his return, he wrote to the Commission and said he thought it was embarking on a course that was unconstitutional, that the planned public investigation was in violation of Article 6, Section 18(f) of the State Constitution, which provides that the Judicial Council will make rules implementing and providing for confidentiality of the Commission's proceedings. But most significant, Mosk had officially notified the Commission in writing before the hearings began that he would not testify in public and would go to court to close the hearing if required to testify. He had, in fact, prepared an application for writ and was ready to go to court before the hearing began.

Whether he would file before the hearings or later was extremely important. Mosk was not the only person who determined the timing of his suit. He was given poor advice by the Commission and he abided by it. Good and reasonable people can argue quite forcefully either that such hearings should be open or that they should be closed. But surely no one would argue that such a hearing can be a just proceeding if part of it is open and part closed. Most people would think it reprehensible if a trial began open and then closed. It simply would not be permitted because of the potential gross injustice that could happen to the accused—actually, to all parties. If a hearing or trial is partially open and partially closed, an accusation by a witness in public may be vitiated during the private hearing. But the exoneration made in private could never be known.

A group of California newspapers filed a friend-of-the-court brief in Mosk's suit, asking that the hearings remain open. Unfortunately, they made their argument hinge, at least in part, on the fact that Mosk had delayed filing his suit until after the hearings were well under way. The claim ignored the record, both of Mosk's early intentions and of the Commission's request to Mosk that he not file his suit until later. Lawyers for the newspapers should have stressed instead the importance of the uniqueness of this one situation—that the right to know should not be chopped off in mid-proceeding. They could have argued that it was unconstitutional for the Commission to hold its investigations in public, but, because this hearing had been open, justice, due process, and the people's right to know required that an exception be made in this instance: this hearing should be permitted to be completed in public so that public accusations partially investigated in public might be completely investigated in public.

Carelessness seemed to have been the most consistent feature of this entire affair, beginning with the original accusations and continuing through the Mosk suit and the remainder of the Commission's proceedings. One of the Commission's most serious errors was its failure to resolve Mosk's questions about the constitutionality of open hearings before the hearings began. Special Counsel Hufstedler was a much-respected person. He had the respect of the commissioners to such a high degree that they seldom countered his opinions and advice. It may be true that not one of them disagreed with his decision before the hearings began to ask Stanley Mosk to delay filing his suit until later, until *during* the hearings. If so, it speaks poorly of the wisdom of the commissioners individually and collectively. Perhaps they relied too much on Hufstedler. That decision was a serious mistake on Hufstedler's part, though he still doesn't see it that way. The commissioners were experienced enough in the law that they should have recognized his poor judgment in that matter, refused his counsel, and instructed him to go to court before the hearings began to resolve the issue of whether the hearings would be open or closed.

Hufstedler told me in the fall of 1981 that at the outset of the hearing the possibility of a hearing that would be part public and part private—which is what eventually occurred—didn't seem likely. "In fact, it seemed very unlikely," he said. This is difficult to understand. For one thing, from the beginning Mosk said repeatedly that he would refuse to testify in public and that he would go to court to have the public hearings declared unconstitutional. In addition, several members of the Commission themselves believed all along that Mosk was right: that what they were about to do, hold a public investigation, was unconstitutional. This meant they could reasonably have concluded there was a high probability that a court would agree with Mosk and close the hearings. In his opening statement at the open hearings, Hufstedler himself had said the old rules on confidentiality (still in existence and superseded by the Judicial Council only for this one investigation) required that investigations "had to remain confidential." In 1981 he told me he still believed that the hearings should not have been public in the first place. But it was his own decision not to settle the open-closed issue before the hearings began that was, in large part, responsible for the chaos that ensued.

The Commission could have responded to Mosk's threat to sue in either of two ways. It could have not discouraged Mosk from filing his suit when he wanted to, before the hearings began. And, had he not been willing to do that, the Commission, on its own, could have gone to court and asked for a declaratory judgment on the issue.

Hufstedler advised against both of these alternatives, and the Commission accepted his advice. His advice goes against the grain of a fairly common belief, namely, that a lawyer should not wait until the end of a case to challenge a critical issue that could affect the outcome of the case. For tactical reasons and for reasons of economy, it is wise to clarify any critical issue very early in the case. It is considered important to do so in order to avert both surprises and quagmires.

There was another factor that motivated Hufstedler and perhaps also motivated the Commission not to settle the constitutionality of open hearings before the hearings began. There was a strong desire to get the show on the road. "The press controversy had reached such a high decibel level by the time the hearings began," Hufstedler told me. "It became highly important to give the press and the public the opportunity to understand this." Ironically, it was this very decision to please an eager press and public by moving quickly that ultimately made it impossible for the public to know—let alone understand— what happened. The press, of course, was merely doing its job when it continued asking questions. However, it was the job of the Commission to set whatever timetable was necessary for it to do its job completely and justly and not rush ahead because the press was eager. Justice, not the press, should have been the Commission's master.

A massive quagmire developed as soon as Mosk filed his suit. I asked Hufstedler why the Commission had not gone to court for a declaratory judgment at the outset and why it had not encouraged Mosk to file his suit at the outset when he wanted to file it. Hufstedler said it is his basic philosophy at all times to "avoid a legal confrontation." When I pointed out that his strategy did not avoid such a confrontation, he replied that he had thought it would. Before the hearings began, he said, he had three alternatives in mind that he thought would solve what became known as "the Mosk problem." First, he thought Mosk might change his mind and testify in public. This implies either that he thought Mosk was bluffing, an unlikely possibility in view of the strong letters and intentions Mosk already had expressed. Secondly, Hufstedler said, "I thought I might be able to persuade him to change his mind." Hufstedler is known as a well-controlled, charming, and persuasive person. Perhaps because of those qualities, he put a lot of weight on this alternative.

His third alternative for solving "the Mosk problem" was extraordinary: "I thought we could use his deposition at the hearing without calling him." Hufstedler said he told Mosk that he might not be called as a witness, that his under-oath depositions could be read into the record. Hufstedler said that at one point Mosk's lawyer, his son Richard, indicated they would be willing for that to happen. The alternative was not suggested to Mosk until the hearings already had started.

If Hufstedler and the Commission had announced that they were not going to call Justice Mosk as a witness and would instead enter his depositions as a substitute for his testimony, there likely would have been a considerable protest from the other justices. All other justices undoubtedly would have thought it clearly unfair that they had to appear for intense and lengthy examination by the seven commissioners and Hufstedler in public if Mosk merely had his deposition read into the record. They had all given under-oath depositions. Mosk was the only justice whom Hufstedler considered not requiring to testify, despite the fact that Mosk himself was being investigated for possible wrongdoing. The unfairness of the proposition is an index of the depth of Hufstedler's desire to avoid going to court about the constitutionality of open hearings.

Justice Clark's testimony changed everything. When he testified that Mosk had told him that he had talked with Justice Tobriner on two occasions and told Tobriner it was obvious he (Tobriner) was holding up decisions because of the election, there finally seemed to be an opportunity to learn the truth. No one's deposition—not Clark's, not Tobriner's, and not Mosk's—mentioned these conversations. Hufstedler told me that after Clark's startling testimony he briefly considered going to Mosk and asking him if he would privately give a supplemental deposition that would speak specifically to the issue that Justice Clark had brought up. But he said he quickly realized that would not work. Mosk apparently did, too. He filed his lawsuit in Los Angeles Superior Court the day after Clark's crucial testimony. Hufstedler said the possible unfairness of permitting one justice not to testify, plus Clark's sensational new testimony, which had to be addressed by Mosk, were factors in his decision not to have Mosk "testify" only by deposition.

This information from Hufstedler—that he had considered not requiring Mosk to testify—leads to an insight not known before: had it not been for Clark's testimony about Mosk's conversations with Tobriner, the hearings would probably have proceeded to their completion in public, with the public fully aware of all testimony and of the Commission's final deliberation and conclusions.

This fact might reasonably encourage people less paranoid than rank conspiracy theorists to wonder about the reason for Clark's devastating testimony about Mosk. Did Clark, with or without Mosk as a conspirator, want to ensure that Mosk would be called as a witness? And did he ensure it knowing full well that if required to testify Mosk would refuse and file a lawsuit that would inevitably close the hearing and prevent the public from knowing what the parties to the crucial conversation, Mosk and Tobriner, actually said to each other? These questions, like many others in this investigation, have never been answered.

"The Constitution of California makes it crystal clear that Commission proceedings are to be confidential," said Mosk in his initial complaint. "If others wish to proceed in the light of clear statutory and constitutional provisions, that is their choice." All other justices by that time had in fact expressed reservations about the constitutionality of public hearings, but none felt strongly enough about the matter to file a suit. Perhaps it is more likely that, except for Justice Richardson, all felt that to file a suit that would attempt to close the hearings would simply be interpreted as confirmation of wrongdoing, or at least of their having something suspicious to hide.

Mosk predicted in his complaint that the public hearing would result in "innumerable grave consequences," including the setting of a "devastating" precedent. He warned that public disclosure of internal memoranda and discussions by justices of pending cases would make it impossible for the court to "function effectively in the future as a collegial body." He maintained that no justice should be compelled to appear in a proceeding that violates the constitution.

As counsel to the Commission, Hufstedler was responsible for arguing the Commission's case. He did so all the way through appeals to the ad hoc Supreme Court. Mosk and his attorneys had agreed with Hufstedler that if Mosk lost his suit in the trial court, Mosk would not appeal his decision. Mosk lost at the trial court when Los Angeles Superior Court Judge Robert Wenke rejected his claim and ordered him to testify at the public hearing. Mosk and his attorneys immediately voided their agreement with Hufstedler and the Commission and appealed Wenke's decision to the Second District Court of Appeal in Los Angeles.

A Court of Appeal panel headed by Presiding Justice Lester Roth, who had long been opposed to judges being investigated by the Commission, ruled in Mosk's favor on 19 July. Justice Manuel was beginning his testimony that day, although the public has never until now learned the content of his important testimony.

As Mosk's litigation progressed, the Commission pursued two tracks simultaneously. Behind closed doors it continued the investigation. At the same time, it continued its court battle to reopen the hearings to the public, intending to recall all witnesses heard in secret if the hearings reopened. It finished hearing all testimony by 27 July, a week after Mosk's victory in the Court of Appeal. But the ad hoc

Supreme Court's decision in the case would not be completed until 18 October, nearly three months later.

When the Commission appealed the case to the Supreme Court, the justices assumed, of course, that they could not sit in judgment on a case that involved an investigation of themselves. Six of the seven thought they should step aside and did so. They were replaced by six Court of Appeal judges. But the seventh Supreme Court justice, Frank Newman, refused to remove himself from the court. Newman denied Commission claims that as a party in its investigation he had an inherent bias and that a fair and impartial hearing could not be heard by him. In papers Newman filed with the substitute members of the Supreme Court, he wrote, "My mind is no more set in this case than it has been in countless cases where in many ways I have had prior exposure to and preliminarily have discussed other complex and challenging legal questions." Newman claimed he was not a party to the investigation, just a potential witness. And "mere witnesses are not parties."

It would take the ad hoc court two months to remove Newman from the panel of judges. He said that though it would be pleasant and comfortable for him to disqualify himself from the special panel, it would be "unprincipled and not justifiable" for him to do so. He said he would take the hard road.

There were arguments to be made in Newman's defense. The vote of the ad hoc court was four to two to remove him, with the two dissenting judges agreeing with Newman that the fact that Mosk might be compelled to testify and that Mosk's testimony might involve Newman, did "not mean that Justice Newman has any interest in whether the Commission is public or private." Despite the Commission statement to the contrary, wrote dissenting Justice John Miller, "it is obvious that Justice Newman is neither a party nor a litigant. . . ."

It was difficult to know whether Newman was pathetic or arrogant. It was certainly difficult to believe what he was doing. Many in the public who were paying either close or peripheral attention to this investigation must have become quite cynical at this point. The Fifth-Amendment right not to testify against oneself is considered a vitally important right. But many people have difficulty understanding it and erroneously insist that only those who are guilty invoke the Fifth Amendment. If that is difficult to understand, it was nearly impossible to understand why Frank Newman would choose to remain seated on the Supreme Court at this time. But there he was. As arguments went on for two and a half hours about whether Newman could legally be a member of the panel, Newman sat in robes on the panel, listening to the arguments and taking notes. It is one thing not to testify against yourself, and another to pass judgments that affect an investigation of yourself.

Though Newman insisted that he had no bias in the case and that he was not technically a party to the case, just a potential witness, it is impossible to think that he did not realize that he was also a potential target of the case. He *was* being investigated. One of the cases being examined was one in which he was the majority author, the *Fox* case. Of all the cases being examined, it had taken longer than any other case to move through the court. He knew very well that the Commission would have a number of questions for him, not only questions about others on the court, but about his own behavior. No matter how innocent of wrongdoing he might have known he was, he must have realized that his claim that he could sit as a judge on a suit to close the investigation of, among others, himself, looked, if not unethical and illegal, then certainly profoundly foolish.

Arguing for Newman's removal, Hufstedler told the ad hoc court that the court should avoid even the "appearance of impropriety. If this court decides with Justice Newman sitting on it that those proceedings should be private proceedings, do you really believe that there will be any faith [in the court]?" Hufstedler asked.

Mosk and his attorneys took no stand on the Newman issue. Their main contention during the arguments on his removal was that the very existence of the ad hoc court was in violation of the law and that the entire ad hoc court should dissolve itself. Mosk argued that an ad hoc Supreme Court in which more than half of the members are Court of Appeal justices is not properly constituted.

In the middle of his litigation, Mosk went to Texas on 14 August to give a speech to the American Bar Association. An ABA public relations officer notified reporters about his speech a day in advance and handed out copies. In it, he angrily attacked the Commission for its decision to appeal his lawsuit to the State Supreme Court. After having violated his own agreement not to appeal the trial court's decision earlier, he now told the ABA that the Commission's appeal of his victory in the Court of Appeal was designed "to further compound judicial humiliation . . . and to titillate the public, with resultant judicial humiliation." At this point, mid-August, it appeared that some judges on the court were quite capable of acting alone to create judicial humiliation. Mosk's speech criticized two commissioners, whom he did not identify, for writing limericks about witnesses and showing them to reporters. "Commission members obviously relish their role on center stage," Mosk said angrily. ". . . Humiliating the court in public appeared to be a barrel of laughs to the Commission."

In his ABA speech Mosk also chided Hufstedler for giving a party for reporters during the course of the hearings. Mosk was right.

Hufstedler had given a party for the reporters who covered the hearing. And it was, at least, in poor taste for him to have done so in the middle of an investigation in which he was going to end up advising the Commission on what their final decision should be. It is one thing to answer questions of reporters; it is another thing to give a party that could be interpreted as currying their favor. If any of the other parties to the investigation—any of the justices, for instance—had given a party for reporters it properly would have been strongly criticized.

In the midst of all this, the Commission itself started to unravel. While the ad hoc Supreme Court was trying to decide what to do about Newman, the Commission lost two members in late August— Kathryn Gehrels and Hillel Chodos. That meant only six members were left to deliberate and that five of them would have to agree on any action to be taken during deliberations. It was never learned why Gehrels left. She resigned from the Commission altogether, offering only a terse public announcement: "As a matter of conscience, I cannot participate in further deliberations of the commission."

Chodos, the persistent questioner, resigned with a blast at Newman and Mosk. He resigned not from the Commission itself, but just from the remainder of this investigation. Writing about his departure from the proceeding, *San Francisco Examiner* reporter K. Connie Kang would describe him as a "man of keen and incisive legal mind" who "will be remembered as one of the few lawyers in the state who dared to speak his mind about Justices Frank Newman and Mosk."

As he left, Chodos said in a lengthy letter that it is basic to the role of the bar in the adversary system that attorneys argue cases before an impartial tribunal. For that reason, he explained, he as a lawyer had to absent himself from the proceedings. For a lawyer to submit himself to a judge sitting in a case in which his own interests are engaged would reflect "dishonorably on the lawyer and violates the principle of the independence of the bar." Chodos apparently was assuming that Newman would not be removed from the ad hoc court, for he wrote his letter in late August when the Newman problem was still unresolved.

"The Commission has already spent more than five weeks in fruitless efforts to obtain a prompt, impartial and final decision on the merits of an alleged constitutional question raised by Justice Mosk, which is itself procedural, rather than substantive," wrote Chodos. To call Justice Mosk's suit merely procedural rather than substantive is inaccurate. The issue raised in his suit was central and one that should have been settled by the Commission itself in advance of the hearing.

Chodos said both Mosk and Newman had used their "vast powers" to frustrate the Commission investigation and had placed themselves beyond "accountability and above the law." The "intricacies of legal procedure" had no utility or significance in themselves. "They only have value to society when they are employed to expedite more efficiently the effort to arrive at a just result on the merits. They should not be allowed to operate so as to postpone or prevent a just and speedy resolution." Chodos was here lumping Mosk and Newman together unfairly.

"It is unfortunate that the Commission members, having given unstintingly of their time and energy, should be prevented by unnecessary and unwarranted litigation delays—instituted and fostered by two members of the Supreme Court—from completing their task in a prompt and orderly way." Chodos sounded like a frustrated and angry juror, but obviously one who felt freer than jurors feel to express their frustration at the length of the trials they must listen to, sometimes for months. They, too, want to get back to their jobs, just as Chodos wanted to get back to his Beverly Hills law practice. On any day of the year there are hundreds of thousands of sitting jurors in this country, most of whom are losing income as a result of their jury duty, and most of whom are having their time on the jury extended by "litigation delays," as Chodos calls them. Any juror—and certainly any lawyer—knows that this is a normal part of the legal process. Some delays are meaningless or even detrimental. But many of them are necessary, even vital, to the concept of due process. In 1981 I asked Chodos if the delays the Commission endured weren't precisely what goes on all the time in litigation. He answered that litigation was prolonged only by "incompetent lawyers who wear suede shoes and argyle socks." A lot of pinstriped corporate lawyers would be surprised to hear that. The remark, as he probably realized, was both elitist and inaccurate.

Commission Chairman Janes issued a statement regretting Chodos' resignation. In it he said, "Mr. Chodos is expressing an understandable unwillingness to abide the apparently interminable procedural quagmire into which the Commission has been drawn. We will sorely miss his keen intellect, boundless energy, and sound advice." When Gehrels resigned just a few days earlier, Janes had said, ". . . In my view if it [the investigation] had been permitted to progress as contemplated by the Judicial Council, whatever the conclusion, this action by Ms. Gehrels would not have been taken."

If anything was clear by late August, after Chodos and Gehrels had resigned, it was that the Commission was getting impatient.

Some humor was needed. It was hard to find it in any of these events. There was much that was ridiculous, but little that was humorous. *Sacramento Bee* columnist Herb Michelson provided some helpful—perhaps insightful—humor in the *California Journal* in the fall of 1979.

Michelson wrote that he was recapping the investigation "for the four remaining Californians still following the 'high court probe'. . . ." Some excerpts from his chronology:

Mid-1978: Somebody named Tanner uses a gun and doesn't go to prison. The Gun Lobby thinks he should go to prison. Armed.

December 1978: The Gun Lobby pushes through a bill which says, in effect, 'Don't use a gun, go to prison,' a logical parameter.

April 1979: The Commission on Judicial Performance orders itself to investigate which of the state Supreme Court justices was at Studio 54 on the day the *Tanner* decision was supposed to be signed. And with whom.

May 1979: The Commission hires as its chief counsel one Seth Hufstedler. He is paid $100 an hour, plus lunch, plus a guarantee that his wife Shirley, already a federal judge, will never have to rule on the *Tanner* case, even if she wants to.

June 1979: The investigation opens in San Francisco, moving after its first week from the Curran Theatre to the Orpheum Theatre because the Curran had previously booked an engagement of 'Ain't Misbehavin'.

July 1979: Chief Justice Bird denies that she has ever used Duncan Hines' Yellow Cake Mix and is supported in this contention by Associate Justice Mathew Tobriner. But in subsequent testimony, Associate Justice William Clark says that he was told by a clerk of Tobriner that a clerk of Bird told a court reporter who was dropping by to deliver transcripts of the *Tanner* decision to a courier of Mrs. Hufstedler that Tobriner indeed prefers Yellow Cake Mix. Betty Crocker!!! (Janes was forced at this point to gavel the entire auditorium into silence.)

Later in July 1979: Associate Justice Stanley Mosk, who originally asked that the investigation run no longer than two weeks because he did not wish to miss the tennis season or be unmentioned in Herb Caen's column for any period longer than that, is called to testify. And refuses. 'The Orpheum,' he says, 'is not my kind of room; my agent prefers a more intimate spot—perhaps a phone booth.'

Very late July 1979: In his third appellate match on the privacy issue, Mosk wins 6–3, 6–2, 7–5, but is required to find a phone booth big enough for both Hufstedler and himself.

Mid-August 1979: Regular Associate Justice Frank Newman refuses to be replaced on the regular acting state Supreme Court, citing the ironclad precedent of Non Feel Likeit.

The Present: Tanner says that if only the investigation can get moving again he'll do anything any judge tells him to do. Tanner says if necessary he will even serve on the temporary state Supreme Court.

In real life, Mosk won his lawsuit and the hearings did not reopen. The ad hoc Supreme Court ruled that the Judicial Council "has authority to adopt rules which provide for confidentiality but it does not have the power to authorize public investigations and hearings before the commission." The court said that when a commission "investigation of alleged judicial misconduct is known to the public, as in the present case, the Commission may report the results of the status of the investigation to the public without violating the constitutional requirement of 'confidentiality of proceedings.'" It would not be clear until the Commission announced the result of the investigation how much mischief could come from its interpretation of this rulng in Mosk's lawsuit.

There would be no more public hearings, only the private hearings. And what the commissioners learned in private, unlike Michelson's column, was not funny.

CHAPTER 10

The Secret Testimony of Justice Mosk

At last, the commissioners had Stanley Mosk in front of them. They could now pursue their most crucial questions, the ones created by Justice Clark's startling testimony:

"At the time of the January [1979] calendar [hearing] in Los Angeles, Justice Mosk . . . said, 'Bill, before election day I told Matt that it was obvious that cases were being held up for filing after election, and I told him that it was obvious, and if it were later revealed he would have to pay the consequences.' " Clark had said Mosk had told him during the hearings that Clark's recollection of his January comments was correct and that, "in fact, I had two such discussions with Justice Tobriner."

Here before them on 24 and 25 July was the feisty, compact justice who Clark said had made this crucial accusation, this accusation that could perhaps bring some clarity to this situation that grew messier by the day. Even as Mosk sat here before them, his case against the Commission was before the ad hoc Supreme Court, where the Commission was opposing his success in the Court of Appeal. But they expected him now, seated before them, to explain this clue, the only important one they had now. He was here before them under the terms he wanted, the terms the Court of Appeal had ordered: secrecy.

Like all other later witnesses, Mosk testified secretly, behind securely guarded closed doors. Only the Commission's executive director, Jack Frankel, the court reporters, Mosk's lawyer, Hufstedler and his staff, and the commissioners heard Mosk's testimony. And all of them were sworn to strict secrecy. Justice Janes solemnly told all of them, "Nothing that occurs in this room is to be disclosed outside this room. All of us are bound by that rule." He would repeat the admonition as each witness began to testify in secret. This is the first time the secret testimony has been revealed.

What Mosk told them was extremely important: *What Clark had said was not true, no such conversations had ever taken place between Mosk and Tobriner.*

It was a striking refutation of Clark's sworn testimony. But the public never heard or read it.

In the secret session, a commissioner asked Mosk, "You made no specific charge to Justice Tobriner, nor did you report to Justice Clark a specific charge that a case was being held up inappropriately?"

Mosk: "I did not."

Clark had claimed that Mosk told him he had told Tobriner the latter would have to "pay the consequences," an implication that Mosk thought Tobriner had engaged in wrongdoing and would have to face an investigation by the Commission that was now investigating the accusations. Mosk was asked if he had said that.

Mosk: "I did not. I would not talk to Justice Tobriner that way."

"Did you raise the role of this commission in your conversation with Justice Clark?"

Mosk: "No. No."

Mosk also said he never mentioned the word "election" in his conversation with Justice Clark. He said he never had the election in mind as far as timing of any decision was concerned, for he was concerned only about whether the *Fox* case was going to be filed before Christmas. In that case, the court had decided that the city of Los Angeles might not light its City Hall windows in the form of a cross to celebrate Christmas and Easter. Mosk was concerned that the opinion might come out just as the city was preparing to celebrate Christmas, and Christians might be offended by the timing. ". . . Good taste . . . that's all I had in mind," Mosk told the commissioners of his conversation with Tobriner about the case. In the spring of 1978 he had brought up the matter jokingly with his fellow justices and said, "Let's not shoot Santa Claus on Christmas eve."

The commission pressed Mosk on what he knew or believed about the delay of decisions. "Do you know of any other information or intelligence which indicates that a case was deliberately held up in view of the election?"

Mosk: "I do not."

"Do you have any other knowledge or information beyond that

which already has been produced or to which you have testified that
the *Tanner* case was held up in order to prevent its being released
before the election?"

Mosk: "No."

"Justice Mosk, did you ever hear a suggestion made in or around
the court that the *Tanner* case should be held up so that the court
would not appear to be responding to the attorney general's charges
or to any outside influences or pressures?"

Mosk: "No."

"In your judgment was the *Tanner* case held up so that it would be
filed after the election?"

Mosk: "No."

The man who was supposed to unlock crucial information by his
recollections of accusatory conversations that he had recounted to
Clark now told the Commission not only that he didn't have such
information but also that he had regarded his conversation with Clark
about Tobriner as a "trivial conversation . . . It didn't occur to me to
have any particular significance."

Mosk recounted what he told Clark. He said he and Clark were
putting on their robes early in the morning of the first day of hearings
at the court's January 1979 calendar in Los Angeles. "This was the
first time I had talked with Justice Clark since I had returned from a
trip to the Middle East over the Christmas holidays. . . . I think Justice
Clark . . . started it by saying something to the effect that 'I assume
that you're not very happy at being back from a pleasant trip and to
come into all the problems that we are facing.' And I agreed with him.
. . . And I think I said that I thought that it was unfortunate that the
Chief Justice had asked publicly for a hearing that affects the whole
court without checking with the court first, and that if she had
checked with the court . . . that the vote would have been 5 to 2 against
having her make the request for the hearing. Justice Clark, as I recall,
said, 'Well, it's done,' but he made some comment about the fact that a
request for a hearing referred only to the *Tanner* case.

"And I said at that point, 'The case that has troubled me has been
the *Fox* case, and I have talked to Justice Tobriner twice and I brought
it up in conference, as you will recall, about the long time it took in
getting the *Fox* case out, and I even told Justice Tobriner I thought
there would be some serious consequences for the court if the *Fox* case
were delayed until the holiday season.' And I continued on, 'There
have been serious consequences. . . . There was a bad reaction when
the opinion was released on the 15th of December. . . . I think the
opinion's right, but what atrocious timing for its release.' And I . . .
told Justice Clark that was the position I had been urging all along.
So, Mr. Willoughby," Mosk said, addressing the commissioner who

had asked him to relate the conversation with Clark, "that's what I meant by consequences."

In his secret testimony, Mosk also disputed the claim that Clark had gone to Mosk before testifying and reviewed the details of their January conversation. Commissioner Willoughby told Mosk that Clark had said that because he "wanted to be very sure of what your reaction was . . . he went over in some detail with you the conversation that he had had in January which included this understanding that your reference about cases being delayed meant to embrace both *Tanner* and *Fox*. Do you recall that happening?"

Mosk responded, "No, I'm sorry. . . . He never sat down. He had his briefcase in his hand and he was hurrying to get over [to the hearing] and didn't go into any details about his conversation. And I was, I guess I was glad that he had called it to my attention because I had completely forgotten about the conversation with Clark, otherwise. . . . But when he mentioned when it took place, I did recall it. . . . He gave me no detail at that time, other than to say he was going to relate our conversation. . . . He said merely, 'If asked, I will tell about that conversation we had in Los Angeles.' I said, 'Fine.' He dashed in and dashed right out."

"There was no effort to renew or refresh the conversation?" Mosk was asked. "No."

After Mosk testified, Tobriner was brought back to the stand. He was asked if he remembered having a conversation with Justice Mosk prior to the election about the consequences that might occur either to the court or to anyone else, if the *Tanner* case was not filed by the election.

Tobriner: "There was never such a conversation."

"To be certain . . . did you hear or have you read the transcript of Justice Clark's testimony about that subject matter?"

Tobriner: "I'm absolutely positive that no such conversation ever occurred."

He was asked if he had any recollection of Justice Mosk telling him prior to the election that he felt the *Fox* case should get out before Christmas. Tobriner said he did. In fact, he thought there had been two or three such conversations between himself and Mosk on that subject. "He felt that the *Fox* case should be moved and that if it were not, that there would be an adverse effect upon the court . . . if the case didn't get out well before the Christmas season," Tobriner recalled in his closed testimony. "I agreed with him that it should be moved as soon as it could be moved."

Tobriner said he explained to Justice Mosk that the case was taking a long time because Justice Newman had written an opinion that "could be better stated." Newman, the newest member of the court, had been Bird's professor years earlier at Boalt Hall, the law school at the University of California at Berkeley. Because of that she was reluctant to be tough on Newman directly about the deficiencies in his *Fox* opinion and asked Tobriner, whom she knew Newman respected, to speak to Newman about possible improvements in his *Fox* opinion. The Chief did write Newman a private memo about the opinion. When he didn't act on it, she began work on a more substantial concurring opinion, hoping that Newman would adopt large parts of it as his own. He did not do so.

After Mosk told his version of the conversations with Tobriner, that he had never accused Justice Tobriner of delaying decisions for election purposes, that he never thought *Tanner* had been delayed, Mosk then began to rehabilitate Clark. It may have been the biggest rehabilitation effort since Sister Kenny tried to wipe out polio.

"Without meaning to help—to try to clear up Justice Clark's confusion, I strongly suspect he is combining two conversations, one that I had with him, and the other that I had in conference," a week after the Los Angeles conversation. Mosk then told the commissioners a story he had told all the justices in private conference. "I started by saying, 'Let me offer a suggestion to any of you who may have held up cases because of the election.' And the Chief Justice interrupted and said, 'If anyone did.' And I said, 'Yes, if anyone did.' And then I went on with this explanation, that I had been with Professor Paul Freund of Harvard in the Middle East. He had asked me what was going on here. I said justices were accused of having held up cases because of the election and his answer was, 'What's wrong with that?' And I said, 'Well, some people seem to think it's wrong.' He said, 'I think that a court, if it has a politically sensitive case before it, has a right and perhaps a duty to hold the matter up until the election has passed . . . I am convinced if the United States Supreme Court had a case before it that would cause either the election or the defeat of a sitting President of the United States it would not release the opinion in October; it would hold it up until after the November election.' And I said, 'Well, suppose, however, it's not the United States Supreme Court where they have life tenure, but it's a judge whose very election depends on this?' And he paused a moment and said, 'Well, that changes the situation a little bit, but not particularly because,' said he, 'the issue in a judge's campaign for re-election is the judge's qualifications or temperament, and not the judge's opinion on a particular case the judge may have rendered. Therefore,' said he, 'if it doesn't involve somebody sitting in jail who shouldn't be there or somebody's property being held up that shouldn't be, I think the court has a perfect right to hold up a case until after the election if it's going to affect the election.'

"So I said to my colleagues, 'I am passing that on to you for whatever it's worth. You may consider that, those of you who will have any problem in the forthcoming proceedings.' " Mosk noted to the Commission that "there was total silence after my presentation."

Mosk said he repeated that story to the commissioners because it was the "only time I have used the term 'cases' in the plural. When I talked to Justice Clark alone I referred only to *Fox*." In fact, not only had he, by his own account, spoken to Justice Clark specifically of his concern about *Fox;* he had also told Clark that he was concerned *only* about *Fox* and that his concern about *Fox* had nothing to do with suspicions of wrongdoing by Tobriner. Still, Mosk testified that "I can frankly understand how he would combine [the] two events."

Mosk's justification of Clark's confusion of the two conversations raised important questions that were not asked at the hearing. Could Clark have repeated the conversation to Mosk—he said he did; Mosk said he didn't—and still come away with such damning false information? How could Mosk say the two conversations—one between himself and Clark, one an account he gave all the justices together—could be easily confused to produce the damaging charge about Justice Tobriner, when, according to Mosk, neither conversation—indeed, according to Mosk, *no* conversation he was involved it—included such an accusation? How could Mosk be so forgiving of the man who had publicly used Mosk's good name and had, according to Mosk's testimony, made him a false public accuser of a longtime friend and colleague? Why would Mosk voluntarily justify to the Commission Clark's serious mistake and spend no time expressing any regret to the Commission about the damage Clark's testimony had done to Justice Tobriner?

When Clark was called back to testify in the private session, he said that he had talked with Mosk after Mosk testified to the Commission. "I said, 'Stan, I hope I haven't misquoted you.' And he said, 'No. Essentially, our recall is the same with the exception of *Fox* on the one hand verses "cases" on the other.

"And he told me he could understand why I might have a different recall, that being that there was a conference following his return from the Middle East in which he referred to a conversation with a professor friend—"

"Freund?" asked Hufstedler.

"Freund." said Clark, "In which the good professor questioned what all of the disturbance was, that he saw nothing difficult with the proposition of timing cases, plural." Clark sounded as though he was trying to crib as accurately as possible from what Mosk had told him about his testimony to the Commission.

Clark maintained, however, that he was still "quite certain" that

Justice Mosk had been talking about Justice Tobriner holding up cases "in reference to the election." He also said he recalled with "certainty" that Mosk had spoken of "consequences." "Whether it was a reference to Justice Tobriner should be prepared or we as a court should be prepared, I'm not certain. But my recall is that it was reference to the person he was talking to, namely, Justice Tobriner."

It would seem that one of these men—Justice Mosk or Justice Clark—was lying, that one of them could have been charged with perjury. Or, at the very least, one was subject to delusion of facts, an unusual aberration for a competent judge.

At least one member of the Commission, Thomas Willoughby, was frustrated by the apparent contradictions in the testimony of Clark and Mosk. He addressed Mosk:

Justice Tobriner is "nearing the end of his career. [He] has this cloud cast over him by first of all the Fairbanks and Endicott [reporters whose bylines appeared on the election-day *Times* story] article, and then by the statement that Justice Clark made, I think in all good faith, in public about the conversation that he, Justice Clark, felt had occurred between the two of you in January. . . . The press picked it up as to imply that there had been a charge, ostensibly by yourself . . . or an allegation, that . . . some cases, and presumably *Tanner* among them, had been delayed until after the election and everybody knew about it. My question to you is, under those circumstances, what's the obligation of a member of a collegial body like the Supreme Court to set the record straight?"

Mosk's attorney, Edward Medvene, interrupted and said he didn't understand the question. But Mosk understood and answered it: "My answer is that all I can do is tell what my recollection is of what happened, and that's what I have done, to the best of my ability."

Willoughby was a non-lawyer on a Commission weighted with lawyers and judges. But often it was his questions that got to the heart of troubling issues.

"What bothers me personally," he said to Mosk, "is that a very serious allegation emerged as a result of those public proceedings which does damage, I think not only to an individual justice, but perhaps to the court as a whole, and from what we've heard you say, that allegation is based on an incorrect recollection of a conversation. How does that mistake that is now out in the public, how does that get corrected?"

"I would suggest to you," said Mosk, that "that's the vice in having public hearings."

Incredulous, Willoughby said, "You mean—I don't mean this to be facetious, but are you saying that Justice Tobriner now has no alternative but to twist slowly in the wind?"

Mosk answered coldly: "I have to repeat my answer. That was one of the vices in having a public hearing in the first instance."

Two years later two members of the commission who heard Mosk's secret testimony still bristled at the fact that Mosk had never done anything to clear the cloud that Justice Clark's testimony had created. "There's nothing," said one commissioner, "that would have precluded Stanley Mosk from publicly saying, 'I have reviewed the testimony Justice Clark gave in public, and I simply want to clear up whatever cloud this has put on my colleague Mat Tobriner. I have a different recollection of that conversation. . . .'" To date, Mosk has never tried to remove the cloud.

No matter what the Commission would do, Mosk could have clarified the fundamental questions raised by Clark's testimony with a brief public statement. Mosk has remained silent on the matter, as has Clark. Clark's silence is understandable. A study of his public statements, including his long testimony, makes it clear that he wanted Justice Tobriner to appear to be tainted, if not guilty, of wrongdoing, despite the fact that Clark gave no basis, even circumstantial, for his innuendo and accusations. Perhaps the explanation for Mosk's silence can be discerned in a comment he made to Tobriner's attorney at the funeral of a mutual friend. The funeral occurred during the hearing and after both Clark and Mosk had testified. Tobriner was already twisting in the wind, and he would continue to do so. Mosk told Tobriner's attorney on that occasion that Tobriner had "brought this all on himself." "This all" began—this charge of wrongdoing by Tobriner—said Mosk, because Tobriner cast the decisive vote for Rose Bird at her 1977 confirmation hearings. It seemed clear that Mosk's hatred of Rose Bird, or at least of her being Chief Justice, transcended his love of justice. He had knowledge that could have brought justice to someone—Tobriner—who, it was now clear, had been falsely accused. While Mosk, as he said, knew nothing about whether the *Tanner* case had been delayed by anyone, Mosk knew, as he testified, that he did not believe it had been delayed. Most important, he knew that, contrary to what Justice Clark had told the world, he himself had never accused Justice Tobriner of delaying *Tanner*.

I asked Tobriner in the summer of 1981 if either Clark or Mosk had apologized to him for what had happened as a result of the public accusations by Clark being answered by Mosk in private. He said neither had. I wrote to Mosk in July 1981 and asked to interview him. "It would appear that your testimony," I wrote, "probably resolved crucial questions that were raised publicly but not resolved publicly." Mosk wrote back: "I regret that I must decline to further discuss the 1979 events concerning this court. All of that has been thoroughly ventilated, and I do not choose to add anything further to the subject at this late date." There had been no public ventilation by Mosk. After his refusal to be interviewed, I obtained the secret testimony from more than one source.

In 1981 I asked Hufstedler if there would be anything improper in Mosk publicly clarifying what was clarified for the commissioners only in private. "It would be quite proper," said Hufstedler, "for Justice Mosk to stand up in public, even today, and say I did have that conversation and here is what was said. He is not gagged."

If the Commission was concerned about "unfair aspersions" on Justice Tobriner, said Mosk's attorney after the Commission completed its questioning of Mosk, then it should also be concerned about the unfair aspersions on Mosk. Noting that some stories had suggested that Mosk may have leaked confidential information to the press, Mosk's attorney said, "He's going to have to live with that the rest of his life. . . . Reputations are, as we all know, a very fragile thing. Takes many years to build up and very little to break down. . . . Tremendous harm, incalculable harm has been done unfairly to Justice Mosk's reputation." It was an absurd statement. If the charges of wrongdoing were true, those who leaked confidential information would be considered whistle-blowers—heroes of a sort. Even if Mosk had not leaked the confidential information, public suspicion that he had done so would not taint him seriously. The only thing that could taint him seriously as a leaker would have been suspicion that he had intentionally given reporters false information or intentionally misled them. No one had suggested that, either publicly or privately. To compare now the damage done by those events to Mosk's reputation to the damage done to Tobriner's reputation was like comparing the weight of a grape to the weight of a watermelon.

But apparently Mosk's attorney, Medvene, was serious. He asked the Commission to issue a public statement at the end of the proceeding that would specifically clear Mosk of any wrongdoing. One member of the Commission noted that this request was particularly ironic in view of the fact that at that very moment Mosk's lawsuit to close the hearing permanently and prevent a full public explanation of the results of the investigation was in the Court of Appeal, moving to the substitute Supreme Court. The Commission had delayed lunch in order to complete Mosk's testimony and spare him from returning in the afternoon. When Medvene finished his plea for public vindication of Mosk, commissioner Hillel Chodos said, "I consider this a matter worth waiting lunch for." Chodos, who had not yet left the Commission, was angry. "If you think that this commission owes a public report of vindication, you had better tell the [substitute] Supreme Court about it this afternoon because if you don't . . . there will be no reports."

Shortly after Mosk left his chambers late in the afternoon of the day before the November 1978 election, he penned a note to the Chief Justice. He congratulated her on the fact that she would easily win the election the next day. The next morning, in addition to Mosk's note, the Chief Justice read the *Los Angeles Times* story that claimed a decision had been held up by Tobriner to help assure her election that day. Two days later at the justices' weekly conference she and the other justices would learn that Mosk was one of the two justices who talked to the *Times* the day before the election.

Mosk testified that his first call from reporter William Endicott came late in the afternoon, perhaps before Mosk finished his note to Bird, before he left for home. Endicott's question was simple, according to Mosk's testimony: "I have this story about the *Tanner* case which is all prepared and ready to go, but is being held up because of the election. Can you give me some comment about that?" Mosk said he replied, "No comment." Endicott called Mosk again during dinner at home. Mosk said Endicott told him in this conversation that the story was completed but that the city desk in Los Angeles wouldn't run the story unless the reporters could get "further confirmation." "Can you confirm or deny the fact that the *Tanner* case is ready for filing but is being held up; that there are four justices of one view and three of another?" "I said, 'No comment.'" Mosk told the Commission.

But when Endicott then said, "Well, we have got this from good sources that this is the situation," Mosk said he responded, "Well, you have remarkable sources." If Mosk's testimony is true, his comment was not the kind a reporter could rely on as confirmation. But, as any child who has played hide-and-seek knows, it's the kind of response that would make you think you were hot rather than cold. A reporter would have to know more. And, according to Mosk, Endicott did want to know more. Mosk said Endicott laughed at his "remarkable" comment and then said, "What I want from you is will you please confirm or will you deny that this is an accurate story?" "And I said, 'No comment.'"

Mosk told the Commission he could not have confirmed anything about the *Tanner* case that day because "I did not know the status of the *Tanner* case on November 6th of 1978." Unlike Justice Clark, Mosk said he was never told by the reporters that he was considered one of their confirming sources. However, Fairbanks told me in the fall of 1979 that the reporters did consider Mosk a confirming source.

Mosk referred twice to Endicott's frustration the day before election at not being able to get past "her boy, Buehl," a gratuitous reference in his testimony to the Chief Justice's executive assistant, lawyer Stephen Buehl. Mosk had made an issue of Buehl's comments to the press less than a month before the election. Mosk was outraged by the fact that Buehl had been quoted as denying gubernatorial candidate Younger's charges that the *Tanner*-case and death-penalty decisions were being delayed. Mosk, according to testimony by other justices, was upset that people might think Buehl was a spokesman for the court as a whole rather than only for Bird. It seemed strange for that to be his concern at that time. It seemed strange that his concern should not be rather whether cases were being delayed improperly, or whether the candidate had lied, or whether confidential information about the court had been given to the candidate. Instead, he was upset that the Chief Justice's aide had looked at the record and had said publicly that the record indicated the charges were not true. His reaction seemed as strange as criticizing someone for hitting a killer bee with a newspaper instead of a flyswatter rather than thanking them for protecting you from the bee.

Mosk's record of reaction to the press is uneven and often strongly emotional. During the hearing, one of the Chief Justice's lawyers had a witness read a memo Mosk had sent the Chief Justice claiming that quotations in a newspaper story that said he was sharply critical of her had been "made up out of whole cloth." He wrote that he intended to communicate his displeasure to the reporter, Endicott. When Mosk testified, he said he was upset that this memo was made public. If the news story was inaccurate, as Mosk claimed, why would he be upset about setting the record straight by having his criticism of the story become public? Even more interesting was Clark's reaction. In the public hearing the day after the memo was read, Clark angrily told the Commission that the public reading of the Mosk memo "I interpret to be only an attack on my colleague, Justice Mosk."

In the spring of 1981, Mosk reacted with vehemence to a story written by *Los Angeles Times* reporter Nancy Skelton. She wrote about a public speech in which he suggested that the golden age of the California Supreme Court had been reduced to a "mere devalued currency." Mosk's reaction was immediate. He sent both a telegram and a letter to an editor at the *Times*. He showed colleagues a letter he wrote to the reporter. He claimed the story had "tortured beyond recognition my talk." In his letter to the reporter he asked if she had been asleep, and suggested that she had decided in advance of the speech to create a controversy. "That you did so is a testimony to your ingenuity but not to your integrity." To respond this way to Skelton's story was highly inappropriate, if not slightly hysterical, for a comparison of her story with the text of Mosk's speech shows that she was scrupulously accurate.

Furthermore, at approximately the same time Mosk made that public speech, he gave an interview to two law professors and made similar observations. "This was a great court under the leadership of

. . . Chief Justices Traynor and Wright. In my opinion it was then the greatest court in the United States, and I felt it was a tremendous honor to serve with men like Traynor and [Raymond] Peters and [Raymond] Sullivan and my colleague, Justice [Mathew] Tobriner. Their contribution to California law was significant. I miss those times very much. I hope in the future our court will ascend to those heights once again." Their article quoting him was published in the *Western Law Journal,* March/April 1981.

Any reporter familiar with the activities of the court in recent years, as Skelton's story indicates she was, would have emphasized precisely what she emphasized. It is news when a longtime and respected member of the Supreme Court makes thinly veiled attacks on his own court and his own Chief Justice. As a matter of fact, many who had socialized with Mosk in recent years knew that his public remarks were mild compared with some of his private statements about Bird and the court.

Mosk was apparently upset that Skelton did not report the 16 recent cases he listed in his speech as "trail-blazing firsts anywhere in the country." Her story was short, and, given the fiery nature of his other comments, it is understandable that she had to dwell on them. Even if she had recited the court decisions that Mosk's speech said were evidence that "the sky isn't falling, Chicken Little, there are only a few clouds," he would probably not have been pleased with the logical conclusion that would have been drawn from his recitation of the cases: The cases he listed, all complicated problems that the court, he claimed, had solved with innovative and important solutions, actually pointed up the fact that under Bird the court was doing approximately the same quality of work it had done before Bird's arrival.

Even after listing the 16 cases that were supposedly evidence of a wise and creative court, Mosk again suggested that something was wrong, that the good that had emanated from the court in Bird's years may have been an accident rather than what naturally could be expected. "Individual justices may come and justices may go," he said, "but the institution as an entity transcends the qualities—favorable or unfavorable—of any individual persons." He said he was confident that if there were barriers to creativity at the court, "that it will continue to overcome them." Mosk seemed compelled to pepper even his favorable observations with insults. He had often criticized William Clark in the past, according to colleagues, but he did so in private. Now his criticism of Bird was both private and public.

Mosk lashed out strongly at the news media in a speech he gave in February 1980, shortly after the investigation was completed, at a judges' symposium in Washington, D.C. Speaking of the "extraordinary power" of media commentators, Mosk said a commentator "who is irresponsible can, by a single thoughtless insinuation, reach millions of persons and instantly destroy, in the name of accountability, the career of a jurist who has devoted his lifetime to the law." If Mosk's testimony was true, he could well have made precisely this statement about his colleague Clark for what he said in his testimony. He never did. Or, he could have made this remark about himself for refusing to clear the name of his longtime colleague and friend Tobriner. Justice, not friendship, should indeed have dictated that he clear Tobriner's name.

Before Mosk left the hearing room, he made a brief speech to the Commission. He again said he could fully understand how Justice Clark could have combined two conversations and come up with the misunderstanding about Mosk's conversation with Justice Tobriner. After making this final effort to rehabilitate Clark while making no apology for the injustice Clark's testimony had done to Justice Tobriner, Mosk told the commissioners that reports of "personal bitterness and divisiveness on the court" were "grossly exaggerated" by the press. He then made a grossly unsubstantiated suggestion, that the press made these alleged exaggerations about the difficulties of the court because the press "sees the judiciary as its enemy." Sounding like an angry parent, Mosk said the press treated the courts this way "despite the fact that the judiciary is the best protector of the press's First Amendment rights that exists."

Justice Mosk left the closed hearing room in possession of one crucial piece of information that he did not reveal to the Commission. He had testified that *Times* reporter Fairbanks came to his chambers to interview him, on 27 February 1979, for a long story the reporter was doing on the fallout from the *Tanner*-case delay stories. Mosk said he refused to give Fairbanks any information about *Tanner* that day. What he did not tell the Commission was what Fairbanks told him that day. In a letter written in November 1979, a little more than three months after he testified before the Commission, Mosk said: "The question is whether Fairbanks was telling the truth to his editors" on election eve. Mosk wrote then that when he expressed outrage to Fairbanks on 27 February for his election-day story, Fairbanks attributed the story to a "breakdown in communications" between himself and Endicott the night they were working on the story. After Mosk's testimony the Commission was back to its original and sole source of an accusation of delay: the *Los Angeles Times* election-day story. It would have been significant to tell the Commission that the writer of the story had admitted to Mosk that the story was flawed, perhaps fatally. Instead of doing so, Mosk kept this information to himself.

CHAPTER 11

As Jurors, the Commission Flunked

The Commission heard its last witness 27 July. That same day it heard Hufstedler and members of his staff summarize the depositions of former Attorney General Evelle Younger and members of Younger's criminal division staff. Then the Commission waited for the ad hoc Supreme Court. It would wait until 18 October to get the decision that permanently closed its doors.

The six remaining commissioners, in six meetings, tackled the mountain of evidence it had accumulated. Testimony by the witnesses filled 4,855 pages—3,869 pages from the public and 986 pages from the private sessions. Though the testimony given in the private session constituted only 20 percent of the total testimony, it was vitally important. "The testimony that we received behind closed doors— especially Stanley Mosk's testimony—was extremely relevant to the final decision that the Commission made on most of the justices," commissioner Willoughby told me. "His testimony was critical in terms of the final decision of the Commission."

When the doors to the hearing were closed, a new hearing was started, technically speaking. All the publicly accumulated testimony was entered as evidence in the new hearing. But the Commission was now in business under its old rules. The primary importance of this was that the Commission was no longer limited to the original areas of investigation—delay of particular decisions and leaking of confidential information. It could now investigate anything and could take action against a judge in the wide area described as conduct "that brings the judicial office into disrepute." Consequently, both the range of the investigation and the range of the potential discipline were broadened by the closing of the hearings and by the forced reversion to the original rules. In contrast to any possible outcome in the public hearings, where all conclusions, including discipline, had to be public, private admonishment of judges was now open to the Commission as a form of punishment.

On Monday, 5 November 1979, the noon news throughout the state announced that the investigation of the court was over. The commissioners had just announced the result: it had decided not to file charges against any justice.

The 2½-page statement was described by reporters as terse. The words that mattered were in the middle of the second page: ". . . The status of the investigation is that it is now terminated and the result hereby announced is that no formal charges will be filed against any Supreme Court justice. . . ."

This had been the most important investigation ever conducted by this Commission. It involved public accusations of improprieties in the State's highest court. The Commission conducted the most extensive investigation of a court ever conducted in the history of the country. Its brief report consisted of 443 words, of which only 29 ambiguous words, 6.5 percent of the document, dealt with the real issues of the investigation. The rest of the report, 93.5 percent, was a litany of petty complaints about the Commission's problems in conducting the investigation.

The document began by announcing that at the outset the Commission had felt it inadvisable to undertake the investigation unless a "full public report could be filed at the conclusion." The report explained that the Commission had asked the Judicial Council for a rule change to permit a fuller report and had, instead, received a demand to hold an open investigation. The Commission said it "remains vitally important that all of the evidence be thoroughly examined and analyzed, and the reasons for any determination be clearly and openly stated." However, the report went on, under the ad hoc court decision in the Mosk case, the Commission "is not only prohibited from concluding the hearings in public but also is prohibited from reviewing or commenting upon the testimony and other evidence, and from public dissemination of the analysis and reasoning employed in arriving at a determination and disposition of the proceedings. We were . . . confined to a 'status report' or an announcement of the 'results' of the investigation. The Commission regrets this limitation but is bound to follow the law as announced by the court."

The statement said that the Commission "wishes to make clear" that its role is limited to judging standards of judicial conduct set forth in the Constitution and that the Commission "is not a general investigative body to review the procedures and functioning of courts nor to recommend improvements in the courts."

The report closed by saying that the investigation had "disclosed certain deficiencies in existing law which have inhibited the Commission in carrying out its duties. Both the public interest and the administration of justice require that these deficiencies be cured."

If ever a public document aroused speculation, this one did. It seemed to answer only one question: Would any justices be charged? It did not actually clear the justices, and its language raised a multitude of questions and suspicions.

If the Commission felt it had to make its report on the results of the investigation brief, why did it spend more than 90 percent of the document complaining about the restrictions placed on it? If it had concluded that a just result was that no charges should be filed against any justice, why did it now emphasize that there was a need for the evidence to be thoroughly examined and analyzed? Such a statement worked against one of the Commission's official functions: to conduct itself in such a way that it would bring the judiciary out of disrepute. Charging justices with wrongdoing would be one way of doing this. Exonerating would be another way of doing this. But simply saying the investigation was ended and then bemoaning the Commission's lack of power sounded as though the Commission felt it might have come to its conclusion with a figurative gun at its head. By saying it was not empowered to review the "procedures and functioning of courts nor to recommend improvements in the courts," did the Commission mean to imply there was a need for an investigation that could perform these functions, or that wrongdoing existed that the Commission was not empowered to act upon? Similarly, when the Commission reported that this investigation had "disclosed certain deficiencies in existing law which have inhibited the Commission in carrying out its duties," did the Commission mean to imply, "Folks, there was a heap of wrongdoing here but we just didn't have the power to get at it, so we are quitting in futility?"

Some people, including resigned commissioner Chodos, told me they thought that was indeed what happened—that the Commission had not considered the evidence at the end, and had simply decided to wash its hands of the whole matter and take no action except to close the investigation. The wording of the report made that interpretation believable. But the wording made quite a variety of speculations believable.

For the publicly accused justices, the questions raised by the report were profound. "No formal charges will be filed" said the report. Did that mean the Commission had concluded there wasn't enough evidence? That the evidence was weak? That the evidence was thoroughly persuasive that no wrongdoing had occurred? The report did not mention any names. Did this mean that the Commission had reached the same conclusion about each justice? Or did it decide to bring no charges for different reasons for different people—some, for instance, because there was no evidence of wrongdoing, others because there wasn't enough solid evidence?

The investigation that had started with such public promise, with the hope of sniffing out any scoundrels and punishing them, had ended pitifully and vaguely. Most of the text of the Commission's report made it sound as though the decision not to file charges was unimportant, that if the Commission had just been given more power, as well as a public forum, it would have revealed not only its decision-making process, but might actually have come to a different conclusion. Far from putting to rest the charges that led to the investigation, the wording and tone of the report seemed to raise more questions than it answered.

This Commission, the first judge-watching commission in the country, a Commission with a fine reputation for being an adequate watchdog of the California judiciary, seemed to be suggesting that a great deal might be wrong at the Supreme Court but that it, the Commission, was powerless to do anything about it.

The confidential letters sent by the Commission to each justice weren't any more helpful in deciphering what had happened. They said: "The Commission has unanimously decided to terminate this proceeding. No formal charges will be filed."

As *The Los Angeles Daily Journal* would put it in a news story a few weeks later: "Whether there were no grounds for filing charges, or whether there were insufficient grounds, remains a matter of speculation among court observers. It is also possible, according to observers, that the commission's decision not to file charges merely indicates that the nine-member [*sic*] panel was unable to muster the five votes necessary to do so, or to exonerate the court."

Press speculation, naturally, was abundant. K. Connie Kang wrote: "The [*San Francisco*] *Examiner* has learned the report is a compromise between members of the commission who wanted to file formal charges against one or more members of the court and members of the commission who wanted to issue a report totally exonerating high court justices from any wrongdoing." This, like much speculation at the time, was wrong.

The *Los Angeles Times* speculated, also erroneously: ". . . It was learned that two of the six members of the commission had argued in favor of formal charges and that they could not persuade the majority to go along. . . . The commission's . . . statement . . . was essentially a compromise between the members who favored formal charges and those who favored a more positive 'exoneration' of the court."

Three days after the Commission's report was released, Assembly Speaker Leo McCarthy, a Democrat from San Francisco who was elected Lieutenant Governor in 1982, called for an investigation of the Supreme Court by the legislature. It was the same threat that, a year earlier, had been partly responsible for the Judicial Council's panicky adoption of an unconstitutional rule. Now, a year later, McCarthy said, "I believe the courts of California are vulnerable. I believe the investigation of the Supreme Court added up to a negative. I think it's important for the legislature—with enormous respect—to review every aspect of the Supreme Court situation." After making his remarks to the press, however, McCarthy took no official steps to press for a legislative investigation.

A San Francisco law professor, P. J. Riga, wrote a guest column in the *Examiner* calling for the resignation of all the Supreme Court justices. He wrote: "As Henry VIII told Thomas More: 'You are my public minister, Thomas, because you are honest; and what is more to the point, you are known to be honest.' As a people, it is sad to say that we can no longer say this of the present members of the California Supreme Court. They all must go."

As Kang astutely put it in an analytical article in the *Examiner* a week after the Commission report became public: "For the public, which paid $510,000 for the probe, the commission report leaves a lot to be desired. It leaves unanswered the questions aroused by the testimony of Justice William Clark, who quoted Mosk as accusing Tobriner of holding up cases before the 1978 election, saying Tobriner would 'pay the consequences' if this were revealed." In another article she wrote that this testimony by Clark was "the strongest piece of evidence offered" during the entire investigation. "Did Mosk, who testified behind closed doors, confirm Clark? Or did he refute Clark's testimony? The public will never know that answer unless some commissioner, or Mosk decides to disclose it."

It was this strongest piece of evidence—Clark's testimony—that retired Army Colonel Earl Huntting, president of the statewide Citizens for Law and Order, used as the basis for his public request a week after the Commission report that the Assembly initiate impeachment proceedings against members of the Supreme Court. Huntting said Clark's testimony about Mosk's conversation with Tobriner about wrongdoing was the "evidence of probable high-court misconduct" that justified impeachment.

After the results of the investigation were announced, politicians would continue using Clark's testimony as "evidence" that there was wrongdoing. Though the Commission probably didn't intend for its report to become a weapon in the arsenal of the right-wing enemies of the court, or of anybody else for that matter, it was as though the report had been tailor-made for them. Because the language was so inexplicit and plaintive, it could be read to mean whatever they wanted it to mean. Many politicians wanted it to mean at least continuing chaos and some wanted it to mean continuing wrongdoing. Some even used it to make the most extreme demand: impeachment.

Although not as sensational as the calls for resignation and impeachment of Supreme Court justices, a statement by commissioner Willoughby had the most profound effect on the public's perception of the Commission's conclusions. In a *Los Angeles Times* story that appeared two days after the report was issued, he was quoted as saying the Commission's refusal to bring formal charges of misconduct against any member of the court should not be construed as an "exoneration." This was no wild-eyed politician out to make hay from the ambiguity of the report. This was one of the authors of the report, a Commission member who during the hearing appeared to be struggling mightily to get to the truth. His public comments left no doubt that there should be doubt about the report. He was quite clear on the matter: "I see no reason the public should accept the result [of the investigation] because we didn't explain it."

The only authoritative statement made publicly that seemed to point to a lack of evidence against the justices came from Seth Hufstedler. He and his staff of lawyers were probably the only people who had seen *all* the evidence gathered in the case, including many interviews and under-oath depositions never seen by the Commission. That fact adds credence to his comments, which were made during an hour-long discussion of the investigation on KQED, the San Francisco public television station, a month after the results were announced. Anchorwoman Belva Davis asked Hufstedler, "Do you feel this was a good resolution?" He responded that though he thought there should have been a public report that would give the public the advantage of all the information that was developed, "I feel the resolution was right that there should not have been charges filed, as the Commission determined."

The show had a tiny viewing audience. Two newspapers wrote stories about it, but, amazingly, both of them, the *Los Angeles Times* and the *San Francisco Examiner,* carried stories about the program that didn't even mention Hufstedler's revealing comment, even his participation. In view of everything that had been said publicly by then, there can be no doubt that his remark was newsworthy. Yet the stories were about the fact that the Chief Justice had referred during the program to the investigation as a year of "harassment," and the fact that Willoughby had said the charges were not an exoneration (Willoughby was not on the program and his comments were not mentioned in it). Bird's comment was taken from this context: ". . . The court itself was able to function as an institution during all this period of time, a period under which it was under investigation for an entire year, two months of it spent almost solidly . . . testifying—members of the court or staff of the court testifying. I think that really is a compliment to the institution itself that under a full year of constant harassment we were able to function and to keep the standards of the opinions that were coming out."

At a fall 1979 meeting of the National Conference for Judicial Conduct Organizations, Seth Hufstedler must have been welcomed as a well-seasoned veteran safely home from the biggest battle any state judicial commission had endured. He gave a keynote address in which he claimed, "During the California investigation, the commission earned the confidence of the people through public proceedings, and that confidence persisted, even when the commission was forced to issue a confidential report." Later, Hufstedler made a similar statement in an interview with me: "Despite the bifurcated [private/public] proceeding, the press and public accepted the results." I thought Hufstedler's comments were made more as a result of wishful thinking and good public relations rather than of his understanding of how the report was received and interpreted. I reminded him that on the very day we were talking in the fall of 1981 another recall campaign against the Chief Justice had been announced and that the inexplicit results of the investigation figured in the complaints against her. I told him that a wide variety of people had told me that they read the report and concluded "We just don't know what the Commission concluded." Hufstedler then agreed that because of the language of the report, "There's no question people can continue to say that. But to the extent that it *has* been accepted, it is substantially because the largest portion was carried on at a public hearing. People were convinced that the Commission was doing a fair and objective job."

But one of Hufstedler's assistants in the investigation, Pierce O'Donnell, a member of his law firm, seemed to have a perception closer to that of the public. Within a few days of the investigation, he gave a speech to the Whittier Bar Association in which he characterized the secrecy that hid the end of the investigation as "odious and unfortunate." He said the "people of California will never get to hear the rest of the evidence and will never get to know the reasons why the Commission members voted the way they did. . . . There is anger when there could have been renewed respect."

The most perceptive press analysis of the Commission's conclusions was in an editorial, "Wet Squib," in the *San Francisco Chronicle:*

"The result of the grand ethical inquiry into the moves, machinations and motives of Rose Bird's state Supreme Court in its handling of the 'use a gun–go to prison' decision is what the British call a wet squib—a firecracker that doesn't go off.

"The California public is left without facts or findings on which to form an opinion and base a conclusion.

"We can hardly imagine a worse outcome for the reputation of the whole court. . . .

"It is astonishing to consider how muddled and futile this inquiry has turned out to be. As we look back, the first mistake, and the one which tainted the whole proceedings, was the decision last January of the State Judicial Council to open hearings to the public. . . .

"Unquestionably, the chief justice was right to ask for somebody other than the court itself to answer the question whether a perhaps politically damaging decision had been willfully withheld.

"But now, a year later, who knows the answer?"

The commissioners, of course, know the answers. They know what they believed individually and as a group. They know why they came to the conclusion that would seem so befuddling to some, so politically useful to others. I found some of the commissioners were willing to provide details of their final deliberations, willing to assess and explain their conclusion. Some spoke for attribution. Some spoke not-for-attribution.

Perhaps none of them felt pleased with what the Commission finally produced, though their reasons for dissatisfaction differed. "The mountain brought forth a mouse," said one commissioner. Another one identified the mouse: "We issued a Mickey Mouse statement. It wasn't fair to anyone."

"I'm not very happy with the way it ended up," said Willoughby. "The Commission wasn't very happy with the outcome. . . . I think it's unfair. We certainly would have liked to have released a statement that indicated what evidence we considered, and why we made our decision."

Commission Chairman Janes told me he thought the Commission did the best it could while "handcuffed." But what would he think of the conclusion if he were not on the Commission, if he were, say, one of the accused? "I think I would be dissatisfied, I don't think there's any question about that. . . . I would be inclined to feel that perhaps everything went for naught. . . . I certainly wouldn't think it was a whitewash, after all the TV coverage and everything. But I would be very dissatisfied because I would feel that there was no answer to the questions."

What did the Commission actually do when it deliberated on each justice?

Its disciplinary options were three: it could file charges leading, after another hearing, either to permanent removal from the bench or to public censure; alternatively, the Commission itself could issue a private admonishment at this stage against any justice.

"We went over the evidence for each judge, with the help of Seth," explained a commissioner. "He would summarize the evidence for Judge A. We'd compare notes. Occasionally we referred to the transcript. We'd go down the list of what Judge A did. Then we'd say, 'What does that tell us? What evidence of misconduct can be attributed to Judge A that is actionable? If it's all true, what does it amount to?' We took them one by one, and we went through each charge. We did it methodically."

On the basis of exhaustive talks with those who were present at the Commission's deliberations, it is possible to say that the results of those deliberations were as follows:

• No commissioner voted to bring formal charges against any justice. Though questions were raised about bringing charges against some, no one argued for charges against anyone.

• The commissioners agreed that there had been no evidence of a plan by any justice to delay any opinion until after the election.

• The only discipline seriously considered against any justice was the weakest possible punishment, private admonishment.

• No justice was privately admonished.

• The only private admonishments considered had nothing to do with the original accusations that were investigated in the public hearing—delay of particular decisions and leaking of confidential court information. Rather, private admonishment was considered in relation to other matters and based on a more general charge in the California Rules of Court, "conduct prejudicial to the administration of justice that brings the judicial office into disrepute."

One could conclude from this that all justices were exonerated on the original accusations.

• Mosk and Newman were the only persons considered for private admonishment. The considerations were based on the fact that some commissioners saw Mosk's lawsuit and Newman's refusal to leave the ad hoc court as attempts to thwart the Commission's constitutional obligation to investigate.

Excluding the last point—who was considered for private admonishment—all of the findings of the Commission could have been made public—even if one gives the narrowest interpretation to the ad hoc Supreme Court's *Mosk* decision that the Commission said prohibited it from explaining its results.

It took a short time for the Commission to reach these conclusions. It was a fairly easy task, almost anticlimactic, said one commissioner. Far more difficult was the decision on what kind of public statement they would release. The overwhelming majority of their deliberative time was spent writing the statement that caused so much speculation, that raised so many questions that were never answered, and that did not explain results.

Willoughby talked about why the Commission's statement was so unexplicit, why it simply said no charges would be filed and then went on to suggest the Commission might have thought there was wrongdoing but could not get at it. He also talked about why he made his public statement that the justices were not exonerated, so adding fuel to the idea that, indeed, there had been wrongdoing but, for some reason, the Commission had been unable to deal with it.

"We were not prepared to say there was no evidence that could support a charge as long as there had been some feeling of wrongdoing by some justices," said Willoughby. That was why he felt it was important to announce that the justices had not been exonerated. I asked him, "But you believe that what you said—that they were not exonerated—applies to some and not to others." "Absolutely," was his quick reply. I suggested that his public statement made the whole thing look fuzzy, as though everybody was at least a little guilty. "Yes," he said, "and that's unfortunate."

There is confusion among the commissioners on whether the possibility of announcing exoneration ever came up. Some of them were angry with Willoughby for announcing there had been no exoneration, in view of the fact that they thought it had never been an issue. But what was an issue was whether they should announce that there was no evidence, say, against Judges A, B, and C on points 1, 2, and 3, and not enough evidence against Judges D, E, F, and G on points 1, 2, and 3. Willoughby would have considered an announcement that there was no evidence against a particular judge an announcement of exoneration and improper unless all had been considered to be without taint on any matter.

"My recollection," he told me, "was that there was a discussion about the meaning of announcing that we were exonerating some and not bringing charges against others. By the time we were having that discussion we knew we weren't going to bring charges against anybody. We wondered if it would be fair to the people that we don't exonerate to announce that we were going to exonerate others."

I asked him to consider an imprecise analogy. Imagine a trial of multiple defendants. The jury decides, after reviewing the evidence, that some of the defendants are not guilty. On the other defendants the jury cannot agree on either guilt or innocence and is therefore a hung jury on those defendants. And then the jury, in its private deliberations, is convinced by one or more of its members that this divided verdict is not fair to those whose innocence or guilt was not clearly established, for they will appear guilty if others are acquitted. As a result, the jury practices jury nullification and ignores that it has determined innocence in some cases, and announces that it is a hung jury on all the defendants. I ask Willoughby if that isn't in effect what the Commission did—decide to leave everybody tainted in order in "fairness" not to draw a distinction between those it believed were completely innocent and those who some believed had engaged in activities that deserved the minor punishment of private admonishment. While not willing to clear those it thought should be completely cleared, the Commission was willing, wasn't it, to taint everyone with its unclear statement? Why, given the weakness of the only discipline considered, and the lack of agreement on that, weren't all cleared?

"The way you put it today," said Willoughby, "makes it sound so logical and so easy, and all I can remember is that it wasn't that logical and that easy at the time."

I told him that while I did not consider any of this easy, I did consider it logical: that persons who are accused publicly and later cleared by an official investigating agency should be told at least privately, and preferably publicly—as the Commission rules permit—that they have been cleared. The right to a fair trial implies the right to know the conclusion of your trial. Yes, this wasn't *really* a trial. But, as nearly all parties who spoke with me agreed, the impact of the investigation on the accused and on the public was the same as the impact of a trial. The major missing ingredient that made it less like a trial was the lack of due process. Part of that missing due process was that neither the justices, who were publicly accused and investigated, nor the public they serve—the public whose rights they protect—were told whether the accused were cleared of the accusations against them.

If the Commission was concerned, as it is required to be, with even the appearance of impropriety in the judiciary, it should have announced that it had concluded there was no impropriety—at least on the original issues under investigation.

The Commission's final compromise statement, designed to cover those who had no evidence against them as well as those who some commissioners thought had some evidence against them on matters unrelated to the original accusations, though not enough to justify any action, read as follows: "It is now terminated and the result hereby announced is that no formal charges will be filed against any Supreme Court justice." This statement had the effect of guaranteeing a permanent assumption of the appearance of impropriety. The

Commission's muddy statement also had the effect of putting all the justices on perpetual parole.

"It seemed to the Commission," said one commissioner, "to be the only equitable solution—to use one statement for all seven, one that would apply to all, cover all."

One commissioner, deeply troubled by the result of the investigation, said, "It all took on a life of its own, it seemed to be some kind of a process that nobody had any control over. . . . I don't know where the controls would have come, but in retrospect I've looked back at the whole situation, and I think it did just take on a life of its own. It was almost like some kind of classic tragedy in which people got assigned their roles and they had to play out their roles, and they had no control over them. And I think that included the Commission. . . . There were all kinds of things that could have happened." The commissioner thinks a while and says, "The Commission could have simply refused to conduct the investigation under the Judicial Council's rule. We could've said, 'Look, we think it's unfair to all parties involved.' We didn't do that."

For the accused, of course, the ramifications of the entire matter—especially of the final inconclusive results—had deep personal ramifications. For some, tragic ramifications. Wiley Manuel was a case in point. Between the election and the beginning of the investigation, newspapers reported that an anonymous source claimed Manuel, at the request of either Bird or Tobriner, had written a dissent a month before the election in order to assist in delaying the *Tanner* decision until after the election. Manuel died in January 1981, never learning that he had been exonerated by the Commission. According to all my Commission sources, every commissioner agreed he had engaged in no wrongdoing. One of the men on the Commission had tears in his eyes as he told me how sorry he felt for Manuel, who had died six months before our interview.

Justice Tobriner mourned Justice Manuel's death. It pained him that someone 53 years old and so new to the court should die. He liked Justice Manuel. Tobriner also felt it was tragic that Justice Manuel had been tainted with accusations of wrongdoing, had gone through the public and private investigation, and had not lived to see his name cleared.

The strongest public accusation of wrongdoing had been made against Justice Tobriner himself. Though other accusations were being investigated, the ever-dominant issue in the press and in the public's mind was whether Tobriner had unethically delayed a decision to help Bird. The question people wanted answered was: Had this distinguished judge thrown away his integrity late in life in order to help a fellow liberal justice—the first woman Chief Justice—win approval from the voters? The question would never be answered by the Commission.

Three justices—Bird, Tobriner, and Manuel—had been framed by people in and out of the court. From the public and private testimony, the commissioners knew that. But the Commission decided to let the accused justices spin in the wind indefinitely. They left the frame in place. It was justice denied. For those who were investigated and who died, it was justice permanently denied.

Perhaps the Commission started to get out of control as soon as the door was closed on the hearings in July. That was when the Commission began to feel it was being assaulted. As one commissioner told me, "We felt we were trying to do a good job, a very fair job. . . . We were trying to abide by what we all thought was an awkward and almost impossible rule the Judicial Council had given us, to hold this preliminary investigation in public. . . . And then to experience this continuing frustration, all this litigation with Mosk, and the appeals, and all that. That was a frustrating, traumatic situation. And then when the commissioners started to resign, Chodos and Gehrels. That was awful for us."

This commissioner agreed that the justices didn't have adequate due process, particularly in their right to a conclusion, but said it wasn't the Commission's fault. "I guess I don't want to sound as though I'm being too defensive, but I think that really was the result of the court's ruling in the *Mosk* case, that's why they didn't get it. . . . We felt an enormous responsibility. We knew we had not moved any cloud away. It was our hope that we could either bring charges against somebody if there was some evidence of wrongdoing or, if there was no evidence, we would clearly state why we felt there was no evidence or not enough evidence, that all the evidence we had was very thin. In the end, we could not do either."

All the commissioners I talked with said their frustration with the court as a whole escalated considerably over the Mosk and Newman episodes. "It was a growing sense of frustration," said one commissioner. The actions of Mosk and Newman clearly were individual actions. No justice besides Mosk brought a suit to declare the open hearings unconstitutional. No justice besides Newman remained on the ad hoc Supreme Court panel or refused to share internal court communications with the Commission. But the Commission saw these justices' actions as representing more than Mosk or Newman. "It was like the establishment was trying to frustrate the Commission because it saw the Commission as the enemy, as a threat," said one commissioner. "So the whole judicial establishment was trying to frustrate the Commission. And at that time it was just kind of mind-boggling to us. When Newman wouldn't remove himself from the court . . . it was really mind-boggling that this could be happening. That was the period I think of as one of intense disillusionment and frustration."

The profound frustration the Commission felt with Newman erupted briefly in an unpleasant exchange between Newman and Willoughby when Newman testified in secret. Newman, both when he gave depositions to Hufstedler and now in the closed hearing, refused to talk about conversations or any other communications with fellow justices. He also refused to turn over internal Supreme Court communications. Newman claimed both an institutional and private privilege not to disclose such communications. Hufstedler had just chastised Newman for refusing to discuss "the basis for your privilege and its scope."

Willoughby stepped in at this point, and asked, "Justice Newman, are you just playing with us—"

Newman: "I don't like that question."

Willoughby: "Let me finish. You've asked us to take very seriously your claim to privilege, and then you play this cutesy little game of 'I won't give you citations.' I find that offensive."

Newman's attorney: "Mr. Chairman, I find the question offensive. It seems to me that's not a proper question. Justice Newman has had a distinguished career before he came on the court. He's a member of a court that's been distinguished up to this point. And I don't think he should be subjected to this kind of question."

Chairman Janes: "It's not a question. It's a statement, and it will stand, as will your remarks."

Later, Newman angered the Commission on two occasions. He said that all other justices who had testified about comments made at a particular weekly conference of Supreme Court justices had testified inaccurately. But then he claimed that his privilege not to reveal internal communications made it impossible for him to reveal what had been said at the conference. Presumably, this privilege also should have prevented him from saying they all were inaccurate. At another point, he described his reaction to the Chief Justice's concurring opinion in the *Fox* case, an opinion that she hoped he would use to improve his majority opinion in the case. He said that he was very busy and was irritated at her for bringing up a new constitutional issue. He said he was irritated, in part, by the fact that "I knew it was going to be a big job for me either to write a memo or to revise the majority opinion to take [it] into account. . . . At some point in November . . . finally, I decided, if my language can be excused, to hell with it. . . ."

I asked each commissioner I interviewed why the Commission's final statement was used primarily to complain rather than to explain the results of the investigation. Why, if they felt the decision in the

Mosk suit limited them to a very brief statement, did they spend more than 90 percent of their brief statement complaining about their frustration with the investigation?

"We were fed up. We had had it up to here," is what one commissioner told me.

Two others confirmed what one put quite succinctly:

"Look, by the time we wrote that statement we were petulant, and the statement was petulant. We were fed up by that time and decided, 'This is all we're going to say.' Why, we could've written fifty pages explaining a whole lot if we had wanted to, but we were sick of it by then. We were especially fed up with Newman and Mosk."

It was a remarkable admission. What was even more remarkable was that the person who said it felt the petulance was understandable, justifiable, excusable, not a bad thing. There was profound irony in this. Some commissioners had contempt for Newman when he said he had concluded "to hell with it" rather than spend more time considering revising the *Fox* decision. But the Commission itself had essentially decided "to hell with it" in this fundamental investigation, this investigation that had rocked public confidence in the judicial system of California as nothing ever had and no event likely ever will again. Through this petulance the Commission would let the public remain—indeed, *cause* the public to remain—confused and, ultimately, cynical about the basic integrity of its Supreme Court.

These commissioners were jurors. They were a jury assigned to judge judges, a highly important obligation in a society that regards the judiciary as the most independent of its three branches of government, a society in which the judiciary is, inevitably, a watchdog on the other branches of government. This agency, the Commission on Judicial Performance, was the watchdog on the watchdog. It determined that the Supreme Court justices were innocent of wrongdoing and then decided not to tell the justices or the public of this determination. It committed this injustice out of petulance and then blamed it on the *Mosk* decision of the ad hoc Supreme Court, the decision that closed the hearings. There is flexibility in the *Mosk* decision as well as in the California Rules of Court that govern release of information about investigations known to the public. While the Commission was not free to release all the evidence, it was free, even obligated, to explain its actions.

If only the Commission had managed to maintain the constant sense of responsibility that the average American juror is expected to maintain. Ordinary jurors spend long hours sifting through evidence, some of it conflicting, some of it extremely difficult to understand. They are told not to let their emotions play a role in their deliberations. They cannot release statements of resentment about the rules of law they are told to abide by. They cannot meet with reporters during a trial, as the commissioners did, and announce that they are tired and angry about the fact that the trial is not progressing as smoothly or as quickly as they wish it would. They cannot tell the public, as the commissioners did, "Don't blame us if this turns out differently than you hoped it would." Instead, ordinary jurors persist patiently and come to conclusions, conclusions that are announced without self-serving statements from them.

I do not doubt that each member of the Commission might be a good and honest person, and that the Commission normally functions well. But for some reason, in this case it functioned in a manner that would not be permitted of the average citizen who serves on jury duty. If a juror said, "Oh, to hell with it," and issued a careless conclusion as a result, it would be unacceptable to the judiciary, not to mention the public. The juror would be dismissed with a reprimand and a mistrial declared. But when the respected and much-imitated California Commission on Judicial Performance became petulant and released a petulant statement, nothing happened. Except for one thing: the Supreme Court remained a punching bag. Those who wanted to believe there had been wrongdoing would continue to say there had been wrongdoing.

It was as though the Commission had been playing a long, complex chess game, keeping track of masses of evidence, thinking carefully, and then coming to conclusions about that evidence. But then, before the chess game ended, the Commission switched games and started to play—well, patty-cake, to use H. L. Richardson's expression. Like pouting children, they said, in effect, "If you—Mosk and Newman—won't be nice to us, we won't be nice to you. We won't tell any of you what our real conclusions were. We'll let you keep spinning in the wind. And we'll tell everybody it's your fault, Mosk, because of your lawsuit, and not the fault of our petulance."

Others were not playing patty-cake. Interestingly, one of the first to step forward after the Commission announced its conclusion was William Clark, the only witness who stood as an accuser during the investigation. A week after the Commission announced its results, Clark said in a press-covered speech at the Rotary Club in San Luis Obispo that it was "obvious that the recent investigation of the high court was inconclusive and that confidence in the court had not been restored."

It was Clark's second major speech criticizing the court. His first speech also had an interesting timing. He gave it less than a month after the 1978 election-day press accusations about Tobriner. That Clark speech was a broadside on the court, a highly unusual thing for a justice to do publicly about his own court. In a speech then before the Rotary Club of San Diego, he called on the public to be wary of "excesses" of courts in general, and particularly of the California Supreme Court. He warned that his court was irresponsibly carving out a separate set of standards in the law that is more protective of citizens and criminal defendants and more restrictive of police and prosecutors than the standards imposed by the U.S. Supreme Court.

In his speech the week after the Commission's report in November 1979, Clark made a curious statement. "Some, including at least one member of our court [whom he did not identify] would attribute our difficulties to a combination of press distortion and the attempts on the part of one or more groups to 'politicize' our courts." It was the comment about the press that was odd. He expanded on it as follows: "In the years that I've been on the court I have seen nothing that I could define as press distortion on the court's activities or opinions."

His comment was curious because one of the clearest villains in this case was the press.

CHAPTER 12

The Los Angeles Times—
Technically and Morally Wrong

The *Los Angeles Times,* the state's most powerful newspaper in the state's most populous city, has had a checkered career. For decades it was the voice of conservative Republicans. No California Republican could hope for success in the state or the nation without the *Times'* blessing. Its national reputation had been poor, nothing more than a mouthpiece for the friends and politics of its owning family, the Chandlers. But in the 1960's it began a major change. To the old *Times'* warriors-for-the-right were added cadres of bright young journalists who transformed the reputation of the paper from one of the country's ten worst (a list it used to make with fair regularity) to one of the country's ten best. The new reputation enhanced its power and it became the bellwether for important news in the entire state, indeed, in the entire West. There was, apparently, a remnant of the "the old *Times*" still surviving in 1978 in "the new *Times.*"

The basic building block, the foundation, of all that happened in the investigation of the California Supreme Court is the *Los Angeles Times* election-day story. Without that story there would have been no ruining of reputations, no investigation that went nowhere, no debacle by the Commission on Judicial Performance, no endless ammunition for those who want to convince the public that the court should remain in perpetual disgrace.

Although others had pushed the story of a delayed *Tanner* decision earlier, it was only the *Times* election-day story that mattered. It claimed to have high-court sources saying what only partisan politicians had been publicly gossiping about before. When pressed by reporters for what they knew, these politicians never came up with anything but suspicions. Now, after the election-day coup by the *Times,* all other stories written on the subject—and there would be hundreds—would flow from this one story.

On the first day of the investigation, Special Counsel Hufstedler began his long opening statement by saying, "Thank you, Mr. Chairman, ladies and gentlemen of the commission. On election day last year, 7 November 1978, the following story appeared in the *Los Angeles Times.* The first paragraph read as follows: 'The California Supreme Court has decided to overturn a 1975 law that requires prison terms for persons who use a gun during a violent crime, but has not made the decision public, well-placed sources said today.'" That story was the reason why the Commission, at that moment, was starting this momentous investigation.

Early in Chief Justice Bird's testimony, she would say, "We are . . . here because a very powerful newspaper was told by so-called informed sources that the Supreme Court had overturned a use-a-gun-go-to-prison law and that it was sitting on Justice Tobriner's desk, ready to go and ready to be filed as of election day. That's basically why we are here. We have faceless and nameless, anonymous accusers."

The targets of anonymous stories often make that kind of response. But sometimes a newspaper has no choice—it must use anonymous sources. Most reporters and editors prefer not to use anonymous sources. A story is far stronger, seems more credible, particularly if it is a story that makes strong, critical charges, if it is backed up by named sources. Otherwise, the newspaper is in the position of saying to its readers: "You should trust us. We wouldn't be printing this unless we were thoroughly convinced that our sources told us the truth. We have done everything we can to verify it." That trust should be handled very carefully. It is a precious trust. The reputations not only of the people destroyed by the newspaper, but the reputations of the newspaper itself and of individual reporters rest on such trust. That is why a reporter must be especially tough with anonymous sources: Exactly what do they know? How do they know it? Who else knows it?

There was a lot of trust in the *Los Angeles Times.* It could use anonymous sources, as it did that election day, and be believed. Over the previous 15 years, it had become one of the largest and most respected newspapers in the country. It had a distinguished Washington bureau. The paper didn't do much investigative reporting. When it did, the reporting appeared to be backed up by solid digging that would withstand vigorous scrutiny. Perhaps that was why all of the other newspapers that did later stories on the accusations against the Supreme Court did little or no investigating themselves to see if the basic accusations in the *Times* story were true. All newspapers—including the *Washington Post* and the *New York Times*—took the *Times* story at face value and used it as their basic building block. Any investigative work that they did later assumed the truth of the original story. It was an impressive show of confidence. Unfortunately, it was misplaced. The basic building block was made of sand.

The *Times* story was so unsubstantiated that the only appropriate place for it to have been published was in the pages of those flashy supermarket tabloids that are read with a grain of salt. In a good journalism school, if the story had been submitted in a beginning reporting class, it would have been elaborately critiqued, given a D and the student told to start over. (Not an F because the spelling and punctuation were fine.)

As one *Los Angeles Times* editor who was present the night the story was edited, but who was not consulted about it, told me, "What we did that night makes what Janet Cooke did seem minor." The *Washington Post*'s Janet Cooke wrote fiction and said it was fact. She had to return a Pulitzer prize in 1981 when her sham was revealed. She brought shame to the *Washington Post* and probably brought a permanent end to her budding career in journalism. She did something unforgivable in journalism: she used fiction without saying so. But the problem she described, addiction of very young ghetto children, is real. The *Los Angeles Times* election-day story wove together the half-truths and false information of its sources, the ignorance of its reporters, and the bias of both sources and —apparently—writers. The end-product was the most sensational story ever written about the California Supreme Court, perhaps about any appellate court. The story set off an unprecedented series of events that put the State Supreme Court on trial and led to the profound manipulation of the public about one of its most important institutions. The episode disgraces American journalism, although there has been hardly any recognition of this fact.

A quick reading of the election-day story, which is what most stories get, suggests at least this: "There's something wrong. I'd better think twice about whether I'm going to vote for Bird today." A more careful reading suggests that it isn't your typical well-reported *Los Angeles Times* story. The target, Justice Tobriner, is described as being a "strong supporter" of Bird (unwritten but obvious clue to reader: therefore, it's likely he would delay this controversial decision for her benefit). But the high-court sources who make the accusation are not only anonymous, they are not described in any way: Are they friends or enemies of the target? Are they court staff members? Nor does the reader learn how the anonymous sources know their information: Is it documented? Did they overhear a conversation? Do they have direct or indirect knowledge of the planned delay? Such information is crucial when serious accusations are being made, particularly when they are being made by anonymous sources. Without such information the readers could judge the veracity of this story only on the basis of whether they trust the *Times*. Readers should never be asked to judge a story on that basis alone.

Like perhaps most readers, I was a casual rather than a careful reader on election day 1978. I read the *Times* story in the *San Francisco Chronicle*. I was just your average puzzled citizen. I had no journalistic involvement with the case until September 1979. The investigation was just about over when one evening I heard San Francisco lawyer-journalist William Turner ask someone at a party, "What do you think of a reporter asking a source, 'Will you throw your coffee cup against the wall in the morning if you read this story in the paper?'" I laughed, imagining the question to be part of a joke the reporter must have had with the source in the middle of an interview. But Turner said the question had apparently been considered important when the *Times* was gathering information the day before the election. I was amused but skeptical that such a question could have been a serious confirming technique.

A short time later, I was called by an editor at *Columbia Journalism Review* and asked if I would be interested in doing a story examining the press coverage of the hearings. I remembered Turner's question and said I was interested. I started at the beginning instead of at the hearings. I read more than a hundred stories that had been written about the accusations, beginning before the election and going through the investigation. I interviewed nearly all of the reporters who had covered the Supreme Court in recent years. I read all portions of the transcript of the hearing that pertained to justices' contacts with the press. Later I would read the entire transcript, public and secret portions.

I started out with a bias. Despite the fact that the investigation had seemed to move nowhere, I believed there probably was wrongdoing, that a decision had been purposely delayed. That forceful statement by Clark, about what Mosk had told him, seemed very important. I thought the secret hearings would unravel who did what. In brief, until I started my research, I assumed the *Los Angeles Times* election-day story was correct. Reluctantly, I started having doubts as soon as I became a careful reader/researcher. After most of my paper research was completed, I talked with the reporters who researched and wrote the election-day story and with one of their editors. By the time I was done talking to them I was shocked.

Columbia Journalism Review was enthusiastic about the story but a space problem prompted an inexperienced editor to shorten by removing most of the documentation and leaving only my accusations against the *Times*. I said this was irresponsible and would make me guilty of the same shoddy journalism as the *Times*. I withdrew the article and it was published in *New West* magazine in November 1979.

Shortly after I started my research I attended a San Francisco meeting of Sigma Delta Chi, the honorary journalism fraternity, where a panel of reporters discussed the then ongoing investigation of the court. The opening speaker was Philip Hager, who had been sent from the *Times* Los Angeles office a month after the election-day story to cover the Supreme Court. Hager gave a chronology of events, beginning with the start of the campaign against the Chief Justice in the summer of 1978. When he got to election day, he summarized the *Times* story and then described it as containing "error" and "misunderstanding." I had begun to suspect that by then from my reading of the story and the ones that followed it. But here was confirmation from the *Times* reporter who now covered the court. When all the panelists were done, I asked Hager from the floor if he would be specific about what error and misunderstanding were in the original story. Hager flushed a deep pink and said he didn't mean to put it that way; he had meant to say that the reporters involved, Robert Fairbanks and William Endicott, simply could have done a better job if more information had been available to them.

Hager's initial comment was correct, I would learn as my research continued. The story contained error and misunderstanding. The story, was, in fact, *based* on error and misunderstanding. And that, it would become clear, was the result of inadequate reportorial techniques rather than the withholding of official information.

The story was written by Fairbanks, then chief of the *Times'* Sacramento bureau. He said a small amount of research for it was done by Endicott, then chief of the *Times'* San Francisco bureau. I interviewed both of them, as well as *Times* managing editor George Cotliar, in September 1979. Among the things I learned from the reporters were the following:

• The *Times* never had anything stronger than speculation by its sources that Tobriner had delayed the *Tanner* decision. None of the sources, said Fairbanks, provided any evidence or knowledge—direct or indirect—that they knew the *Tanner* decision was purposely delayed for political or any other reasons.

• The *Times* reporters did not understand at the time the story was written that the *Tanner* case had not been "decided," or completed, as the story said it had been.

• The reporters never asked the questions about court processes that would have led them to understand what probably was happening to

Tanner—that it was winding through the court's complex pipeline, along with 16 other cases that had been in the line even longer than *Tanner.*

• Fairbanks told me he thought the alleged delay of the *Tanner* decision was an *unconscious* act by Justice Tobriner, that he was delaying it to help the election of Bird, but that Tobriner himself did not consciously know he was doing it.

Could this mountainous scandal possibly have been built on accusations of acts the reporter believed the accused did not consciously know about? If it was an unconscious act, it certainly was something he was not legally culpable of, not even personally culpable of. Our society has not yet decided it is proper—in law, journalism, or psychiatry—to slice someone's head open to learn what they can't tell us. Could this investigation possibly have been started by a story the basis of which was someone's speculation about the accused's unconscious will? Could the people of California possibly have been forced to pay more than a half-million dollars to pursue a "crime" not even the alleged doer could know about? Apparently so.

This revelation from Fairbanks came as we discussed why he had written in March 1979, in a long story entitled "Anatomy of a Duel," that "Tobriner declined to answer questions from the newspaper about the charge—both before and after the story appeared." Fairbanks had told me earlier in our exchange of an interview he had had with Tobriner after the election-day story in which Tobriner had answered questions and denied the accusations made in that story. I asked why he had written in March that Tobriner had declined to answer questions and why he had not described Tobriner's face-to-face denial to him. "Well, I must say I don't always understand my own mind, I really don't."

"What are you saying?" I asked.

"I'm saying that maybe he doesn't understand his own mind either," said Fairbanks.

Asked then if he meant that he thought the alleged delay of the case by Tobriner was an unconscious act by the justice, Fairbanks said, "Yes."

No wonder Hufstedler and his associates could find no smoking gun. According to the belief of the author of the story that led to the investigation, if there was a smoking gun it was inside Tobriner's head and even Tobriner didn't know it was there.

Fairbanks's meeting with Tobriner occurred just a few days after the original story appeared. He and Endicott went to the court and met with several of the justices. "Tobriner absolutely said he didn't do it," Fairbanks told me as he recounted the session. "I was in the court and Tobriner said, 'I want to tell you, I did not do it. I did not do it.'

What do you do when a guy is looking you in the eye and says that?" Fairbanks said to me. Then he answered his own question: "Well, I told him then that I believed him. And I did believe him. And I believe him now." Fairbanks would later write a letter to *New West,* after my article appeared, claiming that it was a "false charge" that "I held a personal conviction that he was telling the truth." Justice Tobriner confirmed, however, that Fairbanks had told him that day that he (Fairbanks) believed Tobriner was telling him the truth.

Several times in my interview with Fairbanks he repeated this important point: the *Times* never had a source who was doing anything but *speculating* about Tobriner delaying the decision. Nobody *knew* anything about delay.

Fairbanks would claim after my article appeared that *Tanner* was on Tobriner's desk on the day before the election and that that fact alone meant he was delaying the decision. That was, of course, no more proof that he was delaying it than it was proof that he was not delaying it. It said only that the case was on Tobriner's desk. Would Fairbanks have written that the 16 other cases that at that time had been circulating in the court longer than *Tanner* were being delayed by all the justices on whose desks they could have been found the day before the election?

The crucial accusing paragraph was:

"The sources said that announcement of the decision is being delayed by Associate Justice Mathew O. Tobriner, who has been one of Ms. Bird's strong supporters against a well-organized campaign to win voter disapproval of her appointment to the court." It was quite clear what the reader was to infer, not that the decision was merely, routinely, lying on Tobriner's desk, but that it was improperly being delayed there in order to protect Bird at the polls.

"We never really knew Tobriner was doing it," Fairbanks told me. He said none of the sources provided any evidence, such as documents, direct or indirect, or knowledge of conversations about a planned delay. Endicott spoke with more certainty about his conviction that Tobriner had delayed the decision. "I'm still certain of that, but it'll never be clear in a million years." Well, that's certainly true if the person accused of withholding it was doing so as an unconscious act. I asked Endicott what criteria he used that day to judge whether he had confirmation from a source or sources, and he said, "You just know when they mean to confirm. I was very sure of it." Fortunately, mental telepathy has never been generally accepted by journalists as a valid test of a source's confirmation.

Fairbanks would say later that the *Times* story didn't say whether Tobriner was improperly delaying the decision. He said readers could speculate about that, but the story didn't. His claim is not very convincing. The reader didn't need a bullhorn to know that the crucial paragraph about delay claimed sources had said Tobriner was doing something improper. As Fairbanks and Endicott and every reader of the story knew, the only reason the story was written—and placed on the front page—was because of the implication of wrongdoing by Tobriner. If the reporters had thought it proper for a decision to be delayed, there would have been no story.

Wrongdoing was suggested not only in the original story, but also in innumerable later stories that appeared in the *Times,* including ones written by Fairbanks. Some of those later stories clearly did not leave room for the reader to speculate. Here is a sample of crucial phrases from later *Times* stories.

23 November 1978: ". . . whether a decision invalidating the law was purposely held back by judicial allies of Chief Justice Rose Elizabeth Bird to help assure her confirmation by the voters . . ."

1 December 1978: ". . . a report that the court opinion was delayed in early November because it might have hurt Chief Justice Rose Bird's chances of confirmation at the polls."

22 December 1978: ". . . defense of Tobriner against claims that a decision overturning the law had been purposely delayed beyond the election to try to insure voter approval of Chief Justice Rose Bird."

23 December 1978: "The court's handling of the case . . . was surrounded by unprecedented charges and denials that the decision was being held beyond the November election to ensure voter approval of Chief Justice Rose Elizabeth Bird."

23 December 1978: "*The Times* reported November 7 that the court had voted to strike down the law and quoted court sources accusing Justice Mathew Tobriner, as author of the lead opinion, of withholding the filing of the decision to aid Ms. Bird, who was under attack from opponents as being soft on crime."

29 December 1978: "Sources within the court charged early last month that the *Tanner* decision was being withheld unethically for political purposes to help assure voter confirmation of Ms. Bird at the November 7 election."

17 January 1979: ". . . alleged improprieties by the Supreme Court. . . ."

19 January 1979: ". . . the decision was intentionally held up by Tobriner to help Ms. Bird."

9 February 1979: ". . . the justice was accused of delaying the ruling beyond the November election for political reasons."

6 March 1979: "Clark struck back after the appearance of an election-day story in the *Times* carrying charges from undisclosed sources to the effect that Ms. Bird's chief ally on the court, Associate Justice

Mathew O. Tobriner, deliberately had prevented a pre-election re-lease of the *Tanner* decision. . . . Its release would have done nothing but harm her chances at the polls." Thus Fairbanks himself, in his "Anatomy of a Duel" story, characterized what *he* had written in his election-day story.

Between election day and 6 March, *Times* news stories repeated the accusations at least twenty-one times, using stronger language as time passed. But the reporters told me that after election day they never had any additional evidence to bolster their original sources' claims that Tobriner was delaying the decision. All claims about delay of the *Tanner* decision derived from the same election-eve sources' specula-tion.

The two reporters had a profound lack of understanding about how the court works. This could have made them easy prey to people who wanted to manipulate them into thinking that a decision had been delayed. But such ignorance, of course, is never an excuse for a reporter. Reporters spend most of their time asking questions be-cause they need information they do not have.

Fairbanks was amazingly candid in my interview with him about his lack of knowledge about the court. "I never covered the Supreme Court and didn't know the names of all the justices. I was getting all this stuff about holding up decisions. Someone would give me this, someone else would give me a little more information. . . . That day I did not know about how the Supreme Court operates. That's one hundred percent correct." He said he didn't even know what the word "decided" meant when used about a court decision. That, de-spite the fact that the first sentence of his story began, "The California Supreme Court has decided . . ."

"I didn't know when the vote is taken on a decision. I just thought that the vote was taken once and that was it. That if they voted last February [at the time of the 1978 hearing], that was it. . . . But I was sure there was a decision. . . . The word 'decision' has a formal mean-ing I didn't really understand at the time, so maybe it wasn't so good to say the court had 'decided.' I realize now that to say a case is 'decided' means that it's final; until it's filed with the clerk, at any point along the way it can change. I didn't understand that that night."

Understanding that that night would have been crucial to under-standing whether what the sources were saying made any sense. En-dicott said it would have been impossible the day the story was being written to learn how the court works, "because Rose Bird runs such a closed court."

Rose Bird, of course, is not the only person in the Supreme Court who knows the way decisions move through the court. Any number of people on the staff of the court, plus former justices and staff members, readily would have told Endicott or Fairbanks this unconfidential information if they had asked for it.

Fairbanks has said that "the details and definitions of court procedures, though certainly important, were not central to us in any case. We were using the word 'decided' in its dictionary sense, meaning that the verdict for all practical purposes had been reached." To write a story that says a court has decided a case and then claim later that you used the verb "decided" in its simple dictionary sense rather than in its legal sense is asking quite a bit of a general public that is perfectly familiar with the latter use of the term.

Two people did raise questions about the election-day story. In early January 1979, Peter Schrag, associate editor of the *Sacramento Bee,* commented in an editorial-page column, "Someday they're going to study the *Tanner* case in journalism schools as a classic example of how not to cover a story." Ed Salzman, editor of the *California Journal,* wrote in February 1979 that if a 22 December article by Fairbanks and Hager was true then "The *Times* owes its readers nothing less than a full explanation. It also owes Bird and Tobriner a formal retraction and apology." The *Times* routinely runs retractions of errors made in news stories. For this story it has never run a retraction or an apology. Nor has its media critic, David Shaw, ever conducted an investigation of the *Times'* election-day story. He has done fine analyses of the quality of restaurant criticism by newspapers, for which he traveled throughout the United States, and of the *Times'* coverage—or lack of coverage—of the unprovoked shooting by Los Angeles police of Eulia Love. When I asked him if he had considered examining the election-day story and its aftermath, Shaw said he had not and he thought any story by him on this subject would be regarded as self-serving on behalf of the *Times.*

The 22 December *Times* story that caused both Schrag and Salzman to think the *Times* was admitting that its election-day story was not correct began as follows: "The fact that four justices wrote four separate opinions in a controversial gun-law case is what prevented the California Supreme Court from issuing a decision before the November election, court sources said Thursday." The story also said, in the third paragraph, "A series of dates tracing the court's handling of the case was cited by these sources in defense of Tobriner against claims that a decision overturning the law had been purposely delayed beyond the election to try to insure voter approval of Chief Justice Rose Elizabeth Bird on the November 7 ballot."

I asked Fairbanks and Endicott if that 22 December story was an attempt to put the election-day toothpaste back in the tube. They denied it. Fairbanks said the story was simply adding information, not diminishing the credibility of the original story. His first comment to me about it was one of frustration. "That story caused me a lot of problems. . . . AP [Associated Press] even put out a story saying we backed off. We didn't. . . . That story was written by a committee. Hager wrote the first part. He wrote the lead. Bill Stahl on the desk [in Los Angeles] changed it. And I approved it without really hearing it when he called to read it back to me. I was really bothered by it. Late that night I called the desk and asked them to change the lead, but they said it was too late."

I asked Fairbanks what had bothered him so much about that story. He replied, "You had to read too far down to realize we were quoting supporters of Tobriner." It was an amazing statement for this reporter to make. In this story official court records, not mere speculation, were being quoted, and Fairbanks was upset that the story didn't immediately, rather than later, notify the readers that the sources who provided the official records were supporters of Tobriner and, therefore, potentially biased. But in his election-day story Fairbanks had not given the reader one hint as to whether the sources making the crucial charge about Tobriner were supporters or enemies of Tobriner or of Bird, the person who was supposed to have profited from the alleged wrongdoing of Tobriner. That those sources were not named was, of course, appropriate. Confidential sources must be protected. But in nameless-source stories, particularly stories like the election-day story, that contain no documentation, labels help the reader evaluate the sources for bias or possible political motive. On election day such qualifiers are especially important, given the possible impact on the electorate.

When I confronted Fairbanks with the fact that he had not seemed to be concerned about this in his election-day story, he acknowledged that his sources then were "opponents" of Bird. But he said he didn't label them as such because he didn't know enough about them the night he wrote the story to label them as opponents or supporters.

"You knew something about Stanley Mosk, didn't you?" I asked Fairbanks, who had acknowledged that Mosk was a source. "Yes, I knew he was no friend of Rose Bird," he admitted. That he would consider saying he didn't know how to describe these sources, including Mosk, was not credible. Just four days before the election, the *Times*—in a story written by Fairbanks—reported that Mosk had refused to accept the Appellate Judge of the Year Award from the California Trial Lawyers Association because the group had endorsed Bird's election. Fairbanks had also reported earlier that Mosk "was known to have been dismayed" by Brown's appointment of Bird.

Assuming that Justice Clark didn't lie under oath and that Senator

H. L. Richardson didn't lie to me, Fairbanks also knew as he wrote the story that it was Senator Richardson, the head of the Law and Order Campaign Committee, the chief campaign against Bird's election, who that very day had paved the way for him to talk with Clark.

Richardson told me he was trying to help Fairbanks that Monday when he called Clark. Early in the day, the justice testified, he received a phone call from Richardson. The Senator, said Clark, then asked him to talk to the press and specifically "referred to either the *Los Angeles Times* or to Mr. Fairbanks by name."

Clark testified that he received his first call from Fairbanks soon after Richardson called to introduce the reporter. Fairbanks, he testified, asked whether the *Tanner* case was decided and not filed—not about whether it was being withheld improperly. According to Clark's testimony, he skated around the reporter's questions, not giving explicit responses.

In a second phone call from Fairbanks, Clark said the reporter told him that the *Times* had talked with Mosk and that Mosk had said they had either "interesting" or "good" sources.

Apparently frustrated by his failure to get direct denial or confirmation from Clark, Fairbanks, according to the justice, said, "Well, let me ask you another question. If in the morning you should read the story that I have described to you, will you throw your coffee cup against the wall?"

Clark testified that he thought his response to the question was a chuckle, "not a yes or no." Fairbanks would not tell me whether he regarded the justice's response—or nonresponse—as confirmation of his story. Clark's later testimony indicated the reporter, months later, told him he had relied on the coffee-cup exchange as confirmation.

It was during a third phone conversation on the same day, Clark testified, that he realized Fairbanks considered him a source. Clark testified: "I received a phone call from him, I believe, just as I was leaving my apartment to go back to the court. . . . If I recall, he said, 'We have filed the story and I want to tell you what we have said about two justices on the court.' . . . He read something that I later recognized in the article."

Hufstedler placed on the screen in the auditorium a blowup of this paragraph from the story: "However, two other justices confirmed that the individual decisions were signed some time ago by all members of the court. The justices could not explain why the outcome had not been announced." "Is that the part he read to you?" asked Hufstedler.

CLARK: Yes. I am not sure that he read both sentences, but read, certainly, the first sentence about the two justices confirming that individual decisions were—I am reading it from your board—signed sometime ago by all members of the court.

HUFSTEDLER: Did he ask you to confirm that statement?

CLARK: No, I don't think he did. He asked—he invited my comment on it. He may have asked if this should be expanded, or would I add to it. But I did not.

HUFSTEDLER: Did he say that you were one of the persons he was relying upon for confirmation of that statement?

CLARK: He may have said something to that effect because that was the impression I was getting, or had gotten, I realized both in the course of the conversation and later talking about it.

HUFSTEDLER: Well, did you say to him, "Now, wait a minute. Don't put me in that category, I am not one of those people"?

CLARK: No. I felt that anything I would say in that regard I'd be reading.

HUFSTEDLER: That is, that you'd see it in the newspaper the next day?

CLARK: Yes.

HUFSTEDLER: Let me ask you specifically if you said three things. Did you say, one, "I will not confirm it"?

CLARK: No, I did not say that.

HUFSTEDLER: Or did you say, "I will confirm it"?

CLARK: No.

HUFSTEDLER: Or did you say, "I have no comment on whether or not I will confirm it"?

CLARK: As I say, my recall is that I can't recall any utterance, and certainly the ones you suggest don't trigger my—any recall.

HUFSTEDLER: All right. What was your mental response?

CLARK: Well, that he was relying perhaps on a coffee cup and whatever else he may have acquired from some other justice to write what he apparently had already filed or was in the process of filing.

HUFSTEDLER: Did you have any intention of being one of the persons who confirmed that statement to him?

CLARK: No.

HUFSTEDLER: On the other hand, did it occur to you as you listened to him that you might well be one of the two justices he was referring to when he said two justices had confirmed that?

CLARK: Yes, I did.

HUFSTEDLER: Did you say anything at all to disabuse him of that possible idea?

CLARK: No, I believe not.

HUFSTEDLER: Justice Clark, we were discussing your three telephone conversations with Mr. Fairbanks on the day preceding the election. You told us that in the course of that third conversation that you thought it likely that Mr. Fairbanks was considering you as one of the confirmers for the story. Did you—why was it that you did not think it advisable under those circumstances to straighten him out then and there that you weren't confirming that story?

CLARK: I felt that to that point it wasn't Clark confirming the story, but rather, I believe, Mr. Fairbanks who was confirming the story by further discussion. In answer to your question, it didn't cross my mind then, but it did later that had I gone into the facts of *Tanner* at that point that it might have been resolved had I, shall we say, gone all the way to point out the—at least the fact that there were four opinions on which, yes, there were seven signatures for a three–three tie and one vote going off on its own.

This did cross my mind that it might have been a story, *but it would not have come out in the light that it did* [my italics]. But this did not occur in the discussion with him. [This seemed to be a tacit admission by Clark that he hoped the story would come out in the light Fairbanks had indicated to him rather than in an honest light.]

HUFSTEDLER: Well, you would not have thought it appropriate to give him any information about the *Tanner* case, I gather?

CLARK: That is correct.

HUFSTEDLER: Well, but you could have said to him, "Just a minute, Mr. Fairbanks. Whatever you do, don't put me down as confirming the story," without giving him any information, couldn't you?

CLARK: Well, of course, what he had read, he wasn't putting me down as a confirmer of the story.

HUFSTEDLER: Well, I thought you told me you suspected that he was using you as one of the two justices who confirmed that individual decisions were signed sometime ago by all members of the court.

CLARK: By reference to me, I mean not by name. [It is frightening to see a justice of the Supreme Court play with the truth so adroitly.]

HUFSTEDLER: No, that's right but you did have the impression that he was viewing you, William Clark, as one of the justices of the court who to him confirmed it?

CLARK: Yes, that was my impression. He was reading back to me what he had written and I felt he was doing so for reaction. But as I recall, I don't think I reacted. In a later conversation with him concerning that, I had somewhat the same feeling.

HUFSTEDLER: Well, I gather that you thought you weren't reacting in a way that would confirm the story to him in your own mind? That was your view, was it not?

CLARK: Yes.

HUFSTEDLER: But at the same time, I think you have told us that it crossed your mind that he might have taken your reaction as a confirmation?

CLARK: Yes. At the end of the conversation I felt that with the coffee cup—I think he repeated the coffee cup, if I am not mistaken. And I don't know in what context in this conversation. As I say, it was very brief.

HUFSTEDLER: Recognizing that you, as you have told us, didn't intend to confirm his story, and recognizing that the thought crossed your mind that he might be taking you as a confirmer of this story, and recognizing that you didn't want to tell him the facts, I still have a little difficulty understanding why it was that you couldn't say to him, "Wait a minute. I am not confirming your story." Why didn't you say that?

CLARK: Well, I think that I had pretty well said that before. It was clear to him, additionally. The story was in. I felt any further discussion would be part of the story. . . . I thought about our conversation and from what he later described to me both in the last conversation that night and a subsequent conversation with him while he was at the court, *he took the coffee cup statement as, in his mind, not my confirming, but his confirming that sufficiently that he could say that two justices, whatever he [sic] up there* [my italics]. [What he wrote "up there" was that "*two justices confirmed* . . ."]

HUFSTEDLER: When you were talking with Mr. Fairbanks during the third conversation, when he told you in effect that he was going to run the story, *did it cross your mind at all that if the story was run it might have some effect upon the chief justice's re-election?* [my italics].

CLARK: I don't recall. *I think it probably did* [my italics], though.

There were hints and innuendos in Clark's testimony about what he said to Fairbanks the day before the election. But as *New York Times* columnist Anthony Lewis has written, "There was certainly nothing that in common English could be called a confirmation." If Clark's own description of his response to Fairbanks is accurate, he was a slippery, if not treacherous, source. H. L. Richardson had said of his campaign against Bird that he wasn't playing patty-cake. Clark wasn't playing patty-cake either—but he *was* playing games.

Clark testified that he could have violated the judicial canons and the strong tradition of not discussing pending cases and explained the whole matter to Fairbanks. "But," he added in an apparent admission that he wanted the story to come out as Fairbanks indicated it was going to come out, "it would not have come out in the light that it did." That's right, it would have been closer to the truth, presumably. Clark, however, could have spoken without violating the canons and tried to get Fairbanks off the track he was on. Clark could have refused to comment. Or he could have said, when he realized he was considered a source, "I am not confirming anything." By that time, after dealing with the press for more than a decade, he had become an expert. But, as he said, "it would not have come out in the light it did." Apparently he liked that false light and wanted to help spread it without having his name directly associated with it.

If Clark wanted the story to come out in the light it did, Fairbanks also desperately wanted Clark to be a source. But in view of Clark's testimony about a conversation a few months later between the two of them, Fairbanks apparently wondered himself if on election eve his "confirmation" from Clark wasn't slippery at best.

Clark said that months afterward, in February or very early March 1979, Fairbanks dropped into his chambers without an appointment and said he wanted to talk with him about a long story he was working on about the entire *Tanner* controversy. "He said one facet that he was considering writing was the coffee cup incident and the confirmation. He handed me a story and he said . . . 'Look at this for accuracy.'"

HUFSTEDLER: Was the essence of it that he had used the coffee cup ploy and that you had responded in a way that he treated as a confirmation?

CLARK: Yes.

HUFSTEDLER: Do you remember with any more particularity what he said about the coffee cup episode in that article?

CLARK: No, except that he relied on the coffee cup as confirmation for his reference to the two judges.

HUFSTEDLER: What further was said?

CLARK: I said, "The portion that you have alluded to in the third conversation with me is not accurate, Mr. Fairbanks."

HUFSTEDLER: All right. What more was said? Did you tell him why it wasn't accurate?

CLARK: No. He responded to the effect, "I think you are right," or "I guess so." . . . As I can recall, I came to the portion of his story, or what he had handed me, which referred to the third conversation. And as I recall, it said, "Clark confirmed that cases had been signed . . ."

HUFSTEDLER: All right. And as I understand it, you told him that was incorrect, that you had not confirmed that?

CLARK: Yes.

HUFSTEDLER: Do you remember whether you had any further conversation with him on that occasion?

CLARK: Only that he said, "I guess you're right, and I probably won't use it." He left the statement on my desk.

The story that Fairbanks left on Clark's desk was the "Anatomy of a Duel" story that appeared in the *Times* on 6 March. When the story was printed it did not say Fairbanks had relied on the coffee-cup incident, nor was the incident even mentioned. Nor did it say that Clark had made it clear to the reporter in March that his November comment that was regarded by the reporter in November as confirmation was not confirmation. The readers, of course, deserved to know that, late as it was. They were never given that information by the *Times*.

In Fairbanks's March story, the "duel" is between Clark and Bird. Fairbanks gave a pre-publication copy of the story to one combatant, Clark, but not to the other, Bird. The story Fairbanks left behind with Clark prompted an unusual attack from Clark during the Commission's hearings. Near the end of his testimony Clark angrily announced that he suspected Chief Justice Bird's attorneys or staff of stealing the Fairbanks draft story from his private files. It was an astounding accusation. Clark publicly demanded that her staff be examined to determine if they had stolen the document. As might be expected, his accusation and demand stimulated dramatic news accounts. "Clark Implies Pilfering of Files in Court Inquiry," was the *Times* headline the next day. One of Bird's attorneys, Harry Delizonna, told the Commission that the Chief Justice, her staff, and her attorneys "know about as much concerning whether that document ever existed . . . or whether . . . it in fact disappeared as we do about the eighteen-minute gap in the Nixon tapes."

Clark simply made the bald assertion. He didn't explain why he thought her attorneys or staff members had taken it. He said he had not seen the story since the day Fairbanks left it on his desk. During a break in that day's hearing, when asked specifically if he suspected that someone associated with Bird had taken the Fairbanks memo, Clark told another *Times* reporter, "No, I have no suspicions in the matter. I would like to determine its whereabouts."

Clark had no suspicions? He had just publicly accused the Chief Justice of having a thief on her staff and asked for an investigation of her staff and her attorneys. And a few minutes later, when pressed, admitted offstage to a reporter that he had no reason to suspect anyone, let alone the Chief's staff. But the damage had been done. Other reporters did not press him and already were rushing to phones to report Clark's latest accusation. It is news when a Supreme Court justice accuses another justice of having someone in her employ who steals papers from a colleague's office.

It was unclear why Clark was so enraged by the fact that the story seemed to be missing from his files. He may have made the charge because he felt he could once again easily arouse sensational sentiment against the Chief Justice without his own deviousness being revealed. If so, he was fairly successful, for he escaped criticism for his trick. Surely his outrage was not intended as a defense of Fairbanks, the author of the allegedly missing stolen story. According to Clark, the story draft contained some claims that the reporter omitted at Clark's request. Given the great importance of at least one of them— that Clark denied in March that he ever confirmed the election-day story—Fairbanks would look at least foolish if that original draft became public. But before this outburst from Clark about thievery, Clark himself had already made that embarrassing information public. He had also demonstrated in his testimony that he and Fairbanks each apparently willingly let the other use chicanery on the eve of election day in order to make sure the story would appear as it did: as an accusation of wrongdoing. According to Clark's testimony, and according to my interview with Fairbanks, each of them knew that the scaffolding on which the confirmation of the election-day story was built had no grounding. Most important, each of them was willing to deceive the public about members of this important public institution. Now, Clark was willing to use the same reckless, headline-grabbing irresponsibility, even in the glaring spotlight of the public hearing.

There were some other unfair elements in the *Times* election-day story. The story referred to Attorney General Younger's earlier accusation that the court was delaying decisions. But the story did not refer to the fact that Younger had retracted his charges. And, though the reporters did not bother to learn the basic information that would have helped them understand whether the decision was being delayed—and, therefore, whether there even was a story—they did spend time learning how law enforcement would react to the accusations in the story. An assistant attorney general was quoted as saying that law-enforcement officials throughout the state would "rise up in anger at the decision. This is really an important law, more than the death penalty. This is really working; people are going to prison. The death penalty is just sitting around."

Fairbanks cautioned me to remember that "this wasn't a new story when we reported it." He noted that both H. L. Richardson and Evelle Younger had made the same charges. That was, of course, irrelevant because Younger had retracted his charges and Richardson, as he himself told me, never had any information about delay. He told me the basis of his claims was completely subjective, "based on how Bird and Tobriner acted in the past. I never had any specific knowledge. I made a projection on her past behavior. I knew she was against the death penalty and that she'd probably be against *Tanner*. I made a projection. I wanted the press to pursue it."

Fairbanks had lunch with commissioner Willoughby just a couple of weeks before the Commission's investigation began in the summer of 1979. "It's my personal conclusion," Willoughby told me, "that a lot of this happened because of a lot of carelessness and a lot of mistakes . . .

back to the beginning. I happen to know Bob Fairbanks because he's worked around the capital here. . . . I was talking to him about this and about the story he wrote. . . . He said to me, 'People are making too much out of that story.' . . . He was somewhat defensive about the story, but he said that the story was the same story that was kicking around for some time. He said all Fairbanks and Endicott did was to kind of piece it together and make some phone calls to some judges. . . . He also told me he had no idea of the box and the movement of the box. . . . He stressed that this wouldn't have made him change the basic thrust of the story, but it might have made him rewrite it slightly to indicate . . . why all the signatures weren't in place. I think that's a tremendous detail to overlook."

I asked Fairbanks if he tried to find out the day before the election if *Tanner* was being treated differently than the other cases that had been before the court as long or longer. Fairbanks said he didn't learn that there were 16 such cases until Hager mentioned them in a December story. But a reporter could not understand a statement that a decision was being delayed unless he or she learned the context of the accusation "delay." It was necessary to ask: How long do decisions usually take to reach completion? Has this one been in the pipeline longer than any other? How does its time compare to others'? How many others have been there longer? If any, how many and how long have they been there? By means of such questions a reporter can begin to establish the veracity of a source's undocumented charges. The reporter, in essence, is trying carefully to establish whether a decision is being delayed, or whether the source is trying to trick the reporter. Such information was not asked for when the election-day story was being prepared. In the meantime, some silly assertions would be made without a context, such as this comment in a *San Francisco Chronicle* editorial: "This case was argued in the Supreme Court last February and should have come down months ago. The question to be answered is, what has happened to it?" The question normally wouldn't be asked, for many cases routinely take longer than *Tanner* had taken by election day.

But Fairbanks told me knowing other cases had been there longer than *Tanner* would have been irrelevant the night he wrote the story. I asked why. "There's a distinction with *Tanner*," he said. "That was not an obscure statute. When [Governor] Brown signed the law, it was a big deal. He praised it. Maybe the average citizen doesn't know it, but the people up here in Sacramento generated a million dollars of free publicity to advertise that law, the 'use a gun, go to prison' ads. It was important; you couldn't judge how they treated it alongside how they treated other cases. . . . None of the other cases had the emotional impact that *Tanner* had," said the reporter who also said he didn't know anything about any of the other cases pending before the court the day he wrote the story in question.

In deciding *Tanner,* the court should have had in mind, he said, the fact that "if you asked the voters of California today if we should hang, draw, and quarter criminals, they might approve that. People are definitely law and order today. She [Bird] wasn't. If she was trying to keep her record from them, that's serious. The voters needed Bird's record."

A year later, it was clear that Fairbanks still did not understand a great deal about how the court worked. Not only did he not understand the internal movement of opinions. He also did not understand that the court must not be concerned with an ad campaign organized on behalf of a law. He also seemed oblivious of the fact that Bird had already been associated with a number of controversial criminal cases released shortly before the election—the *Caudillo* case, for example. There was much evidence that she was not trying to hide her record.

There also was evidence that Bird was trying to expedite *Tanner* rather than trying to delay it. Court records show that, beginning in early June and continuing on almost a weekly basis until 13 December, every "prompter memorandum" written to the justices by the Chief Justice urging that they expedite the completion of particular decisions included the *Tanner* case. Pay no attention to those memorandums, Fairbanks told me. They could, he claimed, be viewed as evidence that Bird was sitting on the case rather than expediting it. How so? "It's like me telling my son to stop chewing with his mouth open," said Fairbanks. "It's a family joke by now. He keeps chewing with his mouth open, and I keep telling him not to do it. I don't really believe he's going to stop. Maybe it was like that with her. She says, 'Oh, there's *Tanner* again.' But the effect is the same as with my son: Nothing happens and I don't really do anything about it."

"My guess," Fairbanks told me, "is that the day before the election was too late."

"For what?" I asked.

"To defeat Rose Bird," said Fairbanks.

If the *Times* story had come out "just one day earlier, Rose Bird would not be Chief Justice today," Richardson told me. Actually, the timing was perfect. Hitting voters with it election-day morning was probably much more effective than an earlier story would have been. If it had appeared a day earlier, Bird would have released her statement denying delay and defending Tobriner before election day. And voters would have had both sides to ponder.

George Cotliar, managing editor of the *Times,* told me it was highly unusual for the newspaper to publish a story with anonymous-source accusations on or near election day. He said the paper had had to make a decision about such a story the day before election day "any number of times. Usually we've not run such stories because the source is not willing to put their name to it, and we've not been willing to get in that bind. There are very few times when you'd run a story like this . . . Election day is the worst possible day to run a political story of this nature. The magnitude is such that it truly could have decided the election. But this was a totally different case, of course." I asked him how it was different. "This was a different case in that this was not a case of a candidate making a charge against his opponent. There was no one who would gain from the defeat of Rose Bird. Besides, these sources were two justices." It is difficult to understand why there were two campaigns being run against Rose Bird if nobody had anything to gain from her defeat.

"Often people come to us and say the other candidate is corrupt," said Cotliar. "But our feeling is that you don't print that at the last second unless the other person is willing to have their name used. But this was a totally different case. The only similarity is that we did wonder a great deal about why they were telling us what they were telling us when they were telling us. But we had two reporters, in San Francisco and Sacramento, working on this. We had two men of the court. We kept going back and verifying. We were satisfied that we had it. . . . When we talked to two Supreme Court justices and got it solid, I decided that we'd print the story. . . . We felt this was as solid as you could have a story."

Cotliar's strong defense of the story seemed almost pathetic in view of the fact that the "confirming" part of the story, the part he seemed to be so sure of, did not confirm the basic accusation in the story: that the *Tanner* decision was being delayed. The "confirming" paragraph simply said two justices confirmed, first, that individual decisions were signed some time ago and, second, that the confirming justices could not explain why the outcome had not been announced.

Fairbanks said he had "several" accusing sources, presumably others besides justices, who, presumably, fell under his rubric "high court sources" in the first paragraph. They, rather than Mosk or Clark, are the sources who really matter, for they made the damning accusation against Tobriner. But it was the unrelated "confirmation" from justices that gave the story credibility with the *Times* editors. I asked Cotliar if it was important to him as an editor whether the source or sources' assertions of delay were based on speculation or actual knowledge. "Very much so," he replied. "If it was speculation we never would've printed the story." All sources, according to Fairbanks in his interview with me, were merely speculating about the delay in *Tanner.* (Fairbanks left the *Times* in late 1982 and became editor of *California Journal,* a political news and commentary magazine.)

Apparently there was a massive breakdown in communication between the *Times'* Sacramento and Los Angeles offices that night. Not only were elementary rules of reporting violated, but when the story reached Los Angeles there were also serious lapses in editorial judgment. A newspaper should be courageous, never afraid to take on the most powerful or prestigious institutions and individuals. But it should also be honest and thorough and not base its stories on prejudiced sources' hunches. This is true whether the target of the story is an unknown person or a respected public official or a major public institution. Whatever language Fairbanks used when he originally transmitted the story, it passed through the hands of at least five editors who made judgments about it before they finally approved it. Any editor who saw the story in its final form had to realize that the apples in the first paragraph were not confirmed by the oranges in the confirming "two justices" paragraph. Yet, Cotliar, the managing editor, refers to the two justices as providing "solid" information. If they did, the *Times* never told its readers about that information, and the two justices, Clark and Mosk, lied when they testified.

The best that can be said is that the *Times'* normally highly professional decision-making process fell into disarray that night. But the results of the story were so serious that a number of sensitive ethical questions naturally come to mind. Given the number of editors at the *Times* involved in passing pre-publication judgment on this story, did high level officials at the *Times* want to publish a misleading story on election day when, as Cotliar said, "the magnitude is such that it truly could have decided the election"? Even if reporters do have clear political intent—and it is not known if that was the case here, although Fairbanks's prejudicial comments raise the question—editors are supposed to spot such prejudices and take extra precautions to make sure stories are solidly based on information rather than only on politically based speculation.

On election day most newspapers and broadcast stations in the state ran the *Times* story, or reported: "The *Los Angeles Times* said today . . ."

But the *San Francisco Examiner* claimed on election day to have its own confirmation of the story from justices: "Two members of the high court have confirmed to the *Examiner* that the decision was reached some time ago, but they could not explain why it has not been announced." But buried in the middle of a 25 November *Examiner* story on Bird calling for an investigation of the court, a sentence begins, "Unconfirmed news reports on election day said. . ." Justice

Clark had testified that early election-day morning the *Examiner*'s Kang had called to ask him if he was one of the two justices referred to in the *Times* story. He said he told her about the coffee-cup question and said he hoped he was not one of the two justices. He said Kang thanked him and hung up.

One of those *Examiner* stories had to be wrong. When I called Kang to ask which one, at first she said she would not talk because she was afraid of being subpoenaed to testify before the Commission. The hearings were over, but the Commission was still deliberating. Nevertheless, she talked a little. When I asked again about the contradiction in the two stories, she said, "It's a hectic business. You know the deadlines of the afternoon paper. You make mistakes." Given the fact that the first story was written on deadline for that day's paper and the other story was not written under the same pressure, the error was more likely in the first day's story, the one that would have affected voters. It was a significant error and, given the fact that the *Examiner* was aware of it, it was strange that it was not corrected until two weeks after the election, and then buried in a downplayed story. But the *Examiner*'s error, of course, was not nearly so grave as that made by the *Times*. I asked Kang if the mistake was made by someone on the desk at the *Examiner* rather than by her. She would not answer, but a source close to Kang later told me that the answer was yes.

After the election-day story appeared, many other stories would add additional details—principally more information about the still unreported opinions in the *Tanner* case. Naturally, reporters looked to see if any other wrongdoing could be found at the court. The *Times'* Endicott apparently thought he had found another purposeful delay—a delay in deciding the *Teron* death-penalty case. He wrote about it twice, once in early December 1978 and again in late January 1979.

Gregory John Teron Jr. had been tried and convicted for a grisly murder in Orange County. The trial was in May 1978. Endicott's first story on the case began, "The California Supreme Court apparently has missed a legally mandated deadline for deciding a death-penalty case on which it will hear oral arguments Tuesday. . . . If it had been decided within the deadline as spelled out in legislation that became law in August 1977, the result would have been filed—and thus made public—the first week in November." That law requires that in all death-penalty cases the Supreme Court must reach an opinion within 150 days after the trial record has been certified to the Supreme Court.

Endicott reported that Orange County officials said the case had been certified 5 June, which meant that the court ought to have completed the decisions before 5 November—two days before the election. Endicott pointed out in his first story that Attorney General

Younger had suggested in mid-October that the court was holding up a death-penalty decision because of its possible impact on the election. As in the election-day story, Endicott failed to point out that Younger withdrew that charge also the day after he made it. Even more significant, he failed to point out that the member of the Attorney General's staff responsible for death-penalty cases at the time, William James, had told reporters that Younger's charge was wrong and that *no* completed death-penalty cases had been sent to the Supreme Court by prosecutors, making Younger's accusation absurd.

Endicott quoted the Chief Deputy Clerk of the Supreme Court, J. L. Kavanaugh, as saying that the record in *Teron* was not complete when it was sent to the Supreme Court from Orange County on 5 June. What Endicott did not do was check the public (and available) record, which would have shown him that the record in the case was not complete and certified until 21 August. Consequently, the 150-day time limit would not expire until 21 January 1979, instead of 5 November. If Endicott had checked the official record, he would have realized that the claim that the court had missed a "legally mandated deadline," the basis of his story, was not true. As it was, coming a month after the election-day story, another story accusing the court of delay was easily believed. By then people naturally thought, "What has happened to the integrity of the Supreme Court?"

Actually, there was something else important about the *Teron* case, and Endicott missed it. Ted Millard, the deputy district attorney from Orange County who gave Endicott information about the case, told me that he and others pushed the *Teron* case through trial because "we wanted a death-penalty case announced before the election. It would've affected the election. If they had overruled the death penalty just before the election it would've really meant something. . . . It would've made a difference in the election. . . . My whole intention was to make them get this decision out on time."

But in its haste, apparently, the Orange County clerk of courts office didn't send the full record to the court. Millard, who successfully ran against an incumbent Superior Court judge in Orange County in the same election, said the *Teron* case record was completed by June and that any requests for additional portions of the record after that were "just gimmicks to stall it." But the official records show an exchange of correspondence in June, July, and August, with the Supreme Court clerk's office asking the Orange County clerk's office for documents that were missing from the record. Finally, on 21 August, the Supreme Court clerk's office received a letter from the Orange County clerk's office saying only then that the record is "now complete." The prosecutors were clever in selecting the *Teron* case to affect the election. The defendant had been permitted to represent himself at his trial. That alone would almost guarantee that the Supreme Court would reject the death sentence and the case would be an effective weapon by the prosecutors in the election.

Apart from the poor quality of the reporting about this alleged delay by the court, the incident raises another question. It was made quite clear to the public in innumerable stories that it would have been highly improper for a judge to have purposely delayed a decision in order to affect the outcome of the election. A judge, if found guilty of delaying a decision to affect the election, could have been removed from the bench. A prosecutor admitted to me that he speeded up a death penalty case for the purpose of affecting an election. Was that improper? The question was never even raised.

Several reporters I talked with said the *Times* had simply been braver than the rest of them. "Oh, yeah, we knew about this delay for weeks," one told me, echoing others about the delay of *Tanner*. This attitude more than anything else was probably responsible for the fact that all other reporters assigned to the story built their stream of stories on the *Times* story without doing their own investigating to test the truthfulness of the original accusations.

Justice Clark testified that, when the *Washington Post*'s Lou Cannon came to see him the week before Cannon's 23 November article, Cannon told him that the *Post* "considered it a big story, not necessarily from the court's standpoint but from the press standpoint. . . . He referred to . . . the working press as having been upset because they felt, as I recall, . . . the story had been around for some time but had not been published. He was referring to the *Tanner* story." I found that when each of the reporters who made this claim to me was asked what it was they knew but didn't publish, it was the same unconfirmed speculation of Younger and Richardson. Not one of them said they had anything stronger than that, and not one of them ever wrote that they had anything stronger than that.

Reporters who cover events in groups sometimes make the serious journalistic mistake of developing a gang mentality. Herd journalism, it's often called. They depend on each other. In doing so, they give up their independence. This has been examined in commentary on military news coverage and on coverage by the White House press corps. Such a mentality also developed at the California Supreme Court. Few news organizations assigned reporters to the Supreme Court to cover it systematically. They sent reporters each time there was a particularly newsworthy decision released. But most decisions were never read and never reported by the press. The only two reporters who paid particularly close attention to both the decisions and the administrative aspects of the court were Kang of the *Examiner* and

Carol Benfell, former editor of the newsletter of the California District Attorneys Association, and in 1978 a reporter for a legal paper, the *Los Angeles Daily Journal*. Other reporters, when sent to the court, tended to rely on the impressions of these two reporters. One problem with that was that though both of them were capable of being good reporters, early in Bird's administration they had developed a strong bias against her that showed in their stories. As the resident authorities in the court press room, they were able to influence other reporters who were less familiar with the court.

Some other reporters shared Kang and Benfell's anger that they could not reach Bird by phone. And that would be given as an excuse for one-sided stories. The fact that Bird herself did not take phone calls but instead had a knowledgeable aide return them—this, plus her having the locks on her door changed—were key factors in the early and persistent descriptions of her as "inaccessible." It was a strange expectation, that the Chief Justice should be available to the press. But good reporters do not simply turn against the source who doesn't personally take their calls; they develop other sources close to the wanted source. Kang and Benfell tended to develop only sources opposed to the Chief Justice. If they had tried to talk to people other than her opponents, for instance, the story about the locks being changed would have included the true reason. Instead, it was reported and then perpetually repeated, as it was during the hearings, as an example of Bird's being paranoid and inaccessible. Routine journalistic diligence would have produced accurate, factual stories about Bird. Instead of reporting that she changed the locks on her door because of being paranoid, for instance, such reporting would have revealed that she changed them because a Court of Appeal justice unlocked her door and entered her office late one Saturday evening and was surprised to find the Chief Justice at work. Had Kang learned and reported the truth about the locks, a story she wrote in *California Journal* entitled "The Locksmith Cometh" might have instead—and more accurately—been called "The Court of Appeal Judge Breaketh In."

Another thing that happens to reporters who cover stories in groups is that they gossip. That is natural enough. The real problem occurs when they start believing the gossip as though they had secured the information through reportorial questioning. For example, when I interviewed reporters who covered the court, several of them told me that part of their reason for believing the *Times* story that Tobriner had delayed the *Tanner* decision was something else they had heard: that Tobriner had gone to all major newspapers throughout the state and asked them to invite Rose Bird to meet with their editorial boards before the election in the fall of 1978. The implication was that this was a political act performed in the hope that they would editorially endorse her. They told this to me, a reporter, as though it was true information. I might reasonably have assumed that they knew this from talking to their own editorial departments. There would not have been anything wrong with Tobriner suggesting that editorial departments meet with the Chief. But by 1979 it would have been considered significant because, had he done so, it would have cast doubt on his testimony that he was not involved in the Chief Justice's campaign. I called the head of every editorial staff of every major newspaper in the state; I also called some newspapers that weren't so major. I asked if Justice Tobriner or anyone representing him had suggested that they invite Rose Bird to meet with them or that they endorse her. Each of them without exception took the question seriously. Those who had invited her traced through their staff members and others how they had happened to invite her. Those who had not invited her also took the question seriously and investigated whether it had been suggested they should invite her. In not one instance had Justice Tobriner or anyone close to him, according to these editors, initiated a suggestion that she be invited to meet with them. One editor did tell me that he realized reporters on his paper believed Tobriner had done that. "It's accepted wisdom, but it's not true," he said.

Several months later, in the spring of 1980, I talked with Preble Stolz, a law professor at Boalt Hall, the law school at the University of California, Berkeley. He told me the same story, offering it as proof of Tobriner's political activity in Bird's campaign. I told him what my research had shown. He said that too many reporters believed the story for it not to be true, and that he intended to report it in a book he was then writing on the investigation, *Judging Judges,* without checking its veracity with the editorial-page editors, those whom Tobriner was supposed to have approached.

Even by some observers in the legal community to whom it is quite clear that the *Times* had no basis for its original story, it is assumed that the *Times* nevertheless did the right thing in publishing the story. Professor Stolz, for instance, blames the entire scandal on faults of character and discipline among the Supreme Court justices and pronounces the press, particularly the *Times*, blameless.

Stolz has written that once the story was filed by Fairbanks, the *Times* editors "had no realistic alternative" but to print it on election day. "Endicott and Fairbanks were not the first reporters to get the lead," Stolz writes, "but they received from at least three justices, as apparently no one had before them, a nondenial of wrongdoing. *They interpreted the nondenial as confirmation* [my italics]. Once the story reached that point, the editors in Los Angeles had no realistic alterna-

tive but to print the story on election day. For the *Times* not to publish
the story would have been interpreted as a cover-up dictated by editorial policy. No newspaper of any pretension to public service could
engage in such behavior." Stolz then asks a basic question: "Should a
newspaper depend for important stories on the failure to deny as the
equivalent of an affirmation?" His answer to his own question is
shocking: "It would be quite wrong to fault the *Times* or Fairbanks for
failing to live up to that ideal since the current generally accepted
ethic of the press is clearly to the contrary."

Most newspaper editors would fire a reporter who confessed to
viewing failure to deny as confirmation. Journalism, like the law, is, of
course, an imperfect discipline. What was surprising to me in talking
with Stolz and some other persons close to the California investigation, was that they had such remarkably low standards for journalists.
Even more surprising was the fact that they approved of these low
standards.

Unfortunately, some reporters who were involved deeply in this
story as it developed have as shallow a view of journalistic standards
and responsibilities as Professor Stolz has. Benfell—the former editor
of the newsletter of the California District Attorneys Association, a
reporter for the *Los Angeles Daily Journal* on election day and during
the investigation, and later a reporter for the *Oakland Tribune*—wrote
in an article in the *American Bar Association Journal* after the investigation:

"Reporters were on the spot. The [election-day] story obviously
could have been a plant, politically contrived to unseat the chief justice. On the other hand, they [reporters] could not take responsibility
for killing a story unless there was an indisputable factual way to know
it was false. If it were true, the public had a right to know of double-
dealing in positions of highest trust, and the reporter's duty lay in
telling the story. *Unfortunately, there was no factual material available* [my
italics]. There was no one who would or could tell reporters then the
facts that emerged from the public hearings: that the high court has
its own unique interpretation of the word 'submitted' [a fact which is
irrelevant to the election-day story]; that a quarter of the cases before
the court take as long, or longer than *Tanner;* that justices frequently
sign an opinion weeks or months in advance of a final decision because that is procedural, not conclusive."

Reporters are on the spot in a case like this only if their fingers get
so sore they can't dial any more phone numbers. If that happens, they
should stop writing. There are 79 people on the staff of the Supreme
Court. Most of them could have, and many of them would have,
provided reporters with a basic description of how opinions work
their way through the court, along with the other information re-

porters needed the day before election day in order to weigh the speculative accusations sources had given them.

Contrary to Benfell's claim that a reporter cannot take responsibility for killing a story unless there is an indisputable factual way to know it's false, any reporter who feels that way is a gold mine for the dishonest source who wants to "get" his or her enemies. If her claim were true, such people could tell a reporter anything and expect a reporter to write a story about it unless it is proved indisputably false. A reporter's responsibility is, in fact, precisely the opposite: to be able to explain why it is true, or to write that a named source claims it is true, or establish the basis on which accusations are made whether sources are named or unnamed. Good reporters and editors kill stories every day that appear to have no basis in fact.

Invalid accusations often do get into the news media when uttered by sources who are inherently newsworthy, such as a governor or the President. Anything people in such positions say is newsworthy. But, even then, the reporter is obligated not simply to repeat their charges but to try to verify or dispute the charges alongside the accuser's comments. Even a prominent accuser should be pressed to explain the basis of his or her accusations. And if this prominent person refuses to provide evidence or describe what kind of basis supports his or her accusations, that refusal should be reported along with the accusations. The stories about Younger's accusations a month before the election demonstrate the importance of this standard journalistic practice. The day after he made his accusations that the court was delaying decisions, he admitted he had no basis for what he previously had said he was "certain of." His backing off was reported. But if reporters had pressed him for supporting evidence when he originally made the accusations, the first story might well have included both his damning accusations and the fact that, as he later acknowledged, he was merely raising questions and was not "certain" of his claims. Much of the American press discovered the catastrophic consequences of the failure to pursue the basis of accusations during the time of the late Senator Joseph McCarthy in the 1950's.

Journalism is not a game of Russian roulette, where sources can choose their target and expect a reporter to print or broadcast whatever they say, whether or not there is evidence of its veracity. Sometimes a reporter just can't get the story verified by the crucial time— say, election day. If so, it is the reporter's obligation to say, "The story's not ready. I don't know enough. There may not be any basis to it. I need more time." Such an admission, after diligent research and the promise of more research, is not shameful, nor is it, as Stolz suggested, a cover-up. It is simply the honest and professionally correct thing to do if the press is to have any credibility. Stolz and Benfell notwithstanding, no responsible journalist would claim that the press has a license to print any charge unless it is proven indisputably false. Most journalists would prefer that an accusation they are writing be as close as possible to being indisputably true. Journalists should be willing to cast doubt on individual reputations and institutions only when the evidence demands it.

The same *ABA Journal* article of Benfell's illustrates the importance of the very simple journalistic procedure of checking documents. She wrote that the Chief Justice issued a memorandum to all members of the court staff telling them they might be held on felony charges for releasing, as Benfell put it, "court processes to the press." That is simply not true. The document was and is available. It prohibits the release of confidential court documents, the same documents that are probably confidential in every appellate court in the country— opinions in process, memorandum related to opinions in process, and documents about activities of the justices' weekly confidential conferences. No one is, or ever has been, prohibited from describing general court processes of the California Supreme Court.

Reporters were told near election day 1979 that a justice "close to the Governor" was delaying a decision that was unfavorable to the Governor, Benfell wrote in the *ABA Journal* article. She said that because reporters had learned how the court operates from the public hearings, their skepticism in 1979 "fell on the teller of the tale, not the court." But she said that because reporters move on to other beats, new reporters will cover the court and, not knowing how the courts operate, may create "another *Tanner* type of story next year, and the next, and the next." This will be true only if future reporters are infected by the same striking lack of basic professional discipline and skill that caused the election-day scandal of 1978.

"Reporters saved the court from another *Tanner* this year," concluded Benfell. "It is time for the court to get a move on and protect itself." It is more accurate to say that these reporters saved themselves from another *Tanner* scandal. There is, of course, no protection from journalists who believe they must run a story unless it can be proven indisputably false. Instead of preaching to the court about protecting itself, journalists involved in this imbroglio should put their own house in order.

Reporting of events surrounding the investigation was generally poor. One got the impression that perhaps only Kang had read the California Rules of Court and the State Constitution's provisions pertaining to the Commission on Judicial Performance. Because reporters were unfamiliar with these basic documents, it was apparently impossible for most of them to understand themselves, let alone explain to their readers, the various events, such as the Judicial Council rule-making, that produced such a confused hearing and end result.

Interestingly, no newspaper assigned a reporter to take the entire transcript of the hearing and summarize and analyze it after the investigation was over. The *Times* and the *Examiner* are the only papers in the state that routinely assign reporters to stories that involve long preparation. The *Times* occasionally runs extensive, sometimes nearly book-length, reports. It would have been the most likely paper to make such an assignment. At some major papers, such assignments are routine at the end of a long trial. An editor will say, "Okay, now pull it all together and tell the reader what it amounted to." No one did that at the end of this major investigation, despite the fact that it was about one of the most important public institutions in the state and was an historic and complex event.

The secrecy of the last portion of the hearing was tantalizing not only in its implications for serious public policy but also journalistically. Accusations had been made in public and answers were made in private. The strange final report of the Commission kept the resolution as muddy as ever. It is surprising that reporters so eager for inside tidbits that in 1978 they printed unconfirmed gossip as news did not try to find the under-oath answers made in the closed hearing. Executive sessions are not new to journalists. They exist in Washington, in every state capital, and in most city councils. And a standard practice in political reporting is to attempt to get some idea of what transpired in secret when the event is of serious import to the public. In this case, the question was not superficial. Was the State Supreme Court worthy of the power invested in it? Numerous people were involved in the closed hearing. Yet no stories told what actually happened there. I discovered that it was not an impossible task. Thanks to more than one source, none of them members of the Supreme Court, I was able to read every word of the closed-hearing transcripts. There are many diligent and talented journalists in California, and I have no doubt that dozens of them could have done the same thing.

For some reason, a few journalists took a proprietary attitude toward the hearing, acted as though they ought to have some authority over what happened in the hearing. Perhaps this was because in many ways the hearing was the creature of news stories so fragile, if not fraudulent, that they needed a great deal of protection. This proprietary attitude reached an extreme point, one commissioner told me, when two reporters approached Commission Chairman Janes more than once and urged him to put Commissioner Jerry Pacht "in his place." Why? Because, the two women were heard telling Janes, Judge Pacht had asked witnesses a few questions that elicited positive information about the Chief Justice and Tobriner. They thought there was no place in this hearing for positive information about Bird and Tobriner. "Those women [the reporters] wanted to see Bird hung and quartered," said the commissioner who overheard their plea to Janes.

When *Los Angeles Times* reporters ask for old *Times* clippings from the newspaper's library, the clippings are delivered to them in an envelope with this disclaimer printed on it:

WARNING TO WRITERS
Use the utmost care when rewriting from clippings. All statements of fact which discredit any person's reputation or business are libelous unless absolutely true. Such facts must be fully verified before publication.

The 1978 election-day story that vilified the Supreme Court is now yellowing and rests in one of those envelopes in the *Times* library. Reporters who draw from the information in those clips in the future would be wise to heed the message on the envelope. Indeed, given the incorrect decision to run the election-day story, it would have been more appropriate for the following disclaimer to have been stamped across the face of the page-one story:

WARNING TO READERS
Use the utmost care when reading this story. The crucial statements of fact are based on speculation. Reading them as fact may be injurious to your understanding of the truth.

The election-day story should not have run unless the *Times* acquired more than speculation about the original accusations. The *Washington Post* probably would like to have run its most crucial Watergate stories before the 1972 presidential election, but it simply did not have enough solid information. It took months for some of the most important Watergate information to be confirmed. The Watergate stories also started with speculation, but something much more solid than speculation had to be developed. That would have required honesty and good news judgment rather than a rush to judgment. Those were professional necessities the *Times*, for reasons not entirely clear, did not use on election eve 1978.

In Lou Cannon's 23 November 1978 story, he wrote that a source claimed that the separate dissent written in October—the one an anonymous source said had been written at the request of Tobriner or Bird as part of a strategy to delay the case—gave Tobriner his grounds for later arguing that the *Tanner* opinion had not been completed by election day. In this story, Cannon also quoted a court source as saying, "Tobriner was technically right but morally wrong.

. . ." It was a strongly condemnatory statement, but it was built on the flimsy sand of the election-day *Times* story. In addition to being irresponsible, the statement is particularly ironic, for, from what is known now about the information known to the *Times* the day before election day 1978, the *Times* cannot claim that it was even technically, let alone morally, right.

Now that the secret testimony is known, that information coupled with other information makes it possible to conclude confidently that the *Times'* election-day story never should have been printed. So massive were the errors and the assumptions that grew out of the original *Times* story that it can be said without exaggeration that the public had no access to the truth.

CHAPTER 13

Fighting Courts Easier than Fighting Crime

Immediately after the Commission on Judicial Performance announced at the end of its deliberations in 1979 that no charges would be filed, those who wanted to discredit the court cried, "Whitewash!" and until Justice Clark left the court in 1981 to become Deputy Secretary of State in Washington, the California Supreme Court continued to be filled with internal tensions. These tensions dissolved with his resignation.

But the tempo of attacks against the court from the outside intensified through 1981 and 1982 with the announced promise that Bird—or what she symbolized to the law-and-order politicians—would be the centerpiece of the 1982 gubernatorial election campaign. She was. The successful Republican candidate, George Deukmejian, who had been State Attorney General since 1978, attacked her opinions and administrative decisions repeatedly and said that if elected Governor he would work to have her defeated when she came up for voter approval again in 1986.

Meanwhile, Deukmejian's friends in the Republican Party announced in 1982 they would try to recall the Chief Justice from office in 1983. But more important, the state Republican Party took the unpredecented step of urging voters to vote against the three new Supreme Court judges who were on the ballot in 1982—Otto Kaus, Allen Broussard, and Cruz Reynoso. It was the first time a political party had asked that a judge be rejected by the voters.

The clouds that were seeded on election day 1978 still hovered as election day 1982 approached.

The dust had not settled on the Commission's 1979 report when yet more biased reporting assailed the court. Such reporting, indeed, continued to be standard practice. One example of it after the Commission investigation involved the retirement of a court bailiff. Though hardly a remarkable event, this became a *cause célèbre,* in both the general news media and the legal press, when the bailiff, Paul Ludlow, held a press conference to announce his retirement. The point of the press conference was to denounce the Chief Justice for not giving him a promotion and to announce, among other things, that her staff had been eating lunch at the long table in her chambers. It was all faithfully reported, with the *Los Angeles Times* story describing the chambers—in its own rather than Ludlow's words—as a "sanctuary."

Ludlow was deeply hurt by what happened to him at the court. He received much public sympathy and understanding. He was also deeply involved with those inside the court who wanted to get rid of the Chief Justice, a fact never explained by the press. He was one of four bailiffs at the court when Bird arrived. He felt he did more work than the other bailiffs, and he wanted his job title changed to assistant office manager and his monthly salary increased from $1,663 to $1,782. Ludlow says he originally made this request in a 5 May 1977 letter to Bird. She claims she never received that letter. Her staff has looked through the files and not found it. Ludlow and she both agree that in the many contacts the two of them had between May 1977 and 27 July 1979, the date he says he wrote a second letter to her asking for the reclassification, the matter was never brought up. And his 27 July letter, submitted to her with copies sent to all justices, mentions no previous letter.

Sorting out what happened in the celebrated Ludlow matter is difficult. Bird said that a study by the state personnel board indicated that his duties were the same as that of the other bailiffs, that compared with the salaries of other Bay Area workers who did comparable work, the bailiffs at the Supreme Court were overpaid. At least one of Ludlow's fellow bailiffs, whom the press failed to talk to, agreed with Bird, thought that Ludlow should not have been given the change in status and pay, and felt that Ludlow's angry public retirement was merely another attempt to embarrass Bird publicly.

The stories that appeared in newspapers throughout the state when Ludlow retired in June 1980 emphasized only the fact that the court was still fighting, and that the justices' disagreement over Ludlow meant that conditions had not changed since the public hearings a year before. Actually, what was surprising was that the court as a whole was involved at all in the Ludlow matter. These seven justices are very busy people, handling the largest case load of any court in the country. Before Bird was Chief Justice it was unheard of, two justices told me, that the court as a whole should tinker with such things as salaries and promotions of bailiffs. Some justices were impatient with their colleagues for wanting to be involved in such matters. "We're acting like a bunch of little boys who want to make the schoolmarm angry," said one of them. In the past, the court had automatically handed responsibility for administrative matters to the Chief Justice. Under Bird the court increasingly assumed that such decisions were not hers to make.

Ludlow had told another bailiff and several other people in the fall of 1979 that he was going to retire. But in November he wrote to the court that, although he had told some people he was going to retire, he did not intend to do so for three years. At this point Justice Clark took up his cause and asked the court for the raise and title that Ludlow wanted. The justices voted 5–2 to give Ludlow what he wanted. Bird and Tobriner voted against his request. Bird vetoed the court's action, pointing to a section of the government code that gives her responsibility for reviewing court employees' salaries. Repeating her previous reasons for rejecting his request, Bird also said it would be improper to grant someone a last-minute raise in order to assure improved retirement benefits.

Ludlow was furious. He got space in the Federal Building to hold a press conference at which he said Bird had "purged" longtime employees from the staff and that "conditions are such that 95 percent of the staff would retire if they were in a position to do so." This extraordinary event, a press conference held by a court employee simply because he did not get a raise, would never have happened except for the events of the previous year. The investigation of the court about delay of decisions seemed to make any act by Bird into a potential controversy. A funny thing happened on the way to making the Ludlow matter a public issue. A *Los Angeles Times* reporter had called Bird's executive assistant to discuss the situation. Informed of the call, Bird asked aide Stephen Buehl to tell the reporter she herself would like to discuss the issues with the reporter. The reporter told her aide he doubted he would be writing a story. However, within a few days a story appeared and Bird had not been interviewed. Was she inaccessible or just made to appear inaccessible?

The same *Times* story referred to another controversy among the justices—the hiring of Laurence P. Gill, a deputy clerk at the U.S. Supreme Court, as clerk of the California Supreme Court. There was sharp disagreement among the justices over whether to promote the then chief deputy clerk, J. L. Kavanaugh, or to hire Gill. Bird had advertised the job nationally and received 300 applications. She recommended that they hire Gill. He was an expert in computer systems, a skill the court badly needed, as it was just beginning to make the transition to computerized office equipment. When she arrived at the court, there was virtually no modern equipment, not even a dictating machine. Gill was hired and introduced word processing to the court. But, before he was hired, there was considerable disagreement among the justices and a dirty anonymous-letter campaign against Gill. Clark, Mosk, and Richardson voted against his appointment and insisted that their votes be made public.

All of the above, except for the anonymous-letter campaign, was reported by the major print news media. The two letters, sent to Bird's executive assistant, Buehl, raised questions about Gill's qualifications and cast aspersions on his character and educational background. Signing "Amicus Curiae," the letter writer claimed to have overheard telephone conversations between Bird and Manuel in California and Michael Rodak Jr., clerk of the U.S. Supreme Court and thus Gill's boss. Bird could not ignore the charges made in the letters; she checked each one and found them all to be false. Both letters had been mailed in San Francisco. Rodak was informed by Bird about the letters, including charges that he had misled her by not being honest about his lack of regard for Gill. Rodak responded by strongly repudiating the claims in the anonymous letter and noting that "I never thought any aggrieved person would go so far as to send you an anonymous letter such as the one you received." Interestingly, the *Times'* sources apparently said nothing about the anonymous letters.

A few months later, the press became interested in the retirement of Miriam Denney, the court's staff person in charge of judicial assignments. In late 1979 her retirement became an occasion for more anti-Bird news stories. She was, in a sense, the dispatcher in the assignment office at the Administrative Office of Courts. She called judges to ask them if they would be willing to sit in a given court during the absence of the judge normally assigned to that court. Over her many years on the job, she had kept a looseleaf notebook with information about each retired judge in the state who was willing to take assignments: when they had retired, where they served before retiring, their address and phone numbers, preferences—some, for instance, weren't willing to go into the Sierra when it was snowing— and each assignment they had taken. It was a log that she kept current. At any time she could look at the notebook and know where to reach a given judge—at his home, or at a particular court where he might have been sitting for several weeks. She had devised a good record-keeping system which would be an important administrative tool for any successor.

That successor turned out to be Beth Mullins, the assistant judicial assignments coordinator. According to Denney, Mullins asked her on her last day of work for the notebook. Denney refused to give it to her and told Mullins she had already taken it home. Mullins asked her to bring it back. "This I refused to do," Denney wrote in a 1,850-word article, "The Case of the Wanted Notebook," that appeared in the *Los Angeles Daily Journal* in February 1980. Denney wrote that the notebook "represents a personal document I prepared only for my own use . . . my bible." It was, though, prepared for her use on the job. What neither Denney nor reporters who wrote about this unremarkable incident mentioned was that all that was wanted was the information in the notebook, not the notebook itself.

When she refused to provide it, her last paycheck was withheld because, as Ralph Gampell, the man who replaced Kleps as director of the AOC, put it, it is standard procedure to withhold final paychecks if an employee is known to retain state property. Eventually, Denney took the notebook to the office, Mullins copied the information after Denney had removed what she regarded as confidential information, the notebook was returned to Denney, and she received her final paycheck. "The fact that Mullins returned my book to me would seem to prove that it was not state property and my checks should not have been withheld," wrote Denney in the largest-circulation daily legal newspaper in the country, concealing either intentionally or unintentionally the fact that it was the data, not the notebook itself, that was state property and was wanted. Perhaps she really didn't understand, for she wrote that when she relented and took the notebook to Mullins, "I asked her why she was so interested in my notebook. . . . I told her that if she had asked me in a nice way . . . I probably would have given it to her." Which is rather like a bookkeeper, upon retirement, saying to the boss, "If you ask me in a nice way, I'll let you have your company records." Incredibly, one staff member who told me about the notebook incident asked, "Why in the world would anyone besides Miriam want to know whether a judge is willing to go into the Sierra when it's snowing?" The answer seems obvious: so as to have access to the same information which Denney had found helpful in her work.

Sometimes the railings against Bird and the Supreme Court—Rosie and the Supremes, one prosecutor called them in the press—have gone beyond the inaccurate and the irresponsible. Some have been gross. Most of the gross comments come in the form of hate mail, the kind of hate mail that politicians and judges often receive. One that came to Bird in 1980 was written across the top of the letters column of a newspaper. The headline at the top of the letters was "The Guilty

Go Free; The People's Wishes Are Ignored." The anonymous letter writer wrote above the column: "This, dear Rosie, is the 'proof of the pudding.' The people are sending you a strong message—'we won't take it any more!' You and your 'criminal coddling apple polishers' are going to get some 'real heated action'—in fact your lives may, indeed, be in danger. Take care, for the 'real people' are almost to the breaking point. Enough said!!!!"

Far more outrageous than the anonymous hate mail are the endorsements of such comments by public officials. While Rod Blonien was an assistant senior attorney general in Deukmejian's office, he put out, at taxpayer expense, canned editorials, many of them attacks on the Supreme Court, that were distributed to print and broadcast news media throughout the state. Thirty people worked in the office turning out material on "crimefighting"—which often meant court criticizing and always meant getting future gubernatorial candidate Deukmejian's name before the public. Such canned editorials are an easy way for an uninquiring or lazy journalist to get quick copy. And, in view of his candidacy for Governor, it was a clever way for the Attorney General to get free propaganda. It is also a public deception since the information is not researched and produced by the people who air and publish it.

Blonien's canned editorials, though often irresponsible, were not gross; as much cannot be said for some of his public comments as the guest on a radio talk show on station KGNR in Sacramento. During this program, which was hosted by Bob Whitten, the following exchange took place:

WHITTEN: We have people held up on death row and I recall the Attorney General is, as I understand it, in favor of the death penalty. What's happening?

ASSISTANT ATTORNEY GENERAL BLONIEN: The hold up has been the Supreme Court. . . . They say the convicts didn't have adequate counsel, that the prosecutor didn't dot the 'i' in this case, or the 't' in that case, technicalities, Bob. People want to know why the murder rate still climbs, and the answer is that we haven't executed anyone yet . . . in over 13 years, and most of the murderers know that if they kill, they won't be executed because the Supreme Court won't carry out the will of the people.

WHITTEN: I just had a grotesque vision of putting Deukmejian and Rose Bird in the ring with gloves and let them settle it there . . . but that wouldn't do either.

ASSISTANT ATTORNEY GENERAL BLONIEN: That's right, Bob, we've just about thrown our hands up in exasperation with respect to the Supreme Court. . . . In the extreme, I guess we could get rid of the legislature and the Governor and save a lot of money by just letting the Supreme Court do everything.

WHITTEN (speaking to a caller): Hello.

CALLER: All of this stuff upsets me, Bob, and you said you'd like to see Rose Bird and Deukmejian in the boxing ring? I'd like to do better. . . . I'd like to see Rose Bird in a dark alley with some of those rapists, and maybe she could get down to the level of the victims and find out what a horrible situation this is. . . . She's up on cloud nine some place.

WHITTEN: You're talking about our Supreme Court Justice Rose Bird?

CALLER: You'd better believe it. And I worked my bottom [bleep] off trying to get rid of her at the last election, too. Maybe I'm too radical.

ASSISTANT ATTORNEY GENERAL BLONIEN: Radical? I think you're midstream. You know what they call Rose Bird's decisions?

CALLER: I know what I call them, but I can't say it over the air.

ASSISTANT ATTORNEY GENERAL BLONIEN: They call them "Bird droppings."

CALLER: Well, my word starts with "B".

WHITTEN: (Laughing in background) Don't say it.

This official, Blonien, was designated by Deukmejian shortly after he became Governor to be his legal affairs secretary. As such, he will play a major role in selecting the judges the Governor will appoint.

Few of the anti-Bird episodes, however, can match a bizarre, possibly sinister, event on an airplane just two weeks before the opening of the public investigation of the court. It was a time when the Chief Justice was under constant scrutiny as the court prepared for this unprecedented investigation.

The Supreme Court was to sit in Los Angeles on Monday morning, 4 June 1980, the first of a few days of public hearings. On Pacific Southwest Airlines flight number 712 Sunday night from Sacramento to Burbank was a woman in a lavender skirt and high-necked blouse that had tiny lavender flowers on it. Her sandy-brown hair was in a bun. She was tall, and appeared to be in her early 40's. Approximately fifteen people on the flight, including a lawyer named Luros who is now a municipal court judge in Van Nuys, thought the woman was Rose Bird. And that is why it was so interesting when this woman loudly and rudely told the stewardess to shut up when the stewardess asked the woman to fasten her seatbelt in preparation for landing. The woman also loudly told the stewardess to go away from her, to go back to her own seat. This naturally attracted the attention of many passengers. Fifteen of them waited at the gate after the flight landed to ask if the rude woman was Rose Bird. Photographs of the Chief Justice had appeared in papers and on television throughout the state in recent days.

Luros was seated in the section where the stewardesses sat during takeoff. Noticing the likeness of the passenger to Bird, he had earlier in the flight asked the stewardess who later was berated by the woman if the Chief Justice was on the flight. She said she didn't know. When the stewardess sat down beside Luros after being told off, she told him she wanted to file a complaint with the Federal Aviation Agency and would definitely do so if the abusive passenger was the Chief Justice. She asked Luros to determine if the woman was the Chief Justice.

The next day, Luros wrote his recollections of what happened after the passenger left the plane. "As I walked up to this individual I noticed that her physical resemblance to the Chief Justice . . . was striking. . . . I inquired, 'Excuse me, are you the Chief Justice?' . . . She replied, 'Yes, I am.' To be positive, I then asked, 'Chief Justice Bird?' And she responded, 'Yes, I am Rose Bird'. . . . I began to refer to her as 'Your Honor.' As I talked with this individual, I stated that I knew that she was in Los Angeles to hear arguments over the next two days, and she stated that this was correct."

Luros told the woman that the stewardess intended to file a report about how the woman had behaved. She told Luros the stewardess had been "snippy" and that she didn't like the stewardess's attitude. "At this point," Luros said, "this individual, who [by then] had repeatedly identified herself as Chief Justice Rose Bird, asked me to do her a favor." She asked Luros to go back and say she was not Rose Bird "because she had enough problems." He said he would do so "inasmuch as I knew that she was sufficiently burdened with running the Supreme Court, and she replied that I was correct." The woman left the terminal and Luros walked to the stewardess and told her it was not Rose Bird.

Luros remained troubled about the incident. The next morning he went to the Supreme Court hearing in Los Angeles. From the back of the hearing room he felt uncertain. The woman on the plane really did look like the Chief Justice. He went closer to the bench and looked carefully at the woman who presided. He concluded that the Chief Justice's hair color was lighter and that her mouth was not the same shape. Later that day Luros called Bird's aide Stephen Buehl, and reported that he had met someone impersonating the Chief Justice.

Actually, the Chief Justice, accompanied by Buehl, had flown to Los Angeles from San Francisco Sunday afternoon and was having dinner with Los Angeles Superior Court Judge Florence Bernstein and Bernstein's husband at the time when the incident occurred on the

PSA flight. They wrote affidavits documenting where they and the Chief Justice were at the time of the incident. After hearing from Luros, Buehl called Mort Rible, the PSA vice president in charge of legal affairs. Rible confirmed that the airlines had been informed by a stewardess that someone on the flight who had acted rudely said she was the Chief Justice. The airlines provided the woman's name and address. The name provided was for a Sacramento woman. Buehl gave her name and address to the state police in Sacramento and they said they would investigate the incident, would talk to the woman. Buehl called the state police twice a week after his first call to them. Each time he was told they had not pursued the matter but would. He never heard from them again about the incident.

In the summer of 1981, I went to state police headquarters in Sacramento and asked Lt. M. O. Townsend if I could see the files on the incident. He went through several boxes of records for the relevant time period and said there was no record. "Apparently it was never assigned a case number," he said. I asked him if it was unusual that there would be no file, no case number, on such an incident. "Oh yes," he said, "any call is assigned a case number if we are going to assign someone to investigate. It's peculiar it's not here." Then he said a strange thing. "That woman sure looked like her." "You remember it? You interviewed her?" I asked. "Oh, I remember it," said Lt. Townsend. "It made all the papers, her picture was in all the papers." His comment was strange because no report of the incident, with or without photographs, appeared in any newspaper or any other news media.

I called the police officer whom Buehl had been told would try to interview the woman. He said he hadn't interviewed her and didn't know if anyone else had. But he said he thought the woman "was just kidding."

It was the woman's dental braces that later convinced Luros that she was not Rose Bird. He told Buehl the impersonator was wearing flat wire braces on her upper and lower teeth, and an inverted U-shaped wire on her lower teeth. When Luros worked his way toward the front of the hearing room that Monday morning, he immediately noticed that the Chief was not wearing any braces on her teeth. What he didn't know was that the Chief Justice had been wearing dental braces of precisely that description until just one week earlier. Did someone ask this woman to impersonate Rose Bird, and in such a negative light? Why was she impersonating her? The answers are not known, but it is impossible to think they are benign.

The most repugnant dirty tricks of all involved false rumors of Bird's impending death. In 1976, Rose Bird's right breast was removed. It seems incredible to think that her cancer would become one of the weapons in her enemies' arsenal, but it did. In the fall of 1977, she had a recurrence, and a small tumor was removed. The news that it was malignant was more traumatic to her than the removal of the breast had been. She had hoped the removal of the breast meant she had licked the cancer. The recurrence was more threatening—the more so because her doctor died of cancer himself within three weeks of removing her second cancerous growth. She found new doctors, read everything she could get her hands on on the subject, permanently changed her diet to include only uncooked fruits and vegetables (the suggestion of a respected researcher), and worked the same long hours she always had. It was after this second operation that she became a lot more reflective about her life. She had always been a person who had very close friends. Now they seemed more precious to her, and she realized that it was her relationships that gave the greatest meaning to her life. That had always been true, but she had not thought much about it. Having carried cancer twice in her body, she now noticed more carefully what was important in her life. She felt very well and, except for a back ache—unrelated to the cancer—that forced her to use a cane occasionally, she was a picture of good health.

Nevertheless, a peculiar thing started happening. In the weeks immediately before election day in 1978, about once a week Bird's secretary would get five consecutive calls from five different reporters. Invariably, they all said that a Sacramento source had told them that Bird's death was imminent and that she was about to resign. The callers wanted to know if it was true. It wasn't. Beginning in May of 1979, and continuing through the investigation of the court that summer, similar calls came in concentrated groups, five or six calls a day every several days. After the hearings Bird's office continued to receive such calls from time to time.

"As you might imagine, it can be very disconcerting, to say the least, to be bombarded by callers asking how soon you are going to die," Bird told a symposium on breast cancer. "One might almost think that someone intended that I give the suggestion serious consideration. . . . If I had not already come to terms with the reality of my disease, I would not have been able to see the gallows humor in all of this. But, thankfully, I can observe along with Mark Twain that the reports of my death are greatly exaggerated."

The meanest of the mean comments about Bird came from, of all people, a State Court of Appeal judge. Robert Kane was appointed to the Court of Appeal by Ronald Reagan. He had written the Court of Appeal decision in the *Tanner* case. It was his decision in this case that was appealed to the Supreme Court in 1978. In the summer of 1979, Kane, a former president of the California Judges Association, re-

signed from the Court of Appeal and went back to private law practice in San Francisco. He said publicly that he was resigning because
the judiciary was in disarray and disrepute. He is supposed to have
said privately that he was stepping down from the bench because he
wanted to make more money in private practice than he could make
as a judge. Four months after he resigned from the bench, he issued a
public call for Bird to resign from the Supreme Court.

Kane's cruelest public attack against Bird came in December 1978
while he was still a judge. It occurred about a month after the election
debacle in 1978, and shortly after Bird had her second recurrence of
cancer. There was a small news story in newspapers all over the state
reporting that the Chief Justice had had a small malignant tumor
removed. A week later Kane gave a speech in which he called for the
removal of "the cancer" at the top of the court.

Amazingly, even after he had been criticized for making such a
comment, he made a variation of it almost a year later, in November
1979, in a speech to the San Mateo County Bar Association: "The
major illness afflicting California's judiciary is not a sore toe in the
form of one judge's actions but a cerebral tumor causing the whole
body of judges to suffer. We need to excise the tumor and get on with
some preventive medicine."

Well, Bird wasn't excised. But as the attack on her continued, it
seemed that even when she initiated reforms long needed, she would
not only be criticized but slandered. The regular timing of the court's
decisions was a case in point.

Reporters and law enforcement officials complained from the
spring of 1978 and into 1980 that the Bird court deliberately tried to
prevent thorough coverage of its cases by releasing many important
ones the day before weekends or holidays. That practice, went the
criticism, guaranteed little or no coverage. There were two problems
with the criticism. First, it wasn't true. A study of the release of decisions showed that Tuesday was the most common day for release of
decisions. Second, if it had been true, the result would likely have
been the opposite of what was claimed—by being released right before weekends or holidays, the controversial decisions would have
generated more attention rather than less. Weekends and holidays
tend to be slow news days, so any controversial decisions would be
likely to get more prominent attention then than on a busier mid-
week day when usually there are more hard news stories to compete
for prominent placement.

But Bird agreed with some members of the press that it would be
better to issue decisions at regularly scheduled times instead of randomly. The U.S. Supreme Court has done this for many years. In
early 1980 she suggested that the court ask the news media through-

out the state for reaction to a proposal that the court file its opinions at two regular times each week, thus making the timing completely predictable. The court approved her plan, though Justice Clark voted against it, saying such a schedule would "delay" decisions. The news media reacted positively to the suggestion and a schedule was set: decisions would be released every Monday at 3 p.m. and every Thursday at 10 a.m. It gave afternoon papers an advantage on one of the days and the morning papers the advantage on the other day. This seemed to be an evenhanded approach. The new release plan also involved having the court clerk's office file each submittal order as soon as it was signed instead of when the case was filed. This meant that reporters would know several days in advance when a pending case was about to be filed and could prepare themselves on the background. It would not please those who wished only for news releases they could rewrite, but it would be a help to those who wanted to write stories based on their own ability to interpret the decisions. Most reporters agreed that the arrangement was helpful.

Amazingly, Attorney General Deukmejian attacked Bird for trying to hide major decisions, by filing them on the day before holidays, a few months *after* the court adopted the new release plan. He made the attack after he himself had written a letter officially endorsing her plan.

On 3 July 1980, the court released what Deukmejian would later call "the most remarkable California Supreme Court decision ever rendered." He was referring to the *Van Atta* decision, in which the court shifted the burden of proof that a defendant is unlikely to appear for trial from the defendant to the prosecution. Under the decision, if the prosecution cannot convince the judge that the defendant is likely to flee, the defendant must be freed on his or her own recognizance pending trial. It was, to put it mildly, a decision that did not warm the cockles of prosecutors' hearts. They claimed the effect would be no less than the abolition of the bail system and the release of massive numbers of criminals, an effect that has not in fact been produced. Deukmejian attacked both the decision, which was written by Bird, and the timing of its release. In a statement released the week after the decision was announced, and in a speech three weeks later to the California Broadcasters Association, Deukmejian said the court had released the *Van Atta* decision on the eve of a three-day holiday either "by malignant design or benign insensitivity," in order to restrict coverage and "consequently . . . public awareness." What was strange about his comment was that the decision had been released at 10 a.m. on 3 July and, at least in northern California, it was impossible to hear a news broadcast that day without hearing about this significant case. That very day the *San Francisco Examiner* ran a page-one story on the case: "Court Orders Reform of Bail System." The next morning's *San Francisco Chronicle* also ran a long front-page story with a dramatic headline: "Ruling on Bail to Free Many Suspects."

When court personnel noticed the day the decision was released that no one from the *Los Angeles Times'* San Francisco bureau showed up to pick it up, despite the fact that the decision had been distributed at a regular release time, someone from the court called the bureau and informed reporter William Endicott that the case had been released. Philip Hager, the reporter who had regularly covered the court since December 1979, was on vacation, and Endicott, the only other reporter in the bureau, was covering two other stories. The *Times* ran a small wire-service story the next day and, inexplicably, in only one edition. Hager returned from vacation the next week and wrote a story on the case, emphasizing opposition to the decision and Deukmejian's claim that the news media had not been able to report the decision because of the court's bad timing of the release. To report Deukmejian's comments without explaining that his claim of lack of coverage was false was, at best, misleading reporting. When Deukmejian spoke to the broadcasters three weeks later, he repeated his attack on the timing of the decision and said, "not even *The Los Angeles Times* picked it up until Tuesday, 8 July" [actually, Wednesday, 9 July]. It would have been more accurate to have said that *only* the *Times* failed to pick up the story immediately. But telling the truth would have made it more difficult for Deukmejian yet again to repeat a charge that critics of the court, particularly of Bird, had been making since the spring of 1978, and that official and unofficial investigations had given the lie to—the charge that the court times the release of decisions for its own political and public-relations gain.

Deukmejian's volley was followed by another critic's claim that the court was releasing its decisions at regular times in order to "purchase" press support. "I suppose that this is believed also to purchase an obligation on the part of reporters to refute or avoid covering criticisms," wrote Roger Grace in the newspaper he edits, *Metropolitan News,* a daily paper of legal news in Los Angeles. "We [journalists] do not need, do not deserve, and should not have preferential or deferential treatment with respect to filings of submittal orders or opinions, nor should we have access to the help of a 'public information attorney.' What we should have is ready access to the members of the California Supreme Court, too many of whom, through cowardice or lack of accountability, snub reporters—and thus snub the public to whom the reporters report." His comment ignores the long tradition and canons that force judges to let their written opinions speak for themselves, not to keep arguing a case by explaining it after it has been completed.

The California Supreme Court, like the U.S. Supreme Court, has not been an object of the affections of the law-and-order politicians and law-and-order officials and lobbies in recent decades. But there is a greater shrillness in the attacks against Bird than has been heard since the peak of the "impeach Earl Warren" cries in the late 1950's. It is difficult to know whether the increased shrillness is related to the fact that the Chief Justice is a woman or simply to the fact that law-and-order politicians, buoyed by recent electoral triumphs nationally and in California, are riding very high. They are confident and sassy. With the fear of crime so high that the retail supply of tear gas was exhausted in California early in 1981 (as was the government's stock of licenses to permit citizens to carry tear gas), the electorate is vulnerable to anything—truth or fiction—that the law-and-order politicians tell them.

Much of the criticism ignores the historic fact that the role of American courts is distinct from that of the other two branches of government, the executive and the legislature. The judiciary, unlike the other two branches, does not and must not look to the will of the majority, save as that will is enthroned in the Constitution, for the basis of its decisions. Judges are in and of the world, and they are naturally affected as human beings by what they read and see. To be sure, their thinking is affected even in ways they do not realize as they come to their decisions. It is their duty, however, not to let the will of the majority—or someone's perceived will of the majority—determine their decisions. Harvard law professor Laurence H. Tribe put it well when he spoke to the Lawyers Club of San Francisco a few days before the Commission's 1979 investigation of the Supreme Court began: "Our Constitution's framers knew that equal justice under law demands a judiciary *not* dependent on political will, royal *or* popular. They understood a crucial paradox: that judges can curb irresponsible action by those in power only if they are themselves freed from accountability to the other branches and insulated from the impulses of temporary political majorities."

The courts are supposed to be the protectors of the individual's rights and the minority's rights no matter what the popular cry might be. This goes against the grain of the basic views of those presently trying to discredit judges in California. Colonel Earl Huntting, the head of the statewide group that monitors judges throughout the state, was asked on a television news program if his goal was "to make judges more accountable to the majority will in this state."

Huntting: "Absolutely. Everything else is."

Interviewer: "Doesn't that mean though that necessarily the courts will pay less respect to the rights of minorities and to civil liberties?"

Huntting: "Well, why should they give more rights to minorities and civil liberties? Why don't they give the rights to the majority of the people of the state of California? Why must it always be to minority groups that they give rights?"

The unique role of the judiciary—its obligation to protect minority as well as majority rights—is easily exploited. It made it easy, for example, for Deukmejian to give the speech he gave in October 1980, a speech lambasting the Chief Justice for being an "elitist" who "disparages the public, virtually ignores the rights of victims, and misunderstands the role of the judiciary." And because this branch of government sometimes makes decisions that the majority would vote against if it could, the judiciary becomes an easy whipping boy when society's most difficult problems are not resolved by the other two branches of government. The public is easily deceived, moreover, when its major sources of information regularly provide either biased or incomplete reports about the decisions and effects of decisions by the judiciary.

To hear Deukmejian and other law-and-order politicians, you would think that Bird personally, and the courts as an institution, have as their chief activity the freeing of the guilty. "The nature of the criminal trial has been altered from a test of the defendant's guilt or innocence to an inquiry into the propriety of the policeman's conduct," said Deukmejian. "Rather than a search for truth, today's criminal trial is a prologue for an appeal." Supreme Court Justice William Clark made a similar claim in a not very subtly named television program about the California Supreme Court, "Inside the Cuckoo Court," on the NBC-owned and -operated television station in Los Angeles in 1980. Criticizing the majority of his court colleagues, Clark said, "The guilt of the particular defendant often becomes irrelevant" as the focus is shifted to the "behavior of the police officer or the citizen having made the arrest and witnessed the transaction." Another participant in the program, a Los Angeles district attorney, said court decisions that limit the search-and-seizure powers of police free the felon because the constable has blundered. "I liken [what's happened in the courts] to cutting your neck to stop a nose bleed."

The official records show that such talk is a sham. Through such rhetoric politicians have convinced the public of a fiction: that judges are soft on crime. The facts show that in California more than 86 percent of all persons charged with a crime are found guilty in the courts. If anything, the rate may be shockingly high. Three out of every four persons charged plead guilty. Of the 14 percent who go to trial, the conviction rate is 75 percent.

The arrest rate is quite a different story. Of all reported crimes in California, 21.9 percent result in arrests. It would not be illogical for those interested in curbing crime to support a court system that convicts 86 percent of all charged persons and to criticize law enforcement officers whose investigations produce arrests in only 22 percent of known crimes.

The response of court critics is that arrests are low because the courts have hamstrung police by, for instance, recently mandating stricter rules on search and seizure. Actually, the arrest records always have been low. Going back to 1959, the official national figures compare instructively with current figures. Seventy-five percent of those charged then were convicted. Despite the imposition of more stringent rules on the arresting officers, conviction rates by the courts have increased, not decreased. Sentences are longer and the percentage of convicted persons going to prison has increased. But nationally the proportion of reported crimes in which arrests and charges were made was 20.5 percent in 1959 and is 18.3 percent now, a relatively constant figure during a time of increasing crime and increasing court convictions.

The fine print of Deukmejian's own official crime statistics report for his first full year (1979) in office as Attorney General, shows that much of the reason for the lack of convictions—which he lays at the door of the courts—comes in fact from the large number of arrests that are made with insufficient evidence or sloppy police work. Deukmejian and others continually claim that it is "soft" judges who let criminals go. He never mentions what his own report reveals: that 11 percent were released by the police and another 14 percent by prosecutors who felt they had no case. These "criminals" were released by police and prosecutors *before* they ever got to a judge. The failure to improve police work receives almost no attention in these days when it is fashionable to blame crime on the courts. Yet a March 1981 study of 2,418 police in seven cities across the nation showed that 15 percent of the police were credited with 50 percent of the convictions; 31 percent of them had no convictions. Undoubtedly, many police are overburdened by the reduction of force size after tax cutbacks. But many police departments also have misplaced priorities: they emphasize credit for number of arrests made and number of arrests cleared rather than number of arrests that lead to convictions. Such a policy promotes sloppy arrests that are easily cleared from the record, rather than "good" arrests that lead to solid cases and likely convictions.

The constant charge that courts specialize in turning criminals loose is also difficult to believe in view of the fact that California has more people in prison per capita than are in prison in any nation in the world except for South Africa and the Soviet Union. The only states with a higher imprisonment rate are several in the Deep South and the District of Columbia. (The District has the highest imprisonment rate anywhere in the world—600 prisoners for every 100,000 citizens.) And California's prison sentences are the second longest in the nation, second only to those in Massachusetts. By March 1981, California prisons contained 24,000 inmates, 104 percent capacity. Longer sentences and more convictions had legislators calling for the building of more prisons, a call in which Governor Brown joined. A similar overcrowding occurred when Reagan was Governor. Ironically, his administration diminished the problem by quietly letting prisoners go before they were eligible for release, a fact that his law-and-order political descendants in California now do not mention.

But, say the court critics, if the trial courts are convicting at a high rate, which they are, it is meaningless. The appellate courts in California, these critics claim, are overturning most of these convictions. Right? Wrong. Such is the common wisdom, thanks to the careless broadsides that are continually made against the appellate courts and reported as fact without inspection of the record.

Occasionally, a criminal conviction is reversed and a new trial is ordered by either the Court of Appeal or the Supreme Court. When such reversals involve a case that is particularly grisly, they naturally attract a lot of press attention. But even in those cases, the accused is almost never set free by the reversal; rather, he or she gets a new trial because of error or illegal activity by the government. Usually the accused is convicted again and remains imprisoned. But the reporting of such cases and of the rhetoric about them has been such that the public can easily conclude that the appellate courts are overturning most criminal convictions that are appealed and are constantly setting free criminals convicted of heinous crimes. But that very rarely happens, despite the myth that it does, a myth that is widespread in California and throughout the nation.

Official figures show that in 88.5 percent of the cases that are appealed to higher courts the decisions of the trial courts are upheld. Of the total that are appealed, 76.3 percent are affirmed in full and 12.2 percent are affirmed with modification. Verdicts are reversed and retrials expected in only 10.8 percent of cases appealed.

In the same May 1981 Sacramento speech in which President Reagan's counselor Edwin Meese called the American Civil Liberties Union a "criminals' lobby," he also called for the elimination of insanity as a defense in criminal trials and sharply criticized exclusionary rules, those requirements established by federal and state courts that require the police not to obtain evidence illegally. For instance, the 1966 *Miranda* decision by the U.S. Supreme Court requires the arresting officer to inform a person that he or she has a right to remain silent, that anything they say may be used against them, and that they have a right to legal counsel. Meese's comments, reflective of those made by his friend and legal client Justice Clark when Clark was a justice of the State Supreme Court, appear to be nothing more than rhetoric. The insanity plea is seldom used and a minuscule percentage of those who use it are acquitted. A 1979 national study by the U.S. Comptroller General of 2,800 randomly selected criminal cases showed results that a public indoctrinated by speeches, such as those given repeatedly by Reagan, Meese, Clark, and Deukmejian, would have a hard time believing: evidence was excluded as a result of exclusionary rules in 1.3 percent of the cases. Of that tiny percentage in which evidence was excluded, 50 percent of the defendants were convicted. The bottom line was that the exclusionary rule had significant impact in less than one percent of prosecuted cases.

In another tough law-and-order speech, in April 1981, Meese said judges on both the state and federal levels should get more involved "in cleaning up their own act than in telling you people [he was addressing the California state sheriffs' association] how to run your jails or in telling the Department of Corrections how to run their prisons." He got a standing ovation when he said, "If judges would spend more time cleaning up trials—making sure that the trial is a search for the truth—and less time trying to run prisons, the criminal justice system would be a lot better. . . . What's needed is a realistic attitude on the part of society towards the laws and law enforcement. We've got to make it clear that criminals are the enemies of society, not those of you sworn to enforce the law. . . . We still have legislators, we still have congressmen, who will do anything they can to pass laws—we still have judges who make decisions—that deliberately and definitely thwart the ability of officers of the law to carry out their professional responsibilities and protect the public."

What is needed is a heavy dose of the truth alongside (or instead of) this rhetoric, which has been so much repeated that it is now presumed to be true. It has swept politicians into office, including some liberal chameleons who are afraid not to jump on the law-and-order bandwagon. It is one thing to be agitated about the rising crime rate, and quite another to point an agitated finger at the wrong party. It is this irresponsibility that has removed several trial judges from California benches and threatens to remove more. What the rhetoric ignores are these facts:

• As crime has increased in the last twenty years, the courts have increased the percentage of convictions from an already high 75 percent to 86 percent.

• Law enforcement, on the other hand, has maintained, despite a dramatic increase in crime, a low record on percentage of persons charged for all reported crimes—18.3 percent now compared with 20.5 percent in 1959.

• Together, the above two findings mean that a criminal's chances of being arrested are only 20 percent; there is an 80 percent chance of evading arrest. But, once in the court system, the criminal's chances of being convicted are 86 percent.

• The failure to arrest has consistently been the biggest problem in getting criminals off the street.

• Exclusionary rules have not diminished convictions—convictions are up. If anything, these new rules, now in jeopardy from the President and stage legislatures, have apparently made the police make better arrests rather than fewer.

As Attorney General, Deukmejian's attacks on the courts, the State Supreme Court in particular, were so incessant as to make one wonder what would have happened if, as the State's chief law enforcement officer, he had spent as much time and taxpayers' money fighting crime as he did fighting the courts.

CHAPTER 14

"We'll Set an Example for the Rest of the Country . . ."

The wave of "law-and-order" bills increases every year in the California legislature. Five hundred separate such bills were introduced in 1981. In the course of debating one of them, State Senator John Doolittle, a missionary-turned-politician who used to work for Senator H. L. Richardson and then was financed by Richardson to run for the senate, said:

"This is an attack on the state courts, and tomorrow we will attack the federal courts."

By spring 1982, the federal courts were targeted. More than thirty bills were pending in Congress, bills that would remove certain social issues—school busing, abortion, and school prayer—from the jurisdiction of federal courts. It is the most blatant attempt in American history to remove significant parts of American life from Constitutional protection.

By 1982 what had begun in California in 1978 as dirty politics, using speculation as the basis for public accusations of unethical conduct by a respected liberal on the California Supreme Court, has become a major movement. A seemingly simple question had faced the voters of California on election day 1978: Had one or more California Supreme Court justices become a judicial crook? As it turned out, that question was a ruse. The real question that was planted that day in the public mind, and carefully cultivated during and after the investigation of the court, was this: Is the entire judiciary a disgrace, a mockery of justice?

What is happening in California, and what politicians there, such as Doolittle, are helping bring to the nation, is a radical movement. It has two basic goals:

• To remove the judiciary from its historical and constitutionally required position as an equal third branch of government and make it subservient to the legislative and executive branches.

• To destroy the fundamental principle of American justice that the accused is innocent until proven guilty. It attacks the responsibility of the court to treat each defendant as an individual whose case is to be tried on the merits of the evidence rather than on the basis of the public sympathy of the moment. This movement would alter American society by making the judiciary subject to political expediency rather than the Constitution.

On the state level, this movement has removed a large portion of a judge's discretion in sentencing. That power is passing from the courts to the legislature. What Maury Koblick, one of Justice Clark's research attorneys, said about the use-a-gun-go-to-prison law in his testimony during the 1979 investigation is true of much of the legislation now being rushed through. It is symbolic legislation intended to play to the audience, intended to glean political approval from a public kept innocent of the real intent of the statutes—no additional public protection against crime but additional votes from an electorate deceived about the real record of the courts and the real record of law enforcement.

Many liberals try to have their cake and eat it too by supporting such statutes. They get credit from conservatives for being law-and-order advocates. At the same time they know that, as in *Tanner,* there may be a loophole—the other statute on the books that was not removed—which in effect eradicates the most extreme goal of the statute (in *Tanner,* the goal of excluding just and proper exceptions to the law's intention, that of sending all gun users to prison). Many of the so-called anti-crime bills are there precisely because of what Koblick said about *Tanner,* a law introduced by Deukmejian when he was a state senator. They are introduced simply to gain favorable publicity. The legislators who propose them know they are not needed, but proposing them makes it appear that the legislators are accomplishing two things: fighting crime and throttling liberal judges.

Pollsters in California say that crime is the make-or-break issue for politicians in the early 1980's. The two who vied for the 1982 Republican nomination for Governor, Attorney General George Deukmejian and Lieutenant Governor Mike Curb, both acted as though Rose Bird was the Democratic nominee. She was the main subject of their speeches. For more than twenty years conservative politicians ran against Chief Justice Earl Warren. Now a generation of conservative

California politicians is running not against their real opponents on real issues but against Chief Justice Rose Bird on the false issue of "soft-on-crime" courts.

During the 1982 governor's race, Deukmejian repeatedly attacked Bird and the courts. He called for Governor Brown's three new appointments to the court to be turned out by the voters. Deukmejian said from the beginning that the courts would be a major issue in the campaign, and they were. Tom Bradley, his Democratic opponent, said he thought the courts should not be an issue in the race. Bradley also said he thought it was wrong to suggest that voters should remove any of the judges because of their decisions. Bradley lost and Deukmejian won. No pollster has assessed the role of public attitudes toward the courts in the votes for Governor, but given the prominence of the issue in the campaign, and the low plurality the three Brown appointments to the court received, it may have been significant.

In the summer of 1981 Deukmejian prepared, at tax-payer expense, a ten-page pamphlet, *Murder and the Death Penalty: A Special Report to the People.* As Peter Schrag, editorial-page editor of the *Sacramento Bee,* put it, the pamphlet is "nothing but pretentious demagoguery." Deukmejian claims in this pamphlet that because the Supreme Court has not permitted an execution in California in recent years, "the citizens of California are four times more likely to be the victim of an unlawful homicide than they were when killers were executed." While that might have been effective rhetoric for an Attorney General trying to sustain constant coverage as he ran for Governor, it is not an assertion that can withstand scrutiny. There is no conclusive evidence that the death penalty is a deterrent and none that the absence of an execution makes a state's citizens four times more likely to be murder victims.

In early 1980, Deukmejian's Chief Deputy State Attorney General, Michael Franchetti, was preparing the Attorney General's annual report. He sent a memo to nine aides saying the report would be "describing the departmental accomplishments of the past year. The theme of the report will be the department's 'responsibility to the public interest.' . . . Each of you is authorized to let your imagination 'run wild.' " It is not clear whom Franchetti was quoting when he put "run wild" in quotation marks. But it is clear that the Attorney General himself let his imagination run wild when he talked about the courts.

Some members of his staff used to say Deukmejian had an EOM— an Event of the Month—some sensational speech or activity that was guaranteed to get him front-page and prime-time coverage throughout the state. For instance, fairly early in his administration he himself appeared very early one morning in Mendocino County to raid marijuana fields. There was Deukmejian, in flak vest and field jacket, accompanied by a posse of armed deputies and a posse of photographers. It appeared, as he merged being Attorney General with being gubernatorial candidate, that Rose Bird and the courts were his EOM—*every* month. Sometimes every week.

Just before he announced he would run for Governor, Deukmejian told the Commonwealth Club of San Francisco that in the 1982 gubernatorial election "the judiciary will be a major issue. The people will send a message to the court in a voice so powerful that even the most unwilling justices will hear it." Less than two weeks later he was in Palo Alto saying Bird was the chief villain in a scheme to isolate the courts from public scrutiny and to coddle criminals. Reporters covering his speeches seldom, if ever, checked the official records to see if his claims about the courts were true. Deukmejian said that if he became Governor he would campaign to keep Bird from being approved by the voters again. She comes up for approval by the voters again in 1986, having been narrowly approved in 1978 to complete her predecessor's remaining eight years. The timing would be propitious. As Governor, Deukmejian is likely to be running for his second term in 1986. He would again have Bird as a key issue in his campaign. And Bird would have a distinction that no judge in California has ever had. She could be a major issue in three consecutive gubernatorial races—1978, 1982, and 1986. Bird's defeat in 1986—or her recall before then—would be a special victory for Deukmejian. As Governor he would appoint her replacement.

The law-and-order enthusiasts have a double standard when judging wrongdoing. They are gleeful when a liberal gets caught. They are blind when one of their own trips publicly. For example, the day I interviewed Senator H. L. Richardson in the fall of 1979, Court of Appeal Justice Paul Halvonik and his wife had just been arrested by Oakland police for possession and cultivation of marijuana. I had not heard the news. Richardson's first comment to me after I introduced myself was "Have you heard about Halvonik?" He then told me all the details, the most interesting of which was that the Halvonik house, the police had discovered after being called to investigate a burglary, was a veritable forest of marijuana plants the judge's wife was cultivating. To Richardson, the Halvoniks were far more than stupid, the label many applied to them. Richardson was beside himself with delight. The Halvoniks were valuable new fodder for him. He laughed and laughed. Halvonik was, of course, a liberal. "Now we've got him," said Richardson, who was looking forward to the trial of Halvonik, who would later plead guilty and leave the bench. Naturally, there was a great deal of press interest in the case, and there was much press commentary on the implications of Halvonik's arrest for the entire judiciary. The claim was that once again a liberal judge had brought the entire judiciary into disrepute. The arrest occurred in 1979 while the Commission on Judicial Performance was still deliberating on its verdict on the Supreme Court.

In striking contrast, the arrest and eventual conviction of another judge provoked hardly any comment. Mono County Superior Court Judge Harry R. Roberts was arrested in July 1980 on a felony charge of assaulting a California Highway Patrolman. Two patrolmen stopped a car driven by Roberts's son. As they gave the son a field sobriety test, the judge, according to the patrolmen, swore at the patrolmen and at one point tried to make a citizen's arrest of one of the officers. Then, according to one of the officers, the judge struck him in the chest and both of them fell to the ground and fought. The officer's wrist was broken. The judge was booked on a felony charge for assaulting a police officer and a misdemeanor charge for interfering with an arrest. Two months later the felony charge was dropped. In April 1981 Roberts was convicted on the misdemeanor charge of interfering with an arrest and fined $500.

A 1972 appointee of then Governor Reagan, Roberts continued to sit on the bench while his case was pending and continued to sit after his conviction. No public debate ensued about disgrace to the judiciary. Indeed, in the same year that the judge was arrested, Senator Richardson's Law and Order Campaign Committee released evaluations of California judges in which Roberts was rated "excellent."

At the same time, San Francisco Municipal Judge Louis Garcia was said by the Law and Order Campaign Committee to be "soft on crime." But the Law and Order Campaign Committee was not heard complaining when Judge Garcia, who died in 1982, permitted a man who police say slugged a bartender and a hotel desk clerk to perform twenty-five hours of community service rather than face trial on two counts of battery and one of being drunk in public. Perhaps they didn't complain because the man was Herb Jackson, District Attorney of Sacramento. Jackson struck the two people at San Francisco's fashionable L'Etoile Restaurant in late 1980 during a dispute over a $92 bar bill left unpaid by some of his friends.

When Jackson applied for the pre-trial diversion program, he asked Judge Garcia to permit him to perform community service because, he said, he wanted to warn Sacramento youngsters about the dangers of drugs and alcohol. "I will talk to kids about drugs, including alcohol, on the playgrounds, in the classrooms, on the streets, and in every other possible setting. And whenever I can fit it into my schedule."

That is not quite what happened. The judge granted Jackson's request. But Jackson worked off his community-service time by going out and telling adults how awful the California court system was. "For at least the past two decades, the Supreme Court has interpreted so many laws that it is difficult to convict a felon without the judge and jury witnessing the crime," he told one group. "The court's decisions have made obtaining evidence such a technical morass that many walk out free on technicalities." In another speech, he told his audience that they "should be encouraged by the election of Ronald Reagan." His election, said the District Attorney, will bring a "change in the attitude of the judiciary from the top down." Returning to his favorite target, the California Supreme Court, he said, "The majority of that court couldn't give a damn about the will of the people of this state. [The people] are aware that criminals often escape punishment and victims never do." Not surprisingly, it is believed that in none of his speeches did the District Attorney criticize the liberal innovation which permits some persons arrested and charged to avoid going to trial by performing community service. Instead, he went from community group to community group, biting the "soft-on-crime" hand that freed him.

Another set of events shows the lack of evenhandedness of law-and-order advocates. When Luis Rodriguez was sentenced in 1981 to die in the gas chamber for shooting to death two California Highway Patrolmen, Yolo County sheriff's deputies wore T-shirts emblazoned with a large noose and the words "Adios Louie." When former San Francisco supervisor and former police officer Dan White was arrested in 1979 for shooting to death liberal Mayor George Moscone and gay supervisor Harvey Milk, some San Francisco police officers wore T-shirts bearing the legend "Free Dan White."

As the decibel level of this kind of rhetoric increases, all judges in California, except those handpicked by law-and-order organizations, face the possibility of being defeated at the polls. For many years, it was possible but unlikely for California trial court judges to be opposed at the polls. Most incumbents ran unopposed. It was traditional to keep a judge on the bench unless his or her behavior on or off the bench had become a public scandal. Extreme unfairness or lack of evenhandedness by a judge would sometimes prompt an attorney in a community to oppose a particular judge. This was viewed as an adequate way, along with the watchdog Commission on Judicial Performance, of keeping the bench free of incompetent judges.

The attacks by strong law-and-order politicians are altering the courts of California in more than one way. Thanks primarily to Richardson and his allies, the idea has been successfully promoted that judges are politicians in the same sense that legislators are, and that "we" should throw "them" out when their philosophy is out of line with ours. In 1980 five out of seven incumbent trial judges who were challenged lost their seats. In all cases previous spending records for judicial races were broken. Five of the seven challengers were deputy district attorneys who ran law-and-order campaigns.

In 1980 the Law and Order Campaign Committee ran a full-page ad in the *Los Angeles Daily Journal* saying LOCC was "looking for a few good judges." It went on to announce that seventy-four Superior Court and forty-one Municipal Court seats could be contested at the June election. Then it listed the names of the incumbent judges, and the procedure for getting into the races. The *San Francisco Chronicle* condemned the ad, noting that "anyone running under the banner of 'law and order' or 'civil liberties' or any other fixed predilection becomes a captive of the slogan. And beholden to a special interest group is exactly what a judge should not be."

In 1981 the right-wing Political Advertising and Consulting (PAC) organization in Los Angeles sent a letter to prosecutors throughout the state. It began: "Dear Prosecutor: I'm sure you are aware that in 1982 over 300 judgeships will be on the ballot throughout the state of California. While many incumbent judges will be retiring or running for higher office, many lenient, soft-on-crime judges will be vulnerable to defeat. No longer are judges simply handpicked by the legal fraternity nor does the electorate merely rubberstamp appointees or Bar recommendations. Campaigns for judicial office have become just that—CAMPAIGNS!" The letter went on to say the faculty for the state would include John Feliz, executive director of Richardson's Law and Order Campaign Committee, and William Saracino, executive director of Richardson's Gunowners of California. The registration was so large that PAC could not accept all applications, despite the fact that the fee for the one-day seminars was $325 a person for each of the three regional seminars.

Some people accuse judges of not wanting to campaign because they want to be "above it all." Some judges are elitist and think they deserve a lifetime trust, no matter what their judicial behavior. But the truth is that campaigning as a judge presents some very real problems that cannot easily be overcome unless the ethics of the judiciary and the very concept of fair justices change significantly. If a legislator goes to a chamber of commerce or a labor union banquet during his campaign, he or she can promise anything. They can say they will lower taxes, provide more community services, bring more industry to town, or outlaw smoking cabbage. But an incumbent judge who attends such a banquet can do little more than thank the group for dinner and kiss a baby. Judges cannot make pledges on how they will decide particular kinds of cases. They can't pledge to send more people to prison, can't pledge to reduce violence on the streets by making tougher sentences or instructing juries differently. About all they can say is that they have been a fair judge, will continue to be a fair judge. That isn't the kind of "rhetoric" that generates a lot of excitement, but judicial ethics require a sitting judge to say little more than that. In the meantime, an irresponsible opponent not on the bench and not bound by judicial ethics can promise to increase convictions and sentences.

There is the problem of campaign money. Raising campaign money, when opposed on the ballot, poses a special problem for judges. If not independently wealthy, where does a judge get it? Until war was declared on judges, they usually had only nominal campaign chests, perhaps $5,000 raised among friends, for a few posters and flyers. They seldom felt it was necessary to blanket their communities or to buy air time on radio and television, the lifeblood of other politicians. Now, full-fledged campaigns mean raising significant amounts of money from a much wider circle of people. A Los Angeles Superior Court judge who in his last campaign spent $5,000 has been told by his political consultant that he will need a minimum of $60,000 to win if he is opposed in the next election. Some judges think raising money for themselves puts them in a quasi-unethical position on the bench. "What would you think if you were a litigant in my court and you knew the opposing counsel had contributed to my campaign?" asks Judge Hollis Best, a Superior Court judge in Fresno County. "Wouldn't you wonder about the fairness of my decision if I had ruled in his favor? I don't think judges' decisions are being influenced by contributions. At least not yet, anyway. Nevertheless, the public thinks that money is contributed to campaigns because the contributor wants something."

Money is less of a problem for the incumbents' opposition, at least for those who had handpicked or approved by Richardson and have his treasures to draw from. In 1980 Feliz announced that the Law and Order Campaign Committee had chosen as that year's first target incumbent Superior Court Judge Richard Calhoun of Contra Costa County. He said LOCC would support Chief Assistant District Attorney Gary Strankman in the race. "We'll spend enough to remove the incumbent if it takes $1,000 or $100,000," said the LOCC's Feliz. Strankman won.

Then there are the campaign lies. Lies, of course, are not new to politics, and they weren't invented by the right wing. Lies and half-truths based on judicial records can be particularly clever and hard to rebut, especially if issued close to election day. A case in point is Pasadena Superior Court Judge Gil Allston. At the time of the June 1978 primary election he was an incumbent Municipal Court judge. A widely respected member of the community and a former Deputy District Attorney, he had a wide range of endorsements. He had a sedate campaign committee that had raised $5,000 and wanted to be very low-key. His opponent was new to the community, had not even given an interview to the local paper, seemed to be doing nothing. Allston's committee thought it would be almost tacky to even acknowledge that there was an opposition candidate. Allston and his committee were shocked out of their complacency the Wednesday before the Tuesday election. That day the district was blanketed with anti-Allston leaflets. One side had a photograph of a policeman looking in a store window with a flashlight. Under the photograph were these words: "The police are doing their job. The courts are not." On the other side, the voter was urged to vote for the opponent instead of Allston. What was most devastating was another message: the opponent claimed that during Allston's time on the bench he had never sent one person to state prison. Incredible. Yes—especially in view of the fact that as a Municipal Court judge he *could not* send anyone to state prison. Municipal Court judges send people convicted in their courts to county jails, and Allston had sent many people to county jail. Allston and his sedate committee got to work fast and spent their $5,000 over the weekend distributing leaflets rebutting the challenger's deceptive claims. Allston won, but by the skin of his teeth. If the leafleting had been done against him on the eve of his election, as the accusations were made on the eve of Bird's election in 1978, Allston would not have had time to counter the false claims with the truth.

Another example of deception. In an evaluation of San Francisco judges, Richardson's LOCC rated one judge as follows: "weak . . . a public defender's mentality . . . a fondness for plea bargaining." The judge, assigned to civil cases, had not heard a criminal case in more than five years.

During the 1978 campaign against Rose Bird, Richardson said "We're not playing patty-cake." Truth or consequences is not his game either.

I interviewed Superior Court Judge Thomas Jenkins at the San Mateo County Courthouse late on a Friday afternoon. He had been hearing civil cases for several months. The following Monday he would start a stint hearing criminal cases. "The law and order people will be in my court Monday morning. One or two people come. Usually they don't tell you in advance, but you know they are there. They monitor you and send the report back to Colonel Huntting." The judge was talking about the statewide monitoring of judges that is done by Citizens for Law and Order, Inc. (CLO). In many communities in the state, retired Army Colonel Earl Huntting, the president of CLO, has volunteers who report back to him on individual judges. They have a notorious record for inaccuracy. Four Los Angeles judges received letters from Huntting in 1980 threatening to go to the news media with information about cases they had handled—too leniently, in the view of CLO. But all the judges said the case summaries were inaccurate.

On the San Mateo County bench, Judge Jenkins told me, judges across the political spectrum see the law-and-order groups as a negative force. "I'm known as a fairly tough judge, but I hope and try to be fair," said Jenkins. "The problem is can you be fair to everyone, including the defendant, when there's an organized group looking at you and, in effect, trying to influence your decision?" Some go so far as to call these court monitors court vigilantes. A group similar to CLO has been formed to pressure judges throughout the nation. In 1981 the Washington Legal Foundation founded Court Watch Project. It writes to judges and demands that they justify their decisions in particular criminal cases beyond what they said at trial or in their written opinions.

"It impinges seriously on the whole concept of fairness," said Jenkins. "Look at the matter of fairness as you instruct a jury. You tell jurors to listen and make judgments solely on the evidence and the law. Law and Order [CLO] suggests a judge should have a predisposition, their predisposition. You tell a jury, 'You are now the judges. Don't act out of sympathy, emotion, prejudice, or bias. Act on the evidence solely as you've seen and heard it in the courtroom.' We tell every jury, 'You must be fair.' There's a suggestion here [from the presence of CLO] that seems to be, 'You should go in with a predisposition.' And even stronger, they seem to be saying, 'We want as judges only those who sentence as we think they ought to.' If a liberal group did this, I'd think it was just as unfair."

One judge, I was told, had told close friends that he recognized, with a certain amount of shame, that he had become a different kind of judge because of the presence of Law and Order monitors in his courtroom. He felt he sometimes gave unjust sentences that he would not have given ten years earlier. He said he did this because he did not want to find himself having to raise money for a campaign the next time his name was on the ballot.

I asked Jenkins if he thought judges respond to the CLO monitoring by becoming the kind of judges CLO wants. "I never had an occasion when it occurred, when they affected a particular case." He pondered the question again. "But over a period of time it has to make things harder with respect to being fair. I'm aware of situations in which judges, knowing Law and Order was there, had great difficulty in arriving at their decision. Now, of course, Law and Order would say that's precisely what they wanted."

Many of the errors that become the basis of CLO's public condemnations of judges are the result of their not understanding the role of either the prosecutor or the judge. "They see what the charges are," said Jenkins, "and they note what I do with the case. . . . What the original charges are may not bear much relationship to the possibility of conviction. Those in Law and Order only know the original charge, say armed robbery with a gun. They are shocked then when they find that most of it's dropped and it's just a burglary and the person gets sixteen months or two years instead of six years."

The arresting officer usually seeks the maximum possible charge. This is because charges can easily be reduced later, but can be increased later only with great difficulty. So the arresting officer usually files charges higher than can be expected to stick. The accused is entitled to be arraigned immediately. Prosecutors often don't know the case when they appear at arraignment, said Jenkins. Inevitably, the higher charges are reduced to match the actual offense—often, if not usually, on the initiation of the prosecutor rather than the defense attorney. The CLO court monitors often do not understand these factors, said Jenkins, and they blame the judge for the lowered charges. This step alone is responsible for many of the misleading and inaccurate claims that judges are soft on crime. "It creates a lot of misunderstanding," said Jenkins.

"In the past," said Jenkins, "if a member of the bar thought you were lousy—not fair, not honest—they ran against you. Now we are subjected to campaigns on the basis of our sentencing. The difficulty is that the charge of being soft on crime is extremely hard to rebut. . . . I'll sentence a thousand people by the end of the year. My average sentence won't mean a thing. . . . There's extraordinary variety from one case to another even though they seem alike. . . . I think what they are doing is anathema to the concept of a fair tribunal."

Some people say that what happened to the California Supreme Court on election day 1978 was the result of seriously unethical activity that never got documented. They say what happened was a crime against the people of California, the people to whom the courts belong. Others say there was no such unethical activity but that ensuing events nevertheless demonstrated that the court was composed, in part, of people whose personalities were so unbending and immature that they should not be part of a collegial body, such as an appellate court.

My investigation and analysis lead me to reject both of these theories. I believe what happened was a well-orchestrated plan designed to bring the court into public disgrace. I believe this plan involved people both inside and outside the court. I believe these people had different reasons for wanting to disgrace the court. A few inside the court staff were simply personally bitter at how the atmosphere at the court had changed under Bird. In their wildest dreams, I doubt that the architects of the plan thought they would succeed, as they did, in getting their rumors and speculation of improper delay into print and on the airwaves on election day.

That accomplishment and what flowed from it—the investigation and the unclear results of the investigation—were an enormous bonanza for those right-wing politicians in California who were willing to use rumor and lies to discredit not just the State Supreme Court, but the entire judiciary. They reaped endless fodder from the initial story, from the year when the Commission sputtered and fumbled as it searched to determine if the speculation that spawned the investigation had any basis in fact. And the inconclusive conclusion of the Commission was their greatest bonanza of all. As long as the final portion of the testimony remained a secret, and as long as the Commission refused to list the details of the results of its investigation, the enemies of the court would be able to say, as they did and still do: "We'll never know what happened." "They tried to hide the truth." "I'll bet Mosk really told the Commission exactly what Tobriner did." The truth didn't matter to those who found the non-conclusion, like the preceding year of accusations and investigation, a convenient weapon. Thanks to that permanently dangling investigation, they could continue to speak as though the accusations were as alive today as they were election morning, 7 November 1978.

I do not mean to suggest that the Commission had any obligation to list its real conclusions simply to defend the court from its enemies, whatever their labels. Rather, simple justice to the accused and to the public should have dictated that the Commission get beyond its petulance and act as responsibly as judges and jurors are required to act in the performance of their responsibilities. Justice demanded that the Commission issue a clear conclusion, not one that would let the original accusations, and more, hang in the air.

Some Commission members told me they concluded that Bird and Clark were simply engaged in childish behavior. Some think that this entire mountain grew from childishness—not from either wrongdoing by Tobriner or from a conspiracy to make Tobriner appear to have been engaged in wrongdoing. Looking at the things Clark had done—and would do during the hearings—it is difficult to see how Bird could perceive his actions as being other than political acts—rather than innocent, childish, immature behavior—aimed at the destruction of the Chief Justice and of the reputation of the court itself.

It is difficult to understand why someone would be considered childish for smelling smoke in the midst of so much fire. It is equally difficult to understand the assessment given these matters by the person the press and legal scholars accept as *the* authority on the investigation, Boalt Hall Law School professor Preble Stolz. His final analysis in the book *Judging Judges* seems to ignore even what he heard during the investigation. He has written that Bird probably assumed that Clark's intention was "to humiliate her." "Although that is possible," wrote Stolz, "Clark's testimony before the commission suggests more that Clark rather drifted into each of these incidents without any conscious design." And Clark's statement to reporter Lou Cannon that he had "decisive" reasons which he would not disclose for not signing a statement that said *Tanner* had been handled properly are seen by Stolz as "nothing more than a kind of rigidity in his thinking." If Clark "rather drifted," Stolz is rather gifted at turning blind eyes of scholar and lawyer toward Clark's actions and attitudes.

Stolz's gentle analysis of Clark is in sharp contrast to his analysis of Bird. In asking for an investigation without consulting with the full court, he said, she "was prepared to sacrifice the core values of a collegial institution for transient benefits of her own design . . . exposing extraordinary indifference to the basic nature of the institution of which she was a member." Stolz has said he thinks Bird suffers from a personality flaw that makes her unfit to be Chief Justice. Given Stolz's lack of acknowledgement of the record of Clark's behavior, one cannot help but conclude after reading the public record of the investigation, let alone the private record, that he suffers from naivete. And that his work suffers from serious flaws in research, scholarship, and judgment.

New York Times columnist Anthony Lewis, in a foreword to Stolz's book, wisely refers to Stolz's analysis as requiring a "suspension of disbelief." Stolz's analysis ignores the facts and attitudes expressed by Clark throughout his testimony. I believe it is the result of one of two possibilities. Stolz could be ignoring the record on Clark's action simply because he has contempt for Clark, believes him to be intellectually incapable of the elaborate plan to discredit the Chief and Tobriner. This would explain Stolz's claim that Clark merely "drifted into each of these incidents without any conscious design." If this is true, it implies a view of Clark as so incapable as not to be responsible for his acts. More likely, I think, Stolz's analysis is, like Clark's *Caudillo* reference in the court's first *Tanner* opinion, politically motivated. Stolz, a former member of the Jerry Brown administration, is known to be quite upset about not having been appointed to the bench by Brown. He is known to have expected to get either a seat on the Alameda County Superior Court or on the Court of Appeal. Not appointed to either, he reacted like a bitter lover. He ridiculed one man who was appointed to the Court of Appeal for getting what Stolz told people he regarded as "my seat."

If one does not take the sum of Clark's actions and perceive a conscious design, one must view Clark as having drifted into an amazing number of accidental actions and comments that just happen to add up to a pattern of maliciousness.

Because most members of the press looked at these events through the same pair of glasses, the public had no way of getting the truth. It had no protection. It was the captive audience of the monotone California press. And the national press merely repeated what the major California press reported most of the time.

Consequently, the public was the biggest loser in all of this. It was deceived and lied to by politicians who used gossip about individuals on the court and misstated the facts about the court's decisions. The public was inadequately informed by reporters—some of whom may have purposely misled their readers, some of whom slavishly reported whatever was said to them by sources without checking official records to see if what was said was true, and some of whom were simply following the leader, in this case the *Los Angeles Times*.

As others have suggested, what happened was a crime against the people, to whom the courts belong. But the crime in question was not the delay of decisions for political purposes, which apparently never happened, nor was it committed by the people originally accused. The crime was the deception of the public about one of its most important institutions. And it was committed by a fairly large number of people, some of them dedicated to what they were doing, some of them unaware of what they were doing.

Three years after the investigation, the Supreme Court was functioning smoothly. The three new Brown appointees, Otto Kaus, Allan Broussard, and Cruz Reynoso, the first Hispanic to sit on the court, were approved, but by narrow margins, when they were on the ballot in November 1982. By then there again was a spirit of collegiality on the court, according to several sources, even when differences were being expressed. But the court continued to be attacked by some of the same external forces that were attacking it in 1978.

All the events that have flowed from that election day 1978 news story have made it possible for a right-wing political movement in California to achieve credibility, and to succeed where Ronald Reagan, as Governor, failed. The notion has been implanted in the public's mind that the judiciary is not an independent branch of government, but rather a branch of government that should be manipulated by, and beholden to, a powerful law-and-order constituency. Through lies and distortions, part of the public has further been convinced that the only obstacle to a crime-free society is the present judiciary.

The nation should view the recent attack on the California judiciary as a warm-up for what will happen nationally. In the last two decades California has been an incubator, a laboratory for political experiments and movements, most notably Proposition 13 tax cuts and Ronald Reagan. The Heritage Foundation, on whose board Edwin Meese sits, has funded a project that aims to use the California attacks on the courts as a model for "reforming" the federal courts. Many members of Congress are anxious to remove key public issues from the jurisdiction of federal courts. And Attorney General William French Smith said in a major policy speech that it was inexcusable that the federal courts have failed to yield to "the groundswell of conservatism evidenced by the 1980 election." His statement was a clear enunciation of the Reagan administration's view that the judiciary is not an independent branch of government but a branch that should respond to political pressures rather than to the Constitution.

Senator Richardson has been clear about his intention to take his anti-judiciary movement to the nation. In a letter soliciting funds and members, he wrote: ". . . We'll set an example for the rest of the country—just as California led the nation on tax reduction with Proposition 13—and lead a *national* [Richardson's italics] campaign against crime and the liberal judges."

Several of the chief troublemakers in the California Supreme Court scandal are now high officials in Washington. There is, of course, William Clark, the President's very close friend and political adviser for many years, who has moved from his position as Deputy Secretary of State to the White House as National Security Adviser. It is widely assumed by both admirers and detractors of Clark that he has a much greater prize ahead of him: an appointment by Reagan to the United States Supreme Court, perhaps as Chief Justice. Other high officials who were involved in the scandal in California are presidential counselor Meese, whom Clark said he consulted as his attorney on matters related to the California court scandal, and Herbert Ellingwood. Without Ellingwood, now deputy counsel at the White House, Republican gubernatorial candidate Evelle Younger probably never would have made public charges that the court was delaying decisions unethically in 1978. Ellingwood, under oath, told investigators that the information he had described to Younger as "solid" and safe to use publicly was, in fact, speculation and gossip.

Beginning with the presidential campaign in 1980 and continuing through the first years of the Reagan administration, these new national officials have been tapping public fears of crime by spreading the same erroneous information about lenient judges' being the cause of crime that they long ago made into daily fare in California. These are, of course, the same officials who speak of the "truly needy" and then establish policies that, as they openly admit, benefit only the truly rich. Perhaps there is a clue here about their lack of understanding, or perverse understanding, of the causes of crime. But in this era of Reagan economics, there seems to be little interest, in or out of government, in exploring what the real causes and cures of crime are, or even in improving police training. This is a time of avoiding, or ignoring, solutions. And the main solution for crime, in this administration's eyes, appears to be to find no solution but, by scapegoating judges, to *appear* to be finding a solution. Meanwhile, an economy is being created that will inevitably make more people so desperately poor that they resort to crime.

The courts of California as a whole were hurt by the damning accusations made on election day 1978. The ensuing speculative reporting hurt many people unjustifiably and misled the public. But probably no one was hurt so deeply as Justice Mathew O. Tobriner, who was accused in the *Times* story of delaying the decision in order to benefit Bird.

A glimpse of the personal anguish the accusations had caused him came through briefly during the public hearing in 1979. A few people in liberal law school circles, particularly outside California, argued that even if Tobriner had delayed a court decision because of the election, it was not an improper thing to do; it was perhaps even a wise thing to do. Tobriner, however, never made that argument. He accepted the sternest approach to the issue: that delaying a decision for purpose of protecting a judge up for approval by the voters would have been wrong. And he vigorously proclaimed his innocence.

What was the public to believe? What is it to believe now? Here was a man who was 75 at the time of the investigation, who had served many years on the court, and who had hitherto enjoyed a sterling reputation for honesty and integrity as both a justice and as an individual. But an impeccable past of service and honesty could not, of course, exclude the possibility that in this one instance this fine man had decided to tamper with the judicial process for a colleague he thought was endangered at the polls. Highly reputable people have been known, even after long years of honesty in public service, to engage in wrongdoing.

A former dean of Harvard Law School, the brilliant late James McCauley Landis, who taught at Harvard when Tobriner was a student there, was a person who seemed incapable of wrongdoing. He was widely respected, and he had been an adviser to three Presidents—Franklin D. Roosevelt, Harry S. Truman, and John F. Kennedy. He was chairman of the Securities and Exchange Commission from 1935 to 1937, director of the office of Civil Defense in 1942. In 1960 he prepared a report for President Kennedy on federal regulatory agencies. In August 1963 he was convicted of income tax evasion.

And then there was Alfred Dreyfus, the French captain who was convicted in 1894 of treason by an *in camera* military court. He was sentenced to degradation and deportation for life and sent to Devil's Island for solitary confinement. Dreyfus, a rich Alsatian Jew, had been accused of turning over secret French documents to the German military attaché in Paris, Major Max von Schwartzkoppen. Dreyfus persistently maintained his innocence, even after failure to be acquitted in a retrial. In 1906 he was given a pardon. But not until 1930, five years before his death, was his innocence clearly established by the publication of Schwartzkoppen's papers.

Was Justice Tobriner, as Landis had been, a man who late in life risked tarnishing an otherwise unblemished record? Or, was he, like Dreyfus, a man falsely accused of wrongdoing?

A thorough examination of the record in this case—both public and private—plus interviews with some who made the accusations and those who wrote the accusations for publication, make clear what was never stated by the investigating agency: Tobriner did not delay any decision of the court for election or any other purposes. He was an honorable man who happened to have the decision on his desk the day before the election and who was used by the people who wanted to see Bird defeated in the election.

There was an early but relatively unpublicized hint that at least some of those who made the public accusations knew nothing about whether a case was being delayed. As Attorney General Evelle Younger was leaving office in January 1979, he told reporters, "The justices are answerable only to God. It makes no difference [to the outcome of the investigation], really, whether the hearings are public or not because there is no way investigators can tell what was on Justice Tobriner's mind." The implication was that the knowledge of planned delay was perhaps known only to Tobriner, and if he chose to lie there would be no way of proving it. In the summer of 1981 Younger told me happily that "we'll never know" whether the *Tanner* case was delayed. But Younger said he still believed it had been.

Inasmuch as politics is often dirty, it was natural that Younger, Ellingwood, H. L. Richardson, and others who viewed the court's decision-making process as purely political, would want one idea to persist: the idea that the public will never know. So where is the key to whether this man is guilty of the accusation made in the *Los Angeles Times* on election day? No matter how honest a man he was, one must try to look beyond his own fervent denials. The clearest evidence that no one had the slightest evidence, direct or indirect, that he was engaged in wrongdoing comes from the reporter who wrote the story, Robert Fairbanks. He told me he believed that Tobriner delayed the *Tanner* decision but that this was an unconscious act on his part, that Tobriner himself did not realize that he was delaying it or that he was delaying it for Bird's election benefit. An accusation based on such an understanding—and particularly one made without any explanation to the public that this is its basis—is a perfectly woven web from which the accused cannot become disentangled. Occasionally one reads of a "perfect crime"; Tobriner was the victim of a "perfect accusation," one so cleverly executed that there could be no defense against it, not even the best weapon he had, his honest word.

Tobriner was a strong man. He did not evoke pity. But any human being enmeshed in such a cleverly constructed trap must be pitied. It was particularly ironic that Tobriner, one of the nation's leading judicial exponents of the preservation of the individual's rights against the overwhelming power of big government, big business, and big labor, would become helplessly entangled in such nasty dishonesty propagated by big politicians aided by a big press.

Tobriner's lifelong perspective on the law was eloquently described by his friend and former law partner, Joseph Grodin, now a justice on the California Supreme Court. Referring to Tobriner as both judge and amateur painter, Grodin had this to say in a 1977 law journal article: "Tobriner paints with expansive perspective. He paints, however, always with individual human beings at the center of the picture. Abstractions, doctrines, and rules are but ways of visualizing and grappling with the human dilemma. That dilemma stems mainly from two sources. One is the tension between the need for society to centralize, institutionalize, organize, computerize, and routinize. The other is the need of individuals to be treated with dignity, with respect for their psychological and physical integrity, and with the opportunity for a maximum of self-expression and self-fulfillment. Tobriner's is not the self-sustaining individualism of the frontier, but the individualism of a society in which human beings are dependent upon one another and upon institutions for their mutual survival."

Grodin quoted from a 1975 Tobriner speech: "We live in an interdependent society; each individual depends for his safety upon the exercise of due care of other individuals. In our crowded cities and on our traffic-jammed highways each of us must necessarily depend upon the carefulness and responsibility of others."

In the over 400 opinions Justice Tobriner wrote in his more than 19 years on the Supreme Court, one of the ones for which he will be most remembered—both by those who approve and those who disapprove of the opinion—is *People* v. *Dorado*. In that 1964 case the state argued that a defendant's right to have counsel present during police interrogation was applicable only if the defendant initiated the request. Tobriner, in his majority opinion, rejected that claim and said such a rule would unfairly discriminate against the average, unsophisticated defendants who do not know their rights and who most need counsel. A year later the U.S. Supreme Court upheld the same right in the famous *Miranda* v. *Arizona* decisions.

Mathew Tobriner was the only child of Republican parents. Though they encouraged his early major endeavors—study at Stanford, then Harvard Law School, and then law practice—they had little understanding of his interest in labor unions. "It was almost like talking about a foreign language to them," Tobriner told an interviewer who did an oral history of him in 1958 for the Institute of Industrial Relations at the University of California at Berkeley. He said he never met a working-class person as he was growing up. But he spent evenings and Saturdays with his mother's father, Samuel Lezensky, and his mother's sister, Josephine Caro. They talked with him a great deal about the Judaic tradition's emphasis on the brotherhood of man. They told him that all people should be concerned with service to humanity. These adolescent conversations with his grandfather and aunt, Tobriner believed, were what guided him almost imperceptibly toward his concern for the poor.

When he graduated from Stanford in 1924, he made a speech that was received by the president of the university with somewhat the same degree of enthusiasm which the right-wing politicians reserved years later for his court opinions. As the Phi Beta Kappa speaker at the graduation, he recalled, "I had the temerity to state that the university, as I saw it, although a wonderful place, had been chiefly a process of learning by rote and turning information back in examination books. I said that I thought students should participate in affairs that were going on in the community generally, that the students should . . . engage in the study first-hand of . . . cooperative marketing associations . . . and labor unions, which were present in the Bay Area, but which Stanford students never did study first-hand. I urged a program, really of much more extensive investigation. . . . But I'm afraid I shocked everybody by saying that Stanford was not a very good place as far as these things were concerned.

"So I left an embarrassing silence after I concluded my talk and was answered quite thoroughly by David Starr Jordan [the president of the university], who said that students should learn the facts first before they gave big speeches like this. I was put in my place, and I shall never forget it! . . . I don't think that he really knew what I was talking about. . . ."

Ten years later, in 1934, Tobriner became a Democrat, taking with him into the party future Governor Pat Brown. The two young lawyers had their offices on the same floor of the Russ building in downtown San Francisco. One of their frequent hallway meetings had what Pat Brown would later call "a profound influence upon my future."

"Franklin D. Roosevelt had been president for two years," said Brown, "and although both Matt and I were Republicans, we were very much impressed with Roosevelt's New Deal and particularly with his fireside chats. On this day Matt told me that he was changing his registration from Republican to Democrat. He said, 'From my many talks with you, I think you have to do the same thing.' I responded, 'Changing your politics is like changing your religion.' His response was a catalyst for my weighing my own convictions about the role of government: 'If you no longer believe in your religion, don't you think you should change?' I weighed the implications of his remarks and then said, 'Let's go together to the registrar's office.' We did just that. We changed our registration and became members of the Democratic Party. . . ."

I spoke to Tobriner in summer 1981, nearly two years after the Commission concluded its investigation and left him spinning in the wind, as one commissioner and other persons put it, and just a few months after Justice Clark, on the evening of a farewell dinner in San Francisco before he left for the State Department, made the false claim to two reporters that Justice Tobriner was again improperly delaying a decision—this time, according to Clark, in order to keep him from leaving the Supreme Court. By that time Tobriner had grown more philosophical, but he still felt hurt about what had happened in 1978. He described his reaction on election day when he first saw the printed accusations against him: "I was furious. I was mad. . . . It was like walking out and getting run over by a drunken driver. So what do you do?" He paused. "You can't vent your spleen at the drunken driver. It doesn't do any good. There's no use being angry about it, being furious. I had a little bit of that, but I'm over it."

He explained that he "got over it" by "recognizing how frail human beings are. . . . Look at the records that I get here [court records of cases]. People kill. They do the most cruel and horrible things. . . . Human beings are apparently motivated by these terrible motives." He said he extended the same understanding to those who lied about his delaying the opinion that he extends to those who commit violent crimes. "We're all human, we're all frail and we are all motivated by self-interest and egotism."

Given the mean way these events capped his long career, he seemed particularly forgiving of those who were willing to destroy him in order to try to destroy Bird. "There's no use in having this anger, frustration, and fury. It's no good in this world. You have to know that everybody is terribly weak. . . . I don't have any hate, no use hating. . . . But it really was a dirty trick, wasn't it?"

A few months before he retired from the court in January 1982, Justice Tobriner said of his future retirement, "I'm afraid it's going to be rather lonely." He had relished the daily excitement of his work as a jurist. It was a sad statement for someone who was—in the words of Rosabelle, his wife of 43 years—an inveterate optimist. During one interview he told me he would rather die than do to someone else what was done to him on election day 1978.

Justice Tobriner died in April 1982, just three months after he retired from the court. Many who respected him attended lunches and dinners in his honor shortly after his retirement. He himself was a reluctant guest at such events. Public adulation, then as always, made him uncomfortable. He was a truly humble person. Nevertheless, he appreciated the respect and admiration shown during these final days of his life. He was comforted by this. It was particularly comforting in view of the fact that he knew his integrity had been left spinning in the wind. Those who used him to discredit the court never attempted to untangle the rope of lies that led him to be accused.

As Justice Tobriner's replacement, Jerry Brown appointed a Court of Appeal justice, Cruz Reynoso. Reaction to the appointment of this first Hispanic on the Supreme Court was in much the same spirit as the most violent opposition to Tobriner in his last years on the court. But it was, if possible, even more strident and venomous, and clearly heralded continued attacks on the Supreme Court. When Reynoso was appointed, two other Court of Appeal justices, George Paras and Hugh Evans, both Reagan judicial appointees, wrote letters so vehement and hate-filled that they seemed indicative of a freedom to express racism that would have been publicly unacceptable a few years earlier.

In his letter to the commission that had to vote on Reynoso's nomination to the court, Evans called Reynoso a "true racist." Paras called Reynoso a "professional Mexican."

"To put it very succinctly and very bluntly," Paras wrote in a letter sent to Reynoso and then to the commission that would vote on his appointment, "you have been a pain in the ass. . . . You must ever champion the 'oppressed,' meaning those who so designate themselves, such as criminals, handicapped, welfare recipients, demonstrators, 'minorities,' and miscellaneous other have-nots.

"It is this dedication not to justice and law but to the poor and oppressed that has prevented you from realizing your potential as an effective judge. In virtually everything I saw you do, this was your motivation. . . . Your attitude treats justice as synonymous with victory for the have-nots, a nice socialistic philosophy first proclaimed by Karl Marx many years ago and now still espoused by those who euphemistically call it a 'redistribution of wealth.'"

Reynoso had been executive director of California Rural Legal Assistance, a federally funded organization that aided the rural poor, when Reagan was Governor. Reagan had tried to eliminate the organization. Later, Reynoso was a law school professor at the University of New Mexico.

Within a few days of Reynoso's confirmation to the court, the court ordered the use of a reapportionment plan drawn up by Democrats for the 1982 U.S. Congressional and state-legislative elections. Three days later the Central Committee of the state Republican Party announced it would put substantial resources behind a move to recall Bird from the court. The recall would be her punishment, they said, for authoring the reapportionment decision. This recall effort, unlike earlier ones, seemed very serious. It would have the power and resources of the Republican Party behind it. A short time later, the Republicans said they would wait until 1983 so Brown would not be able to replace her if the voters threw her out. The Republicans also said they would consider targeting Justice Frank Newman for recall. Within three days of that announcement, the Governor announced that Newman, who had voted with the majority on the reapportionment decision, had told Brown he would retire from the court in 1982.

Throughout the 1978 accusations against Tobriner, those who would discredit the courts and destroy them as a co-equal third branch of government, enshrined Rose Bird's name in ink and film as an enduring symbol of "what's wrong with the courts."

A lot of California judges were not enthusiastic about Rose Bird's appointment to the Supreme Court. Not only did she not belong to the old-boy network that other Supreme Court justices had come from; she was not even part of the state's old-girl legal network, young as it is. She had been a public defender, a part-time professor at Stanford Law School, a respected member of the Brown cabinet, and active in the State Bar Association. But she never cared about her status in the legal profession, about whether she would circulate among the elite of the profession or make a lot of money. Yet she now sits at the top of the legal pyramid. Jerry Brown did a number of mindless things as Governor. Appointing Rose Bird to the Supreme Court was not one of them, despite what those liberals who wanted her job have said, and despite what those conservatives who dislike both her public-defender background and her court opinions would have the public believe.

This book is the story of how the New Right, including people who are now high White House officials, cleverly and with a lot of good luck (read: an unquestioning press) created an image of a court that is responsible for many of the ills of society and that, therefore, should be discredited and removed from office. It is a story of the use of innuendo and lies to destroy the reputation of a court. Along the way, reputations of honest people were besmirched, if not ruined. Some of them have died, reputations still in question.

This California story is important for the country. Some have dismissed the attack on the courts in California as yet another kooky California episode, something that, like hot tubs and hula hoops, will pass. But they are wrong. It is true that a former advertising agent, State Senator H. L. Richardson, has been the chief architect of the campaign against the California Supreme Court and against other judges. But far more is at stake. This attack has succeeded because of good salesmanship and, one could say, violation of truth-in-advertising laws. And, if the 1982 California election is any indicator of whether the public has bought the goods, the attack has become a movement. The three new, Brown-appointed Supreme Court judges on the ballot—Otto Kaus, Allen Broussard, and Cruz Reynoso—were approved by the voters by very small margins. The only Supreme Court justice who ever did worse at the polls was Rose Bird on the morning of the election-day *Los Angeles Times* story in 1978.

Those who do not share the far-right views of H. L. Richardson, and those who value truth and fairness and the Constitutions of California and the United States, should look beyond any residues of sexism or elitism that may play a role in their failure to recognize what the law-and-order constituency has done to Bird. She may have moved too fast on some changes she made. But most of them have turned out to have been positive. As long as people dwell on petty complaints about Bird they continue to feed the special-interest groups that attack her. It is important that all who are not far-right realize that an attack against Rose Bird is an attack against them, against the judiciary as a whole, both in California and in the nation.

If this seems like extreme rhetoric, perhaps the words of the Law and Order Campaign Committee's executive director, John Feliz, will attest to its veracity. He told me: "I'm as angry at Mathew Tobriner and Mosk and Newman as I am at her. But the press has made a symbol of her. . . . The governor turned her into a symbol of embattled feminism [by merely appointing a woman]. . . . Until her the press didn't talk about the court. Until her the press was part of the good old boy network. They were incestuous with the court. . . . *We use her because it's easier to grasp a symbol. . . . She is no different than the men on the court. She is simply a convenient focus. She's a perfect symbol."*

These people could be called Bird-hunters. Bird is their unwilling and accidental decoy, in the sense of "one who leads another into danger, deception, or a trap." Bird is the decoy used maliciously to lead the public into thinking that the way to solve the crime problem is to blame the courts. As the evidence has shown, this is a dangerous trap indeed. It solves no problems and serves no constituency, but it gains considerable political mileage for the New Right and denigrates the basic concepts of justice.

"It's headhunting time again" began one newspaper editorial about a new recall attempt against Bird in 1981, an effort headed by a man who has publicly insulted both Italians and Jews by coining a new ethnic slur: Jew-woppie. The term "headhunting" was appropriate for its political symbolism. But it is also particularly chilling in this instance, for some former court staff members—and perhaps some outside the court, too—actually do hope for Bird's death, failing a successful recall.

In the summer of 1981 three former employees of the court told me they had heard the Chief Justice had just started to wear a wig. They said they were sure she was having cobalt treatment for her cancer, thus the loss of hair and need for a wig. "That means she's in pretty bad shape," said a woman, not doing much to hide her joy. Bird, however, has never had cobalt treatments, is not losing her hair, and does not now nor ever has worn a wig for either cosmetic or medical purposes. In fact, her cancer seems to be in remission. But some persist in hoping otherwise. "Everybody says she's much sicker than we really know," a former member of the court staff told me rather happily. "We assume her illness will take care of the whole problem."

But in case it doesn't, and in case a recall campaign doesn't work, there's a contingency plan. Another former staff member who left the court in great bitterness and who keeps in touch with people still at the court and continues to work with those who want to remove Bird from the bench, sounded both ominous and hopeful as he told me, "We're watching her very, very closely. We are hoping that she will commit a major boo-boo to cause another investigation." His voice was fervent, his face intense, as he added: "And this time we will get her."

Index

Index

(Note: The mention "Commission" refers to the Commission on Judicial Performance.)

A

Administrative Office of Courts (AOC), 59, 246; Bird's refusal to delegate authority to, 55–58
Agriculture Labor Relations Act (ALRA), 8, 11–12, 128
Allen, Richard, 37
Allston, Gil, 268–69
American Bar Association (ABA), 6, 103, 167, 174–75
American Bar Association Journal, 61–62, 236–38
American Civil Liberties Union, 258
Arteaza, Daniel M., 15–16
Associated Press (AP), 219
Avakian, Spurgeon, 94

B

Balderman, Evelyn, 107
Ball, George, 37
Benfell, Carol, 233–34, 236–38
Bernstein, Florence, 249–50
Best, Hollis, 268
Biden, Joseph, 32–33
Bill of Rights, U.S., xviii
Bird, Ann, 14
Bird, Rose Elizabeth, xii, 31–32, 38; actions construed as "childish," 272; appointment and confirmation as Chief Justice, 4, 8–18, 22; blanket-assignments policy of, 60; as Brown's Secretary of Agriculture, 7–8, 53, 128; and busing, 131; campaigns for recall of, 3–5, 198, 242, 282, 284; cancer of, 63–64, 73, 250–52, 284; Clark and *Caudillo* position of, 87, 116, 118–19, 125, 128–31, 138–41, 144–48, 155–58, 273; Clark's relationship with, 53, 64, 66, 70–71, 118–20, 127–32, 158, 225–26; Commission's failure to clear name of, 204; criticizes Brown, 65; defends Tobriner, 83; Deukmejian's attacks on, 242, 253, 254, 256, 262–64; early life and career, 14–15; election-day denial of *Los Angeles Times* story, 83; and *Fox* case, 113, 182–83, 205; hate mail of, 246–47; and hiring of Gill, 245; impersonated on PSA flight, 248–50; judiciary's hostility toward, 9–10; Kleps and AOC and, 55–59; *Los Angeles Times'* reaffirmation of charges against, 216–17; *Los Angeles Times* 22 December 1978 story and, 218, 219; Ludlow's grievances and, 243–44; media treatment of, 60, 66–67, 71, 234, 240, 243–45, 247, *and see: Los Angeles Times*—1978 election-day story; memorandum on release of court documents to press, 238; and moonlighting by staff attorneys, 71–72; Mosk's relationship with, 9–10, 53, 71, 160–61, 163, 186, 188–90, 219; and 1978 elec-

287

come of Commission hearings, 195–98; politics of, 209; pre-election-day coverage of 1978 election, 80, 149; Skelton article on Mosk speech, 189–90; and *Van Atta* decision, 254

1978 election-day story: 80–83, 99, 111, 121, 124–25, 138, 163, 185, 188, 191, 209–31, 240–41, 274, 277–78; Benfell *ABA Journal* article on, 235, 236–38; Bird's refutation of, 83; Clark and, 219–26; "communications breakdown" and genesis of, 191, 230; Cotliar's defense of, 228–30; first questions raised about, 218; H. L. Richardson and, 219–20; Hager on, 213; lack of understanding of court procedures and, 213–14, 217–18, 227, 228, 236–37; Mosk and, 163, 188–89, 191, 219, 220; reporters' assumptions about accuracy of, 233–34; Stolz on, 235–38; stories reinforcing charges of, 216–17; text of, 80–81; timing of, and election outcome, 228; 22 December 1978 story and, 218–19; Willoughby on, 226–27

Love, Eulia, 218
Ludlow, Paul, 68–70, 243–44
Luros (lawyer), 248–50

M

McCarthy, Joseph, 237
McCarthy, Leo, 196
McComb, Marshall, 25–26, 40–44, 48, 64–65; Clark and, 41, 45
McGuigan, Patrick, xvi
Madison, James, xi, xiii
Mahoney, Roger, 11–12, 16
Manuel, Wiley, 10, 54, 67–69, 109, 111, 117; death of, 203; and MediCal abortions, 65; and *Tanner*, 88, 122–23, 110–11, 113, 122–23, 125, 142, 144–50, 155, 159, 203; representation of, at Commission hearings, 107; testimony at Commission hearings, 123, 146–50, 172; views on *Tanner* of, 86
Marcus, Gerald D., 107, 166
Marks, Milton, 77–78

Marler, Fred, Jr., 84
Medsger, Betty, initiation of research by, 212–13
Medvene, Edward, 107, 185, 187
Meese, Edwin, 19, 21, 27–29, 31–32, 37, 46, 275; criticizes criminal justice system, 258–59; as Clark's attorney, 107, 275; speculates on *Tanner* delay, 128, 143–44
Metropolitan News (Los Angeles), 254
Michelson, Herb, 22, 176–78
Milk, Harvey, 82–83, 260
Millard, Ted, 232
Miller, John, 173
Miranda v. *Arizona*, 259, 279
Morris, Richard C., 48, 49, 62, 124; and Clark's *Caudillo* footnote, 155–57; at Commission hearings, 107
Moscone, George, 82–83, 260
Mosk, Richard, 107, 160, 162, 171
Mosk, Stanley, 17, 44, 69, 103, 120, 171, 272; attacks news media, 190–91; career and reputation of, 160–63; Chodos' criticism of, 175–76; Clark's testimony on "accusation" of Tobriner by, 143, 159–60, 163–66, 171–72, 179, 184–86, 196–97, 212; considered by Commission for private admonishment, 200; criticizes Hufstedler, 174–75; Jerry Brown and, 160; and *Los Angeles Times* election-day story, 163, 188–89, 191, 219, 220; opposed to investigation of justices, 94, 95, 103, 104; opposes Gill appointment, 245; Pat Brown and, 161, 162; relationship with Bird, 9–10, 53, 71, 160–61, 163, 186, 188–90, 219; relationship with Clark, 160, 162, 189, 190; relationship with Tobriner, 160, 184–87, 190, 191; on past greatness of California Supreme Court, 189–90; sues for closing of Commission hearings, 104, 166–78, 193, 200, 205–7; views on *Tanner* of, 86, 108

at Commission hearings: 113, 179–91; defends Clark's confusion, 183–84, 191; on *Fox* case, 180–82, 184; indifferent to cloud over Tobriner, 185–87, 191; re-